STORIES OF
THE SAHARA

SANMAO

Translated from the Chinese by Mike Fu
With an introduction by Sharlene Teo

BLOOMSBURY PUBLISHING
LONDON · OXFORD · NEW YORK · NEW DELHI · SYDNEY

BLOOMSBURY PUBLISHING
Bloomsbury Publishing Plc
50 Bedford Square, London, WC1B 3DP, UK

BLOOMSBURY, BLOOMSBURY PUBLISHING and the Diana logo are trademarks
of Bloomsbury Publishing Plc

First published by Crown Publishing Company in Taiwan in 1976

First published in Great Britain 2019, published in agreement with Georgina Capel
Associates Ltd. c/o The Grayhawk Agency

Excerpt from Li Shangyin's 'The Brocade Zither', used with the kind permission
of the translator, Chloe Garcia Roberts

Excerpt from Xin Qui's 'The Ugly Page/Picking Mulberries' and from Ma Zhiyuan's 'Autumn
Thoughts' used with the kind permission of the translator, Andrew W. F. Wong,
www.chinesepoemsinenglish.blogspot.com, February 2012, August 2010

Excerpts from Bai Juyi's 'Farewells on Grassland' used with the kind permission of the
translator, Hugh Grigg

Excerpt from 'Climbing' by Du Fu (*Facing the Moon*, Oyster River Press, 2007), translated by
Keith Holyoak and used with the kind permission of the publisher

A catalogue record for this book is available from the British Library

Library of Congress Cataloguing-in-Publication data has been applied for

ISBN: HB: 978-1-4088-8187-3; TPB: 978-1-4088-8188-0; EBOOK: 978-1-4088-8186-6

2 4 6 8 10 9 7 5 3 1

Typeset by Newgen KnowledgeWorks Pvt. Ltd., Chennai, India
Printed and bound in Great Britain by CPI Group (UK) Ltd, Croydon CR0 4YY

MIX
Paper from
responsible sources
FSC® C020471

To find out more about our authors and books visit www.bloomsbury.com
and sign up for our newsletters

STORIES OF
THE SAHARA

Foreword

By Sharlene Teo

The Sahara is the largest hot desert in the world and among the most sparsely populated, spanning 103,000 square miles of dunes and flatlands. How did a fiercely cosmopolitan Taiwanese woman end up living in one of the harshest territories on earth? What compelled her to move there? And once she got there, what happened?

Stories of the Sahara, the book that answers these questions, has captivated millions of readers to date. First published in Chinese in 1976 to rapturous success, Sanmao's memoir and travelogue launched its author as a literary celebrity across Asia. Initially serialised in the Taiwanese *United Daily News*, the candid intimacy and liveliness of Sanmao's writing cemented her status as an enduring cultural icon and figure of quixotic fascination. Coming to public attention during the prohibitive atmosphere of 1970s martial-law era Taiwan, Sanmao's free-spirited itinerancy enthralled readers and demonstrated an exciting model of Asian femininity that centred personal agency, resourcefulness and reinvention.

Across the collection, Sanmao the chimerical protagonist-narrator presents herself as trendsetter and rule-breaker, cool girl and mystic, pensive romantic and comic heroine, globetrotter and housewife. She's a singular polyglot who refuses to be confined to the limitations of a single category. She's an unreliable but compelling narrator who embraces contradictions – evinced by her plain but assured prose style that shifts from farcical to sombre registers, scatological to highbrow, ludic to deadly serious, often within the same page. There is a wide thematic and emotional range to these pieces; from the high tension and suspenseful dread of 'Night in the Wasteland' and 'Seed of Death' to the ruminative melancholy of 'Looking for Love' and the absurdist comedy of 'Nice Neighbours' and 'The Desert Bathing Spectacle.'

Reading *Stories of the Sahara* is a transporting and entertaining experience: the reader is brought up close to Sanmao's individuality and independence. As its bestselling popularity attests, readers were drawn to Sanmao's intrepid literary persona, her zest for life and insatiable taste for adventure. Although ubiquitous in the contemporary age of social media and commercialised feminism, Sanmao's unabashed self-aggrandisement and position of gung-ho empowerment was ahead of its time. Her confidence veers on radical. Here is a woman without any medical training who has no compunction assuming the mantle of the local pharmacist or medicine woman. The roguish resourcefulness and wit of the *Stories* bear the thrill and jaunty energy of the picaresque, as does the memorable cast of characters – from the lovelorn grocer Salun to the enigmatic Sergeant Salva and the tragic Shahida.

'Day after day, a black sheep like myself, who never even grew up in the desert, strives to dispel the misery of these long, leisurely years with artfulness and pleasure,' Sanmao writes in 'Hearth and Home', one of the essays that instantiates *Stories'* thematic preoccupations with identity, alienation, community and exile. There is a world weariness and sense of melancholy that undercuts and arguably contradicts Sanmao's self-aggrandising and buoyant narrative tone. Her narrative persona is outgoing, neighbourly, empathetic and social. Yet she is plagued with abiding feelings of isolation. Beholding the wasteland, she states: 'it was hard not to feel some measure of loneliness. But, by the same token, to know that I was wholly alone in this unimaginably vast land was totally liberating.'

Sanmao's appealingly direct voice combines 'artfulness and pleasure' with an undeniable curiosity about the natural world and its inhabitants. Every story conveys this infectious capacity for wonder. She sees the humour and anecdotal potential of challenging conditions – describing life in the desert as 'an unfailingly colourful experience' – and finds the sublime in the quotidian: 'scattered pieces of driftwood looked like modernist sculptures'. In this way, *Stories'* vivid, searing evocations of desert places and spaces, both awe inspiring and hostile, transported readers who lacked the resources to travel. Her accounts of living alongside the Sahrawi, the indigenous people of the Western Sahara, are oftentimes playful and occasionally dangerous and heartbreaking. She describes cross-cultural encounters and the process of adapting to a new community with the empathy and respectful observance of a self-described 'black sheep' and lifelong outsider.

Sanmao was born Chen Maoping in China in 1943 and raised in Taiwan, and throughout her life she travelled to over fifty-five countries. She drew her pseudonym from the famous and beloved long-running Chinese comic strip character Sanmao, a wandering orphan so malnourished that he has only three hairs on his head. Explaining her rationale for adopting the moniker, Sanmao said: 'When I came across

Sanmao, the orphan wandering in the streets, I realised there were a lot of poor children struggling to survive. When I began to write, I decided to faithfully record the lives of ordinary people whose voices go unheard. So I chose this name.' There are three different identity modes to Sanmao: Chen Ping, her preferred personal name, Sanmao the literary personality, and Echo, the English name she gave herself in order to honour her art teacher.

Sanmao studied in Germany, the United States and Spain, where she met her future husband, José María Quero. Their progressive and bohemian partnership – founded on a shared adventurousness and José's devotion to Sanmao's uniquely independent spirit – forms the emotional underpinning of *Stories of the Sahara*. As detailed in 'The Marriage Chronicles', José's wedding gift to Sanmao is 'a camel skull, white bones neatly assembled, with a huge row of menacing teeth and two big black holes for eyes.' To a delighted Sanmao, this unconventional and macabre artifact 'was just the thing to capture my heart' and 'José was worthy of being called my soulmate.' Their differences in nationality and personality are demonstrated to comedic effect across several stories, but so too is the mutual respect, humour and tenderness of their relationship.

Sanmao is refreshingly frank about her feelings for her husband: 'I had never been passionately in love with him. At the same time I felt incredibly lucky and at ease.' From near-death experiences to domestic episodes deploying ludic resourcefulness to handle the deprivations of desert life, *Stories of the Sahara* transplants the pragmatic challenges and compromises of marriage to an exotic setting. Their love story with all of its domestic foibles and cross-cultural misunderstandings is at once relatable, to deploy the millennial buzzword, and prescient of the increasing ubiquity of transnational relationships in an increasingly globalised world. Their romance is both glamorous and mundane, deeply romantic and humorously practical.

José and Sanmao moved to the Spanish Sahara after she read a feature about it in an issue of *National Geographic* and felt inexplicably and decisively drawn 'toward that vast and unfamiliar land, as if echoing from a past life.' The passages describing its breathtaking scale are written with a mixture of awe and morbidity: 'the deathly still landscape was like a grim and ferocious giant lying on its side. We were driving along its quietly outspread body.'

Is the desert the panacea for 'a lifetime's homesickness' or is it a metaphor for the restlessness and longing that is germane to Sanmao's wandering spirit? The desert conveys infinity and mortal threat, boundlessness and the risk – and opportunity – of getting lost. It is a palimpsest of mirages and myths of rescue and no return. Eclipsing romantic love, Sanmao reflects upon how 'deep in my heart, the Sahara desert had been my dream lover for so long ... I'd expected a scorching sun, but instead found a swathe of poetic desolation.'

While *Stories in the Sahara* abounds with moments of companionship and cameraderie – between Sanmao and José, as well as with the Sahrawi community, these essays are deeply concerned with the isolating and poetically desolate compulsion of wanderlust. 'I wanted a taste of many different lives, sophisticated or simple ... a life plain as porridge would never be an option for me,' Sanmao opines. 'In this life, I'd always felt I wasn't a part of the world around me. I often needed to go off the tracks of a normal life and do things without explanation.' Her quest for self-fulfilment and self-expression is incommensurate with a stable sense of belonging. To the lifelong traveller, the impulse to discover new experiences means that one place is never enough. As the wistful lyrics in her famous song 'The Olive Tree' go, 'Do not ask me where I'm from/ My hometown is far away/ Why do I wander around/ Wandering afar, wandering'.

Tragedy has a tendency to eclipse the light of a life's work, romanticising everything, lending every line an air of pathos and bittersweet resonance. José died in a diving accident in 1979, and a few years after, in 1981, Sanmao settled down in Taiwan where she taught and published more than twenty works including the acclaimed Chinese screenplay *Red Dust*, before committing suicide in 1991. Walt Whitman famously said that we contain multitudes. As the following essays demonstrate, Sanmao possessed a deep understanding of the engagement of the self with the granular and cosmic; in her world, connection and isolation, joy and pain, as well as splendour and melancholy existed side by side. 'Whether in a few short days or over the long span of a life, everything disappears in due time: tears, laughter, love, hate, the ups and downs of dreams and reality. On the sand, pure white like snow, there was no trace of the dead. Not even the nocturnal wind could carry aloft their sighs.'

Sharlene Teo, May 2019

Contents

CONTENTS

A Knife on a Desert Night

When I first arrived in the desert, I desperately wanted to be the first female explorer to cross the Sahara. The thought of it used to keep me up all night back in Europe. My previous experiences travelling through various countries wouldn't be of much use since there was no civilisation to speak of in the desert. After thinking it over for nearly half a year, I decided to go anyway and scope it out once I got there. Of course, I couldn't very well go without any plan whatsoever. It wouldn't do to simply strap a large canteen to my back and parachute out of a plane. So I began in Spanish territory, in the capital of the Sahara Desert: El Aaiún. I found it hard to believe that this was a capital city. It was clearly just a small settlement in the middle of the great desert, with a handful of streets, a few banks and a couple of shops. The desolate scenery and atmosphere reminded me of the towns in Western films. The usual flourishes of a capital city were nowhere to be seen.

The home I rented was outside of town. It was a shabby little place, but the monthly rent was even higher than what was standard in Europe. There was no furniture. I spread straw mats on the ground as the locals did. I bought a mattress to sleep on in the other room. And with that I was all settled for a while. I did have water. There was an oil drum on the roof. Every morning around six or so, the city government would deliver salty water collected from deep wells in the desert. I don't know why it was so salty. You used it to wash your face and bathe. As for drinking water, you had to buy it by the bottle.

Life here was unbearably lonely for me at the start. I didn't know how to speak Arabic and my neighbours all happened to be indigenous people of the Sahara – Africans. Very few of the women knew Spanish, though the children could speak it haltingly. There was a street right in front of my house, and beyond that was the endless desert, smooth and soft, full of serene mystery, stretching out all the way to the edge of the sky. It was a yellowish orange colour. I thought the surface of the moon probably looked pretty similar to this place. I loved how the desert was stained red at sunset. Every day as the sun went down, I'd sit on the roof until the sky was totally dark and feel an immense loneliness, out of nowhere, deep in my heart.

I initially planned to rest for a while and then travel through the desert. Unfortunately I didn't know many people, so I had nothing to do except go and hang out at the police station in town every day. (OK, I'll admit, I had no choice. The police station had confiscated my passport. They were always trying to deport me.) I paid a visit early on to the deputy director, a Spaniard.

'Señor, I would like to go to the desert, but I don't know how to get there. Can you help me?'

'Desert? Aren't you in the desert right now? Why don't you lift your head up and look out of the window?' He spoke without raising his head himself.

'No, I want to make a trip like this.' I waved my hand over the map that hung on the wall and pointed to the Red Sea.

He looked me up and down for almost two minutes. 'Señorita,' he said. 'Do you know what you're saying? This is not possible. Please get on the next plane back to Madrid. We don't want any trouble.'

I became agitated. 'I won't cause any trouble for you. I have enough to cover living expenses for three months. I'll show you. The money's right here.' I grabbed a handful of dirty bank notes from my pocket and shook them at him.

'Fine. None of my business. I'll give you residency for three months. After that, you must leave no matter what. Where are you currently living? I need to register you.'

'I live outside of town in a house with no doorplate. How to explain… I'll draw a picture for you.'

And thus I settled down in the great Sahara Desert.

I don't want to complain repeatedly about my loneliness, but I almost couldn't get over how tough it was during that initial period and thought often about heading back to Europe. Amid that endless stretch of sand, it was so hot during the day that water could scald your hands, while night was so cold that you had to wear a heavy coat. Many times I asked myself why I insisted on staying here. Why had I wanted to come to this long-forgotten corner of the world all by myself? As there were no answers to these questions, I continued to settle in, one day at a time.

The second person I met was the retired commander of the desert corps, a Spaniard who had been living in the desert for most of his life and had no desire to repatriate. I asked for his advice on travelling into the desert.

'Señorita, this is impossible. Consider your circumstances.'

I stayed quiet, but I must have obviously looked dejected. 'Come and look at this military map,' he said, calling me over to the wall. 'This is Africa. This is the Sahara Desert. The dotted lines are roads. The rest, you can see for yourself.'

I already knew. I'd looked thousands of times at many different maps. On the retired commander's map, apart from a few dotted lines in the Spanish Sahara, there were only the borders between countries. The rest was completely blank.

'What are these roads of which you speak?' I asked.

'The roads here are the tyre tracks of people who've travelled before. When the weather's nice, you can see them. Once the sandstorms get intense, they disappear.'

I thanked him and left, my heart heavy. I knew I was overestimating my abilities. But I couldn't just let it go. I'm a stubborn person, through and through. To keep from getting discouraged, I went to find some locals to ask their advice. The Sahrawi people are natives of this huge desert; they'd surely have their own ideas.

There was a public square outside of town, crowded with camels and Jeeps, goods and goats. I waited for an old Muslim man to finish praying, then asked him how I could cross the Sahara. This old man spoke Spanish. As soon as he opened his mouth, a crowd of young people gathered around him.

'You want to go to the Red Sea?' he asked. 'I have never been in my whole life. Nowadays you can fly to Europe, change planes and get to the Red Sea safe and sound. No need to cross the desert.'

'Yes, but I want to get there by going through the desert. Please advise.' I spoke very loudly, worried he hadn't understood.

'You must go? Alright then! Listen carefully. Rent two Jeeps so you have an extra in case one breaks down. You will need a guide. Once you are fully prepared, you may as well try!'

This was the first time someone had told me I could give it a shot. 'How much does it cost to rent a Jeep per day?' I pressed. 'How much for the guide?'

'Three thousand pesetas per day for the Jeep, another three thousand for the guide. Then there is food and gas.' Great. I added it up and figured basic expenses would be 180,000 pesetas for a month.

No, that wasn't right. I needed to rent two cars, so the total would be 270,000 pesetas. This didn't include equipment, gas, food or water. I'd need at least 400,000 pesetas per month or it wouldn't work.

I fingered the few large bills in my pocket, feeling discouraged. 'It's too expensive,' I said grudgingly. 'I can't afford to go. Thank you.'

As I was about to leave, the old man said, 'There is also a way to do it without spending much money.'

Hearing this, I sat back down again. 'What do you mean?'

'Go with the nomads. They are a very friendly people and travel to wherever there is rainwater. This will save you money. I can make introductions.'

'I'm not afraid of hardship. I can buy my own tent and camel. Please help me. I can go right away.'

The old man laughed. 'Nobody knows when they might go. Sometimes they stay in one place for a week or two. Sometimes they stay for months. It depends on whether their goats have enough to eat.'

'How long does it take for them to cross the desert each time?'

'Hard to say. They are very slow. Probably ten years or so!'

Everyone who heard this laughed, but I couldn't bring myself to join in. That day I walked for a long, long time, all the way home to where I was staying. I'd travelled incredible distances to the desert just to linger in this little town, it seemed. Good thing I still had three months left. I might as well settle down first and then make plans.

My landlord's family paid me a visit the day after I moved in. A big group of boys and girls were crowded in front of my door. I smiled at them, scooping up the smallest in my arms. 'Come in, everyone,' I said to them. 'I have snacks for you.'

They awkwardly glanced at a plump girl who stood behind them. She was truly beautiful, with large eyes, long eyelashes and very white teeth. Her skin was a light brown. She wore a deep turquoise fabric around her body and also covered her hair. She walked over and touched her head to my face, then took my hand. '*Salaam alaikum.*'

'*Salaam alaikum,*' I said back to her.

I liked her a lot. Among this group of little kids, the girls all wore long African print dresses in splashy colours and their hair was done up in a ton of snake-like braids. They looked amazing. Some of the boys wore clothes, while others were naked. None of them had shoes on. A pungent smell emanated from their bodies. Their facial features were all very attractive, even if a bit grimy.

I eventually met the landlord himself. He was a policeman who spoke excellent Spanish. 'Your wife is very beautiful,' I said to him.

'That's odd,' he replied. 'You didn't meet my wife!'

'Then who was that plump and pretty girl?'

'Ah! That is my elder daughter Gueiga. She is only ten years old.'

I stared at him in shock. Gueiga looked very mature. I would have guessed her to be around thirty. I really couldn't believe it.

'Señorita, you must also be a teenager? You can be friends with my daughter.'

I scratched my head, embarrassed and unsure of how to tell the landlord my age.

Once I got to know Gueiga better, I asked her, 'Gueiga, are you really only ten years old?'

'What year old?' she said.

'You. How old are you?'

'I do not know!' she said. 'I can only count to ten on my fingers. We women do not care about our age. Only my father would know how old I am.'

Eventually I discovered it wasn't just Gueiga who didn't know how old she was. Her mother and the neighbouring women didn't know numbers, nor did they care about their own ages. All they cared about was how plump they were. Plump was pretty here; who cared how old anyone was?

Within a month of settling down, I had managed to meet many people. I had both Spanish and Sahrawi friends. Among them was a young Sahrawi man who'd graduated from high school, a remarkable feat. One day, he told me happily, 'I'm getting married next spring.'

'Congratulations. Where is your fiancée?'

'In the desert, living in a *khaima*.' (A tent.)

Gazing at this handsome youth, I hoped he would conduct himself differently from his clansmen. 'Tell me, how old is your fiancée?'

'Eleven years old.'

I cried out when I heard this. 'And you've had a high school education? *Dios mío!*'

This made him pretty mad. 'What is wrong about this?' he said, looking at me. 'My first wife was only nine when she married me. Now she is fourteen, with two children.'

'What? You have a wife? How come you never mentioned it before?'

'What is there to say about women...'

I glared at him. 'You're planning to marry your quota of four wives?' (Muslims here can have up to four wives.)

'I cannot. I do not have the money. Two is fine for now.'

Not long after this exchange, Gueiga went crying to her own marriage. It was customary to cry on this occasion, but if I were in her place, I'd probably cry bitter tears for the rest of my life.

One day around sunset, I heard the honking of a car outside my door. I ran out to see who it was and found two of my new friends, a married couple, waving at me from their Jeep. 'Get in, let's go for a ride.'

They were both Spaniards. The husband was serving in the air force around here and had a modern 'camel'. 'Where to?' I asked as I was climbing into the backseat of the Jeep.

'The desert.'

'For how long?'

'A few hours, then we'll come back.'

Even though there was sand all around us, they felt the need to break out and go somewhere far away, I guess. We followed the tyre tracks of another car into the boundless desert. The sun was sinking, but it was still very hot. I felt a bit sleepy and my eyes glazed over for a moment. The next thing I knew … wow, just incredible: two hundred metres ahead was a big lake, flat as a mirror, with a few trees nearby.

I rubbed my eyes. It felt like the car was flying towards the lake as fast as it could. From the backseat, I gave my friend who was driving a smack on the head. 'A lake, *viejo*! Do you want us to die?' I screamed. He ignored me and stepped on the gas. I looked at his wife, who had a strange smile on her face. The car wasn't stopping and the lake was drawing nearer and nearer. I hugged my knees and let them drive on.

I had heard that there was a lake not far into the desert, but I hadn't expected it to be here. Lifting my head slightly, I saw the lake was still there. I hugged myself tightly again and covered my head. The car drove for another hundred metres or so before coming to a stop.

'Hey, open your eyes!' they shouted. I raised my head and saw an endless wasteland. The setting sun stained the entire land blood red; a wind blew sheets of sand into the air. A horrible, frightful scene appeared before my eyes. Where was the lake? There was no lake. The water had disappeared. And there certainly weren't any trees. I gripped the car seat tightly, afraid to make a sound. It was like a terrifying story from *The Twilight Zone* come to life.

I jumped out of the car, kicking at the ground and then touching it with my hands. It was all real, but how did that lake just disappear? I hurriedly turned to look at the car. The car hadn't disappeared. It was still there, along with my two friends who were doubled over with laughter.

'I get it. That was a mirage, right?'

My hair was still standing on end after I got in the car. 'Pretty scary. How come it looked so close? The mirages in the movies always look so far away.'

'Oh, there's so much more than mirages. Take your time to get to know this desert. There are weird things aplenty.'

Afterwards, whenever I saw something, I didn't dare trust my own eyes and always had to go and touch it. Of course, I couldn't tell other people that I'd been spooked by a mirage. 'I'm short-sighted,' is all I would say. 'I have to touch things to be sure.'

I was washing clothes with the door open when the landlord's goat ran in and ate the only flower I'd managed to cultivate with fresh water. Well, it wasn't really a flower, but the two green leaves had been growing quite healthily and the goat ate them both up in one bite. I chased it out to give it a good whacking and ended up falling over. Furious, I ran next door to yell at the landlord's son, Bashir. 'Your goat ate the leaves that I planted!'

At fifteen, the landlord's son was the oldest of the children. 'How many leaves were there?' he asked, looking down his nose at me.

'There were only two leaves and he ate them both.'

'You're mad about two leaves? Why bother?'

'What? Are you forgetting this is the Sahara, where not a blade of grass grows? My flower—'

'Forget about your flower. What are you doing tonight?'

'Nothing.' I really had no plans when I thought about it.

'I'm going to capture aliens with some friends. You want to come?'

'A flying saucer? You mean there's a flying saucer coming?' My curiosity was piqued.

'Yes, that's right.'

'Muslims shouldn't lie, kid.'

He held up his hand and swore that there really was one. 'There is no moon tonight, so it will probably come.'

'Yes! Count me in!' I blurted out, feeling excited and scared at the same time. 'You're going to capture them, huh?'

'As soon as they come out, yes! But you should wear men's clothes, local men's clothes. I do not want to take a woman there.'

'Whatever you say. Lend me a turban and a thick coat.'

So that night I walked with Bashir and his group of friends for nearly two hours. We reached a place in the desert where there were no lights whatsoever, then sprawled on the ground. It was pitch-black all around us. The stars twinkled coldly like diamonds. The wind hurt like a slap in the face. I adjusted my turban to cover my nose, only exposing my eyes. Then, when I was nearly frozen to death from the wait, Bashir suddenly struck me.

'Shh, don't move. Listen.'

Woo, woo, woo, it sounded like the rhythmic hum of a motor coming from all directions. 'I don't see anything!' I cried.

'Shh, don't yell.' Bashir pointed. In the sky not far from us, there was a flying object lit up in orange, slowly coming our way. Even though I was focused on the flying object, I was so nervous that I dug my hands into the sand. The strange thing flew in a circle and moved away. I exhaled a big breath. Then it started flying back, still slow, but lower in the sky.

The only thing I wanted in that moment was for it to go away quickly. Capturing aliens, my foot! We'd be lucky if they didn't abduct us. The UFO didn't descend; I lay there, limp and unable to move, for a long time. In spite of the intense cold, I was sweating all over.

It was broad daylight by the time we got home. I stood in front of my house and took off the turban and coat to return them to Bashir. My policeman landlord was just getting in.

'Hey, where have you guys been?'

When Bashir saw his father, he ran back inside like a dog with its tail between its legs.

'We're back!' I replied to the landlord. 'We went to see a flying saucer.'

'This kid was playing a trick on you and you fell for it?'

I thought for a second. 'It was real,' I told him. 'An orange object, flying slowly. It wasn't a plane. It was very slow and flew low.'

The landlord contemplated this for a moment. 'Many people have seen this thing,' he said. 'It has been coming often at night for many years. No one can explain what it is.'

I felt a twinge hearing him say this. 'So you really believe what I just saw?'

'Señorita, I believe in Allah. But that thing in the desert sky truly exists.'

Even though I'd been awake and freezing all night, I couldn't get to sleep for a long, long time.

Another night I was leaving my friend's after having eaten roasted camel and it was already one in the morning. 'Just sleep over!' they said. 'You can go home tomorrow morning.'

I thought about it, but 1 a.m. wasn't that late, so I made up my mind to walk. An uncomfortable expression came over the man of the house. 'We can't see you home, though.'

'No need to worry,' I said to them, patting my boots. 'I've got *this*.'

'Got what?' he and his wife asked in unison.

I raised my hands dramatically and, in a flash, revealed a shiny knife. The wife let out a yelp. We all laughed for a good while. Then I bid them goodbye and walked off on my own.

It was forty minutes to my home, not a long journey by any means. The annoying part was that you had to pass through two big cemeteries on the way. The local Sahrawi don't use coffins. They wrap people who've died in white cloth, place them in the sand and put a stone tablet on top so the dead people don't sit up in the night.

There was moonlight that evening. I sang the military song of the local desert corps at the top of my lungs while marching ahead. Eventually I realised it might be better if I didn't sing, as it would make me an easier target. There were no lights in the desert. Apart from the moaning wind, I heard only my own footsteps.

The first cemetery emerged crisp and clear beneath the moonlight. I walked past the seemingly endless lines of graves with great caution so as to not step on anyone in eternal rest. The second cemetery posed more difficulty, situated as it was on a slope. To get home, I had to go down a hill where the dead people were densely packed beneath the ground. There was practically no path to follow. Not far in the distance, a few dogs were sniffing here and there. I knelt down to pick up stones to throw at them. The dogs howled and fled.

I stood on the hill for a while, looking in front and then behind me. I felt scared because no one was around. But if a person did come out of the wilderness, I'd be even more scared. What if something came that was not a person? Wah, my hairs began to stick up one by one. I didn't dare let my imagination run wild. Once I was almost out of the cemetery, what do you know, there was a shadow moving on the ground before me. At first it was sprawled forward, then struggling up with arms raised towards the sky, then falling back to the ground. A moment later it was struggling up again, then falling again.

I kept calm and bit my lip, standing still to collect myself. Eh? The shadow was also no longer moving. Looking closer, I saw that it was scraps of cloth around a body. It was clearly something that had crawled out of a grave. I crouched down, my right hand feeling for the handle of the knife in my boot. Gust after gust of strange, heavy wind blew. The wind carried me, in a trance, closer to the thing by a few steps. The thing struggled to rise again under the moonlight. I glanced behind me to assess the situation. It would be an uphill retreat, hard to move fast. Better just to charge forwards. So I hesitantly took a few steps. As I neared that thing, I screamed and quickened my pace, flying past. Who would have expected that when I screamed, the thing also started letting out short screams – *ahh, ahh*, in a voice that was much more miserable than my own.

After rushing forward a dozen steps, I froze and came to a stop. It was a human voice! Looking back, I saw a man dressed in local garb, standing there looking panicked and helpless.

'Who are you? How shameless can you be, hiding out here to scare a woman. Have you no integrity?' I wasn't afraid now, cursing at this guy in Spanish.

'I, I...'

'A thief? Come to rob graves in the middle of the night, have you?' I don't know where I got the courage, but I strode over to him to take a look. What a surprise! It was some kid, not even twenty years old, his face covered in sand and soot.

'I was praying at my mother's grave. I was not trying to scare you.'

'Still won't admit it.' I gave him a shove.

He was close to tears. 'Señorita, it is you who scared me. How unjust. You scared me. I…'

'Scared you? If only!' I found it absolutely ridiculous.

'I was deep in prayer when I heard someone singing in the wind. I listened more closely, and then it wasn't there any more. Then I saw the dogs howl and run away. When I put my head down to pray again, you appeared at the top of the hill with your long flowing hair. I was scared half to death and you came rushing at me, screaming…'

Now I was beside myself with laughter, staggering around, stepping above the dead people. Once the laughter subsided, I told this guy, 'Such a scaredy-cat, yet you come out to pray in the middle of the night. Go home now!'

He bowed to me and walked off.

I realised that I had one foot on his mother's left hand. Looking around, the moonlight was gone but I thought I saw something crawling over by the edge of the cemetery. I cried out quietly and told myself to run. I ran all the way home in one breath, bursting through the front door. I leaned my back against it, catching my breath, and looked at my watch. Somehow I had made the forty minute journey in just fifteen minutes.

Just as my friend had said, 'There are weird things aplenty in the desert. Take your time discovering it!' Tonight, I'd really had enough.

Originally published in Woman's World #3,
December 1974

A Desert Diner

It's really too bad my husband is a foreigner. To refer to one's own husband in this way undoubtedly seems a bit exclusive. But since every country has language and customs completely unlike the next, there are some areas in our conjugal life where it's impossible to see eye to eye. When I first agreed to marry José, I reminded him that we differed not only in nationality, but also in personality. Perhaps one day we might even argue to the point of physical confrontation. 'I know you can be moody,' he replied. 'But you've got a good heart. Fight as we may, let's get married anyway.' So we finally tied the knot seven years after we first met.

I'm not involved in the women's lib movement, but I wasn't willing to toss aside my independence and my carefree spirit. I made it extra clear that I would still do things my way after marriage. Otherwise we should scrap the whole idea. 'All I want is for you to do things your way,' José told me. 'If you lost your individuality and flair, I wouldn't see any point in marrying you!' Great to hear such things from the big man himself. I was very pleased.

As the wife of José, I oblige him in terms of language. My poor foreigner, he still can't tell the difference between the Chinese characters for 'person' and 'enter' no matter how many times I teach him. I let him off lightly and speak his language instead. (But once we have children, they'll learn Chinese if it kills them. He's all in favour of this idea, too.)

Let's be real: the housewife's top priority is the kitchen. I've always loathed chores, but cooking is something I take great pleasure in. Give me some spring onions and a few slices of meat and I can whip up a dish in a flash. I quite relish this form of artistry.

My mother in Taiwan was devastated when she found out that I was moving to the barrens of Africa because of José's work. José is the breadwinner in our household so I had to follow my meal ticket. No room for argument there.

Our kitchen was dominated by Western food in those early days of marriage. But then assistance came to our household via airmail. I received vermicelli noodles, seaweed, shiitake mushrooms, instant noodles, dried pork and other valuable foodstuffs in bulk. I was so overjoyed I couldn't keep my hands off it all. Add to that list a jug of soy sauce sent by a girlfriend in Europe, and the Chinese restaurant in our household was just about ready for business. A pity there was only one non-paying customer to be had. (Eventually we had friends queuing up out of the door to come and eat!)

Actually, what my mother sent me really wasn't enough to run a Chinese restaurant, but luckily José has never been to Taiwan. He saw that I had the cockiness of a master chef and began to have confidence in me.

The first dish was chicken soup with vermicelli. Whenever he gets home from work, José always yells, 'Hurry up with dinner, I'm starving!' All those years of being loved by him counted for naught. He clamours for food without even giving me a second glance. At least I won't have to worry about my looks going. Anyway, back to that chicken soup and vermicelli. He took a sip and asked, 'Hey, what's this? Thin Chinese noodles?'

'Would your mother-in-law send thin noodles from such incredible distances? No way.'

'Well, what is it, then? I want some more. It's delicious.'

I picked up a noodle with my chopsticks. 'This? It's called "rain".'

'Rain?' He was dumbfounded.

Like I said, I do as I please in marriage and say whatever comes to mind. 'This is from the first rainfall of the spring. After mountain rain freezes over, the natives tie it up and sell it by the bundle to buy rice wine. It's not easy to come by!'

José still had a blank expression on his face. He scrutinised me, then the 'rain' in his bowl, and said, 'You think I'm an idiot?'

I brushed his question aside. 'You still want some more?'

'I still do, you charlatan,' he answered. Afterwards he would often eat this 'spring rain' and to this day he still doesn't know what it's made from. Sometimes I feel sad that José can be so stupid.

The second time we had 'ants climbing a tree', or vermicelli with ground meat. I fried the noodles in a saucepan, then sprinkled shredded meat and juice on top. José is always hungry when he comes home from work. He chomped right into the noodles. 'What's this? It looks like white yarn or plastic.'

'It's neither,' I replied. 'It's nylon like the fishing line you use, processed white and soft by Chinese people.'

He had another mouthful and gave me a small smile. Still chewing, he said, 'So many weird things. If we really opened a restaurant, we could sell this one at a good price, sheesh.' That day he ate his fill of upgraded nylon.

The third time we had vermicelli was in a Northeastern style pancake, the noodles minced very fine along with spinach and meat. 'You put shark fin in this pancake, right?' he said. 'I heard this thing is pretty expensive. No wonder you only put in a little.' I laughed myself to the floor. 'Tell your mum not to buy any more of this expensive shark fin for us. I want to write to her to say thanks.'

I was deeply amused. 'Go and write to her now. I'll translate! Ha!'

One day, just before José got home from work, I remembered that I still had some dried pork he didn't know about. I pulled it out of hiding and cut it into little squares with scissors. Then I put the pieces in a jar and bundled it up in a blanket. It just so happened that he was a little congested that day and wanted to bring out an extra blanket for bed. I was sitting nearby reading *Water Margin* for the umpteenth time, having forgotten about my treasure for the moment. He lay in bed with the jar in his hands, peering at it left and right. I looked up and, oh, what a disaster! He had discovered King Solomon's treasure. I snatched it from him. 'This isn't for you to eat!' I yelled. 'It's medicine... Chinese medicine.'

'My nose is all stuffed up, so this Chinese medicine will be perfect.' He had already put a handful into his mouth. I was furious. I couldn't very well demand that he spit it out, so I kept silent. 'It's pretty sweet. What is it?'

'Lozenges,' I snapped. 'To soothe a cough.'

'Lozenges made from meat? You think I'm an idiot?'

The next day, I discovered that he had taken more than half the jar's contents to share with his co-workers. From that day onwards, his co-workers, even the Muslim ones, would always pretend to cough when they saw me, hoping to extort some pork jerky. (I didn't give any to our Muslim friends; that would be immoral.)

At any rate, married life is all about eating. The rest of the time is spent making money in order to eat. There really isn't much more to it. One day I made rice balls, or sushi, you could say, with rice and pork floss wrapped in seaweed. This time José refused to eat it. 'What? You're actually giving me carbon paper to eat?'

'You really won't eat it?' I asked him gently.

'No, no way.'

Excellent. I was more than happy to eat a pile myself.

'Open your mouth and let me see!' he demanded.

'See, there's no colour stain. I used the opposite side of the roll of carbon paper. It won't dye your mouth.' I was used to bluffing every day, so I could easily come up with this kind of nonsense.

'You're full of hot air, you trickster. I hate you. Tell me the truth, what is it?'

'You have no clue about China,' I replied, eating another roll. 'I'm so disappointed in my husband.'

He grew annoyed and snatched up a roll with his chopsticks. Adopting the expression of a tragic hero embarking upon a path of no return, he chewed and chewed and swallowed. 'Yep, it's seaweed.'

I jumped up and exclaimed, 'Yes, you got it! You're so smart!' I was about to jump again when I received a knock on the head from him.

When we had eaten most of the Chinese goods, I grew reluctant to serve from my Chinese restaurant. Western dishes came back to the table. José was really surprised but happy to see me making steak when he came home from work. 'Make mine medium rare. And are you frying potatoes too?'

After we had steak three days in a row, he seemed to have lost his appetite. He would stop eating after just one bite.

'Are you too tired from work? Do you want to take a quick nap and eat later?' Even this old lady could still play tender.

'I'm not ill. I just think we're not eating well.'

Upon hearing this, I leapt up with a roar. 'Not eating well? Not eating well? Do you know how much this steak costs per kilo?'

'It's not that, mi mujer. I want to have some of that "rain". The food your mum sent us tastes better.'

'Alright then, our Chinese restaurant will operate twice a week. How about it? How often do you want it to rain?'

One day, José came home and said to me, 'Wow, so the big boss called me in today.'

'A raise?' My eyes lit up.

'No—'

'No?' I grabbed him, sinking my nails into his flesh. 'Did you get fired? Oh, we're doomed! Oh my God, we—'

'Let go of me, you psycho. Let me finish. The big boss said that everyone at the company has been over to eat at our house except for him and his wife. He's waiting for you to invite him over for Chinese—'

'The big boss wants me to cook for him? I won't do it! Don't invite him. I'll happily do it for any of your colleagues, but it's unethical to invite your superior. I'm a person of integrity, you know, I...' I wanted to go on about the moral character of the Chinese people, but I couldn't explain it clearly. Then

I saw the expression on José's face and realised I would have to choke down my morality.

The next day, he asked me, 'Hey, do we have any bamboo shoots?'

'Plenty of chopsticks in the house, all made out of bamboo.'

He gave me a dirty look. 'The big boss wants bamboo shoots with shiitake mushrooms.'

Amazing, this boss must truly be well travelled. Can't underestimate these foreigners. 'Alright, invite the two of them over for dinner tomorrow night. I'll come up with some bamboo shoots, no problem.' José looked over at me with great affection. It was the first time since we got married that he had gazed at me so amorously. What flattery. Too bad my hair was a tangled mess and I looked like death that day.

The following night, I prepared three dishes ahead of time and kept them warm at a simmer. I set up the dinner table with a red cloth diagonally overlaying a white cloth and a candle holder on top. It was a lovely arrangement. Everyone enjoyed themselves thoroughly at the meal. Not only were the dishes perfect in presentation, aroma and taste, I had also cleaned myself up nicely and went so far as to put on a long skirt. When the boss and his wife were getting ready to leave, they told me, 'If we ever have an opening in public relations, we hope you can fill in and be a part of the company.' My eyes gleamed with joy. All this thanks to bamboo shoots with shiitake mushrooms.

It was already late after we sent them off. I immediately took off the long skirt in favour of a pair of ripped jeans. Tying my hair up with some bands, I began furiously washing bowls and plates. I felt so much more at ease, both physically and spiritually, back in my Cinderella get-up. José was very satisfied. 'Hey, the bamboo shoots and mushrooms were really tasty,' he said from behind me. 'Where'd you get the bamboo?'

'What bamboo?' I asked, while doing the dishes.

'The bamboo shoots from tonight's dinner!'

I broke out into laughter. 'Oh, you mean the cucumber stir-fried with mushroom?'

'What? You… You can fool me all you want, but you dare pull that on the boss—'

'I didn't fool him. It was the most delicious meal of bamboo shoots with shiitake mushrooms he's had in his life. He said so himself.'

José scooped me up in his arms, getting soapy water all over his head and beard. 'You're the greatest!' he said. 'You're like that monkey, the one with seventy-two transformations. What was his name? What…?'

I patted his head. 'The Great Sage, Equal of Heaven, Sun Wukong! Don't go forgetting his name this time.'

The Marriage Chronicles

I.

One morning last winter, José and I were sitting in a park in Madrid. It was incredibly cold that day. I was completely bundled up in an overcoat, covering everything below my eyes except for a hand that was tossing bread crumbs to the sparrows. José wore an old heavy jacket and was reading a book on sailing.

'Sanmao, any big plans for next year?' he asked.

'Nothing special. After Easter, I'd like to go to Africa.'

'Morocco? Haven't you been there before?' he said.

'I've been to Algeria. Next year I want to go to the Sahara Desert.'

José had one great virtue. No matter what Sanmao did, even if others considered it crazy, he would see it simply as par for the course. This was yet another reason I was very happy to be with him.

'What about you?' I asked him.

'This summer I'm going sailing. It was tough having to study and then do military service. I'm moving on to a new chapter.' He raised his hands and clasped them behind his neck.

'And the boat?' I knew that he'd wanted a small boat for quite a while.

'Jesús's father is lending us a yacht. Next year we're going to the Aegean Sea to go diving.'

I believed José. He always did everything he said he would.

'How long are you planning to stay in the Sahara? What will you do there?'

'Well, I was thinking at least six months, maybe a year. I want to get to know the desert.' I'd harboured this fantasy ever since I studied geography in childhood.

'Let's go sailing. The six of us, including you. Can you make it back by August?'

I pulled the overcoat down from my nose and looked at him excitedly. 'I don't know the first thing about boats. What kind of work would you have me do?'

'You can be the cook and the photographer. Besides that, you can handle my finances. Are you up for it?'

'Of course I want to, but I'm afraid I won't be back from the desert by August. What should we do? I want to do both.' How I wished I could have my cake and eat it, too.

José seemed a little upset. 'I've known you for so long,' he cried. 'And you're always running around! It took me forever to finish my military service, and now you want to go it alone again. When are we going to be together?'

José rarely had any complaints about me. I gave him a strange look, tossing bread crumbs into the distance. The sparrows had all been scared away by his thunderous voice.

'You're really set on going to the desert?' he asked me again.

I nodded emphatically. I was completely clear on what I wanted to do.

'Fine.' He spat this word out and then continued to read. José was usually very talkative, which I found annoying. But he would refuse to open his mouth whenever there was a real issue.

Who knew that by early February, José would have quietly landed a job (looking specifically in the Sahara Desert), packed his suitcases and ended up in Africa before me.

I wrote him a letter to say:

You really don't have to endure this harsh desert living for me. Besides, even after I come, I'll probably spend most of my time travelling around. We wouldn't be able to see each other regularly…

José replied:

I've thought it through. To keep you by my side, I'll have to marry you. Otherwise I'll never be able to rid myself of this suffering. Can we get married this summer?

Even though the letter was quite plain, I found myself reading it over and over again. Eventually I put the letter in my trouser pocket and went out on the streets for a long walk. I had made up my mind by the time I got home.

In mid-April, I gathered up my belongings, checked out of my Madrid apartment and arrived in the desert of the Spanish Sahara. At the time, José was living in company housing and I was in the small town of El Aaiún. There was a distance of almost a hundred kilometres between us but he came to see me every day.

'Great, now we're all set to marry.' He was radiant in his happiness.

'Not right away. Give me another three months to look around. We can get married when I return.' At the time I was looking for a Sahrawi guide to take me across the great expanse of desert to westernmost Africa.

'That's fine, but we need to go to the courthouse to find out about the paperwork. And also deal with getting you naturalised.' We had already agreed that I would have dual citizenship after marriage.

So together we went to the local courthouse to figure out how we could get married. The secretary was an old Spanish gentleman with a head of white hair. 'You want to get married?' he said. 'Ay, we haven't dealt with that yet. You know the Sahrawi here get married following their own customs. Let me peek through these legal manuals…

'Civil marriage, hmm,' he continued while browsing. 'Here it is. For this, we'll need a birth certificate, a single status certificate, proof of residence, an official court notice… The señorita's documents will need to come from the Republic of China government, which then have to go through the Chinese embassy in Portugal for translation and verification. After that, the documents get notarised by the Spanish consulate in Portugal, followed by the Spanish Ministry of Foreign Affairs, then forwarded here for review. Upon completion of the review, we post the notice for fifteen days before sending the bulletin to the courthouse of your previous domicile in Madrid…'

I've always harboured an intense distaste for filling out forms and dealing with bureaucracy. I was irritated just hearing what the secretary read out to us. I said to José quietly, 'See how much paperwork there is? So annoying. Do we really want to do this?'

'Yes. Keep quiet for now!' He was really quite antsy. He asked the guy, 'Could you tell us how long it'll be before we can get married?'

'Ah, ask yourselves that question! Once you get all your documents in order, then we can make the announcement. It takes one month for the announcement to go out in two places. Besides that, we have to mail things back and forth. I think three months should be about right.' The secretary slowly began gathering up the manuals.

José got all worked up listening to this. Wiping sweat from his brow, he ventured hesitantly, 'Can't you help us get this done faster? I think the sooner we're married, the better. We can't wait…'

In the midst of returning a book to its shelf, the secretary man shot a furtive glance at my waistline. I'm pretty intuitive about these things. I knew he had misunderstood what José meant, so I cut in, 'Señor Secretary, speed doesn't matter to me. He's the one with the problem.' I realised right after saying it that this might confuse things further, so I shut my mouth.

Grabbing hold of me with one hand, José said to the secretary, 'Thank you, thank you. We'll be on our way to take care of this. Goodbye for now.' After these words, he dragged me briskly down the three flights of stairs in the courthouse. I couldn't keep myself from cackling as we flew out the door and finally came to a stop outside the building.

'What's this "he's the one with the problem" business?' he cried angrily. 'As if I were pregnant.' I was laughing so hard I couldn't even answer him.

2.

Three months passed quickly. During this time, José was toiling away to earn money. He set about building furniture, all while moving his things to my house day by day. I, on the other hand, was running around the tents of the native nomads with my backpack and camera. I encountered various strange and colourful customs, took down notes, collected and arranged slides and became friends with many Sahrawi. I even began to learn some Arabic. Those were happy and rewarding days.

Of course, our most demanding work was applying for each and every document required for marriage. It was the bane of my existence. Even now, thinking back on it riles me up.

Since my place of residence wasn't marked, I rented a mailbox down at the post office. It took about an hour to walk into town and check my mail each day. Within three months, I got to know the majority of the town's residents, especially those at the post office and courthouse. We became friends since I was visiting them every day.

One sweltering, unbearably hot day, I was back at the courthouse. The secretary man said to me, 'Well, it looks like the paperwork in Madrid is all wrapped up. You can get married now.'

'Really?' I couldn't bring myself to believe that this grand struggle with bureaucracy was finally over.

'I've arranged a date for you,' said the secretary, all smiles.

'When?' I asked urgently.

'Six p.m. tomorrow.'

'Tomorrow? You said tomorrow?' I probably sounded in-credulous and not altogether happy.

The old secretary man seemed a bit cross at me for being ungrateful. 'Didn't José say he wanted to do this as fast as possible?'

'Yes, thank you… We'll come by tomorrow.' I drifted downstairs as if in a dream and sat on the stone steps outside the post office, staring off into the desert.

Then I noticed the driver for José's company rolling by in a Jeep. I ran up to stop him. 'Are you going to the office, Muhammad Saleh? Would you mind passing along a message to José? Please tell him that we're getting married tomorrow and he should come into town after work.'

Muhammad Saleh scratched at his head, perplexed. He asked, 'How come Señor José does not know he is getting married tomorrow?'

'He doesn't know,' I answered emphatically. 'And I didn't know either.'

Upon hearing this, the driver looked at me with an expression of fright and drove off swerving into the distance. It was then I realised that I'd misspoken again. He must have thought that I'd been dying to get married and lost my head.

José didn't wait until after work to come flying over. 'It's really tomorrow?' he asked in astonishment as soon as he arrived.

'Yes, it's true. Come on, let's go and send a telegram home.' I dragged him out the door again.

Apologies for giving you such short notice. We didn't know in advance that tomorrow would be our wedding day. Please forgive...

José's telegram was long enough to be a letter.
Me, I sent my telegram to my father and wrote:

Getting married tomorrow. Sanmao.

Just a few words. I knew that my parents would be so delighted and comforted when they received this news. They'd been suffering for many years because of this wanderer. I had really let them down.

'Hey, what are you wearing tomorrow?' José asked.

'Don't know. Something simple.' I was still considering my options.

'I forgot to ask for the day off,' José said, sounding vexed. 'I still have to work tomorrow.'

'Go ahead, our wedding isn't until six in the evening. If you leave an hour early, you should make it back in time.' I didn't see any problem with someone going to work on their wedding day.

'What should we do now that we've sent our telegrams?' He seemed to be in a kind of stupor that day.

'Let's go home and build furniture. The table needs to be nailed together, and I'm still missing half of my curtains.' I really couldn't get why José had to act so strange.

'Do we really have to work the night before we get married?' Apparently he wanted to start the celebrations early and goof off.

'Well, what do you want to do then?' I asked him.

'I want to take you to see a movie. Tomorrow you won't be my girlfriend anymore.'

So we went to the only cinema in the desert to see a brilliant film called *Zorba the Greek*. I guess it was our way of saying goodbye to the single life.

3.

The next day, I was taking a nap when José knocked on the door. I had worn myself out carrying a bucket of fresh water back home. It was already 5.30 in the afternoon. 'Get up!' he cried as he came in. 'I have something for you.' He was quite excited, holding a large box in his hands.

I leapt up and ran over in my bare feet to snatch the box from him. 'It must be flowers!' I said.

'How could flowers grow in the desert? Oh, please.' He seemed a little disappointed at my guess.

I tore feverishly at the wrapping paper and opened the box. Wow! Two eye sockets of a skull stared up at me. I pulled this surprise gift out with some effort and took a proper look. It was a camel skull, white bones neatly assembled, with a huge row of menacing teeth and two big black holes for eyes.

I was overjoyed. This was just the thing to capture my heart. I set it on the bookshelf, clucking and sighing in admiration. 'Ah, splendid, so splendid.' José was worthy of being called my soulmate. 'Where did you dig this up?' I asked.

'I went looking for it! Walked around the desert for ages. When I found this intact, I knew you'd love it.' He was quite proud of himself. It was genuinely the best wedding gift possible.

'Quick, go get changed,' he said, looking at his watch. 'We're almost out of time.'

I had lots of pretty clothes that I usually never wore. I took a look at José, who was wearing a dark blue shirt and had trimmed his beard. Alright then, blue it was. I found a light-blue dress made of hemp. Even though it wasn't new, there was something simple and elegant to it. A pair of sandals would suffice. I let my hair down and put on a wide brimmed straw hat. With no flowers to be had, I went to the kitchen to grab a bunch of coriander and pinned it to the hat. I didn't own a purse so I had nothing to hold. José looked me up and down. 'Lovely. Bucolic. You look beautiful in this kind of simple get-up.'

And so we locked the door and stepped out into the desert.

From where I lived, it took almost forty minutes to get into town. We didn't have a car and so had to walk the whole way. Beneath a vast and borderless sky, we were the only tiny figures crossing a wide expanse of yellow sand. A quiet desolation surrounded us. The desert was beautiful beyond words in that moment.

'You might be the first bride to walk to her wedding,' said José.

'I would have liked to ride a camel, whooping all the way into town. Can you imagine how majestic that would have been? Too bad, really.' I sighed.

Before we had even reached the courthouse, we heard people saying, 'They're here, they're here.' A stranger jumped in front of us and took a photo. I was startled. 'Did you hire a photographer?' I asked José.

'No, it's probably the courthouse's doing.' He suddenly became nervous.

When we got upstairs, we saw that everyone in the courthouse was dressed in suits and ties. Compared with them, José looked like he had just come along for the ride.

'Oh crap, José. Look how formal they are! This is crazy.' The thing I fear most in life is this kind of pompous ceremony. It looked like there was no escape this time.

'Bear with it,' José encouraged. 'We'll have tied the knot soon enough.'

The secretary man was dressed in a black suit and a silk bow tie. 'Come, come, this way.' He pulled me into the assembly hall without giving me time to wipe the sweat from my face. Looking around, I saw that this small room was filled with familiar faces. Everyone was grinning at José and me. God! How did they all find out?

The judge was very young, probably around our age. He wore a robe of black satin.

'Sit over here. Please, sit.' We were like puppets being manipulated. José's sweat was trickling down to his beard.

Once we had taken our seats, the secretary man began to speak, 'Under Spanish law, there are three points to which you must abide after marriage. I will read those now. Number one: after marriage, both parties must cohabit...'

When I heard this, I thought it was just pure rubbish! Absolutely ridiculous and uncalled for. I started to laugh to myself. I didn't pay a bit of attention to what he said after that. Eventually, I heard the judge call my name: 'Señorita Sanmao.'

'What?' I snapped to attention.

I heard a chuckle from the audience.

'Please stand.'

I rose slowly.

'Señor José, please stand as well.'

So long-winded. Why not just say, 'Would you both please stand?' This would also have cut down on our suffering.

I noticed then that the young judge's hands were trembling as he held a piece of paper. I nudged José to look. This was the first time the desert courthouse had performed a marriage. The judge was even more nervous than we were.

'Sanmao, do you wish to become José's wife?' the judge asked me.

I knew I was supposed to say, 'I do.' Instead I ended up replying, 'Yeah!'

The judge laughed. He asked the same question to José, who answered firmly, 'I do.'

Once both of us had spoken, the judge seemed like he didn't know what to do next. The three of us stood in silence. Finally, he blurted out, 'OK. You're married now. Congratulations!'

As soon as I realised this awkward ceremony was over, I livened up immediately and swept my hat off to use as a fan. Many people came up to shake hands with us. The secretary man was especially happy, almost as if he were one of our parents. Suddenly, someone cried out, 'Hey, what about your rings?'

I had the same thought. What about the rings? I turned to look for José, but he had already gone into the hallway. 'Hey, did you bring the rings?' I called.

José was very happy. 'Here,' he boomed. He took his ring out and slipped it onto his finger. Then he went to find the judge. 'Judge!' he called. 'My family register! I need my family register!' He had totally forgotten that I also needed a ring.

The wedding was over. There wasn't a single decent restaurant in the desert, but neither did we have the means to host a dinner. Everyone dispersed, leaving just the two of us unsure of what to do with ourselves.

'Why don't we stay overnight at the Hotel Nacional?' José proposed.

'I'd rather go home and cook. One night at that kind of hotel is a week's worth of groceries.' I wouldn't stand for wasting money.

So we traversed the desert once more on our way home.

There was a large cake in front of our door. When we got inside, we took the cake out of the box and a slip of paper fell out: *Congratulations on your marriage!* It was from a group of José's co-workers. I was really touched. We were truly blessed to be able to eat fresh cake in the desert. Even more precious were the two figurines in wedding garb on top of the cake. The bride in white silk even had eyes that could open and close. My inner child surfacing, I grabbed them and yelled, 'The dolls are mine!'

'No contest there!' said José. 'Would I even try to take them from you?'

He cut a slice of cake for me and finally slipped a ring onto my finger. It was only then that our wedding was officially over. And this was how I got married.

Apothecary

I don't really like to see a doctor when I'm ill. That doesn't mean it's rare for me to get sick. In fact, it's kind of the opposite. I'm too lazy to get checked up because I'm constantly dealing with minor afflictions. I've made it to middle age thanks to my prized possession, a big cardboard box of medicine that I take everywhere. Having relied on it for so long, I feel like I know a thing or two about curing minor ailments.

Last year during my travels across the great desert, I gave two aspirins to an old Sahrawi woman to relieve her headache. While I was still lodging in her tent over the following days, an endless stream of people came by, dragging their children or elderly along to ask for medicine. The only things I felt comfortable giving them were antiseptics, anti-inflammatory creams, painkillers and the like. But they proved incredibly effective for these nomadic people who were so removed from modern civilisation. Before I went back to the little town of El Aaiún, I'd left behind all the food and medicine I had on me for the impoverished Sahrawi in their tents.

I hadn't been in town that long when my African neighbour came looking for painkillers to cure a headache. I remembered there was a government hospital in town, so I wasn't planning to give her anything. I suggested she see a doctor instead. It turned out that the women of these lands all belonged to the same club as me, refusing to see doctors when they were ill. But their reasons were quite different from mine. Since the doctors were men, these women who'd spend the rest of their days beneath their veils would rather die than be examined by a male medic. Helpless in this situation, I grudgingly gave my female neighbour two painkillers.

From that point on, women from all around came looking for me to treat their ailments. Who knows how the word spread. Besides medicine, I would occasionally give them some Western clothes, which made them even happier. More and more people began seeking me out. My thinking was this: if they would rather die than see a doctor, I might as well lend a hand with non-fatal diseases. It would relieve their suffering and, at the same time, ease the loneliness of my life in the desert. Wasn't that killing two birds with one stone? I also realised that the majority of women and children to whom I gave medicine recovered right away. So I gradually grew more bold, even making house calls from time to time. José thought that I was healing the sick as if playing with dolls. He was often gripped by a cold sweat on my behalf. To him, I was just messing around; but he didn't know that behind this seeming carelessness was a great compassion.

Our neighbour Gueiga was ten years old and close to being married off. Half a month before her marriage, a red boil appeared on her inner thigh. At first it was the size of a coin, hard to the touch and without pus. Due to swelling, the skin at the surface was bulging and shiny. Her lymph nodes were also swollen and hard as seeds. When I saw her a day later, the boil on her thigh had grown to the size of a walnut. The girl was in such pain that she could only lie moaning on her ragged mat.

'No question about it, she has to see a doctor,' I told her mother.

'This region cannot be shown to a doctor,' her mother answered adamantly. 'She is getting married soon.'

I had no choice but to give her a topical cream, as well as a specific treatment for inflammation. Her condition hadn't improved after dragging on for three or four days. 'Can we take her to a doctor?' I asked again, this time to her father.

The reply was the same. 'Definitely no.'

Then I remembered the soybeans at home. There was no other option. Might as well let the Africans try some Chinese medicine. So I went home to grind the beans. José saw me in the kitchen and stuck his head in to ask if I was making food. 'It's Chinese medicine for Gueiga to put on her skin,' I replied.

He was dumbfounded for a moment. 'What does that have to do with beans?' he asked.

'It's an old trick I saw in a Chinese medicine manual.'

Upon hearing this, he looked very disapproving. 'These women won't see a doctor, but they'll still trust you. Don't bite off more than you can chew.'

I poured the soybean paste into a small bowl. 'I'm an African witch doctor,' I proclaimed as I headed out to Gueiga's house. That day I applied the soybean paste on Gueiga's red swelling and put a gauze on top. The boil had softened by the next day. I put on some fresh soybean paste, and by the following day there was yellow pus beginning to show beneath the skin. The next afternoon, large amounts of pus oozed out, along with a little bit of blood. I applied more medical ointment. She was completely fine within a short amount of time.

'She's cured,' I told José smugly when he came home from work.

'Was she cured by the soybeans?'

'Yes.'

'You Chinese are so mysterious,' he said, shaking his head uncomprehendingly.

A few days later, my neighbour Khadijatu came calling. She said to me, 'My cousin came in from the desert. She is staying in my home, near death. Will you come see?'

As soon as I heard that she was near death, I hesitated. 'What illness does she have?' I asked Khadi.

'I do not know. She is weak and dizzy. Her eyesight is slowly getting worse. She is very skinny, about to die.'

The way she described it was so vivid. I was already starting to feel intrigued when José heard our talking from inside the house. 'Sanmao, mind your own business,' he yelled, very agitated.

I had to lower my voice. 'I'll come in a little bit,' I said to Khadijatu. 'I can't leave until my husband goes to work.'

Once the door was shut, José began scolding me. 'And what if this woman actually dies and they blame you for it? If she won't see a doctor, then she deserves it!'

'They just aren't educated. It's quite sad...'

I knew José had a point, even though I was trying to talk convincingly. But my curiosity was strong, and I was gutsy. I wasn't willing to budge. José had to go to work. He barely had one foot out of the door when I slipped out behind him. I went to Khadi's house and saw a young girl, thin as a bundle of sticks, lying on the ground. Her eyes were deep black holes. I didn't feel any fever when I touched her. Her tongue, her fingernails and the whites of her eyes seemed to be a healthy colour. When I asked her where she didn't feel well, she couldn't speak clearly. Khadi had to translate from Arabic. 'Her vision is blurry. Her ears will not stop ringing. She does not have the strength to stand up.'

I had a sudden stroke of inspiration. 'Your cousin lives in a tent out in the desert?' I asked Khadi. She nodded. 'She doesn't eat very well?' I pressed.

Khadi said, 'She has almost nothing to eat!'

'Wait a minute,' I said. I ran back home and poured out fifteen maximum-strength multivitamins for her. 'Khadi, can you spare to slaughter a goat?' She nodded excitedly. 'First give your cousin these vitamins, three times a day. Besides that, prepare some goat stew for her.'

Within a week and a half, the cousin that Khadi had described as near death paid me an unexpected visit. She lingered for a good long while before returning home, seemingly in good spirits. José laughed when he came back and saw her. 'What's this? You saved someone from the brink of death? So what was the disease?'

'No disease,' I replied with a chuckle. 'Just extreme malnourishment!'

'How did you figure that one out?' José asked.

'I gave it some thought.' To my surprise, I realised that he now seemed quite proud of me.

We reside on the peripheries of the small town El Aaiún. Few Europeans live here, and José and I take great pleasure in getting to know the locals. The majority of the friends we have made here are Sahrawi. I don't have much to occupy my time, so I host a free women's school at home. I teach the local women how to read numbers and distinguish coins. The more advanced ones move on to arithmetic (along the lines of one plus one equals two). I have between seven and fifteen female students; they're always coming and going. You could say this school is pretty free and easy.

My students weren't very focused one day during class and ended up fumbling along my bookshelves. It just so happened that they discovered the book *El Nacimiento de Un Bebé*. This book was in Spanish and had many diagrams and drawings. There were also colour pictures depicting how women became pregnant all the way through to the baby's birth, with clear explanations for everything. My students were immediately fascinated, so I set aside the arithmetic and taught out of this book for two weeks. They would shriek and whoop looking at the pictures, as if they had absolutely no idea how a life was made. This was in spite of the fact that quite a few of my students had three or four children of their own.

'What a strange world,' José said. 'A teacher who's never given birth explaining to mothers where children come from.' He couldn't keep from smiling.

'Before they could only give birth, but now they know the ins and outs of it. I guess this kind of thing is easier to do than understand.' At least these women could gain some more common knowledge, even if this knowledge wouldn't make their lives easier or healthier.

One day my student Fatima asked, 'Sanmao, will you come when I give birth?'

I stared at her completely dumbstruck. Fatima was someone I saw nearly every day, yet I had no idea she was pregnant. 'You… How many months along are you?' I asked.

She couldn't count, so she didn't know how many months. I finally convinced her to take off the large piece of fabric that wrapped her head and body, revealing just the long dress beneath. 'Who helped you the last time you gave birth?' I knew that she had a three-year-old son already.

'My mother,' she answered.

'Why don't you ask your mother to do it again? I can't help you.'

She lowered her head. 'My mother cannot come now. She is dead.'

When I heard this, I shut my mouth. 'How about going to the hospital?' I tried. 'Don't be afraid.'

'No,' she refused immediately. 'The doctors are men.'

I looked at her stomach. She was probably around eight months pregnant. I spoke to her hesitantly. 'Fatima, I'm not a doctor. I've never even had a baby myself. I can't assist in this birth.'

She suddenly seemed close to tears. 'I beg you, it is so clear in your book. Please help me, I beg you—'

My heart was softening at her supplication. But even after some thought, I still couldn't agree to it. I steeled myself and told her, 'No, don't beg me like this. If anything happens, it'll be on my hands.'

'It will be fine. I am very healthy. I can give birth. I just need you to help a little...'

'Let's talk about it another time!' I said, skirting the issue.

A month passed. I had long since forgotten about this matter. Then one day at dusk, a little girl I didn't recognise came knocking on my door. When I opened the door, all she could say was, 'Fatima, Fatima.' She didn't know any Spanish.

I came out, locking the door behind me, and spoke to the girl. 'Go and tell her husband to come home. Do you understand?' She nodded and ran off.

I went to Fatima's house to take a look. She was in pain, sweating on the ground. Her son was crying by her side. There was a pool of sweat on the mat Fatima lay on. I scooped up the small boy and carried him off for a neighbour to look after. Then I dragged a middle-aged woman back with me to Fatima's home. The locals here are very uncooperative and have little compassion for each other. When the middle-aged woman saw Fatima in such a state, she started cursing me in Arabic. She turned around and left. (Only later did I find out that the locals considered witnessing childbirth to be unlucky.)

'Don't be scared,' I told Fatima helplessly. 'I'm going home to get something. I'll be right back.' I dashed home and ran immediately to the shelf to get that book. Opening it to the page on childbirth, I leafed through it in a hurry, thinking to myself, *Scissors, cotton, alcohol, what else? What else do I need?* Only then did I notice that José was already home. He was staring at me with a puzzled look on his face.

'Aiya, I'm kind of in a pinch,' I said quietly, trembling. 'I'm not so sure I can do this.'

'Do what? Do what?' José couldn't help but absorb my anxiety.

'Assist in a birth! Her waters have already broken.' I had the book in one hand and a large bundle of cotton in the other as I searched all over for a pair of scissors.

'You're insane. I won't let you.' José snatched the book from me. 'You've never given birth. You'll be the death of her!'

I felt more clear-headed than before and started putting up an unconvincing argument. 'I have this book. I've seen documentaries about childbirth—'

'I won't let you.' José came and forcefully grabbed hold of me.

With things in both hands, I could only jab him in the ribs with my elbow. Amid this struggle, I cried, 'You have no compassion, you cold-blooded animal! Let go of me!'

'No, I won't let you.' He held on to me stubbornly.

While we were jerking this way and that in our fight, Fatima's husband appeared in the window looking bewildered. José let go of me. 'I won't allow Sanmao to assist in this birth,' he said. 'She'll harm Fatima. I'm going to find a car now. Your wife will have her baby at the hospital.'

In the end, Fatima went to the government hospital and gave birth to a little boy without a hitch. The Spanish government waived the fee because they were locals. After her release, she was extremely proud of being the first woman in the region to give birth in a hospital. The matter of the male doctors was not brought up again.

One morning, I was up on the roof hanging clothes when I realised that there were two new baby goats in the little pen that our landlord had constructed up there. I was overjoyed. 'Come up here and see!' I called out to José. 'Two adorable little baby goats.'

He ran up to take a look. 'These kind of baby goats would be perfect for roasting,' he said.

I was shocked. 'What the devil are you talking about?' I asked him angrily. I shooed the goats over to their mother. Then I noticed there was a large, heart-shaped object still connected to the doe. I guess this was the placenta? It was so gross. Three days later, this viscera was still hanging from her body.

'Let's slaughter and eat her!' my landlord said.

'If you kill the mother, how will the babies survive?' I came up with this excuse quickly to save the goat.

'With her placenta hanging out like this, she will die anyway,' said my landlord.

'Let me see if I can help. Don't slaughter her yet.' These words rushed out of my mouth, though I had no idea how to care for a doe. I mulled it over at home until an idea came to me. I got a bottle of wine and went up to the roof. Then I grabbed the doe and forced the wine down her throat. As long as she didn't drink herself to death, I'd have half a chance at solving things. This was a technique that I'd once learned from a farmer and remembered all of a sudden.

The next day, the landlord said, 'She is saved. The dirty things in her stomach all came out and all is well. May I ask how you saved her? I truly give thanks to you.'

I laughed and said softly, 'I forced her to down big bottle of wine.'

'Thank you very much!' he said again.

As he walked off with a helpless look on his face, it hit me that Muslims couldn't drink alcohol and so, of course, neither could his goat.

This old witch doctor could work her magic on almost anyone. Only José was afraid of me. He usually never gave me a chance to treat him. But I wanted nothing more than for him to have confidence in me. One day his stomach hurt, so I gave him a pack of powder called Siron-U and told him to drink it with water.

'What is it?' he asked.

'Why don't you give it a try first?' I said. 'It's very effective on me.' I forced him to down a packet.

Afterwards, still not quite comfortable, he examined the medicine's plastic packaging. He couldn't understand the Chinese, but there was some English on it – *Vitamin U*. 'Is there such a thing as vitamin U?' he asked grumpily. 'How does it help stomach pain?' I didn't know either. I grabbed the package to take a look. It was as he said. I laughed hard. Sure enough, though, his stomach pain eventually subsided.

I actually really enjoyed being a veterinarian. But after the incident with Fatima giving birth, José was frightened out of his wits. So I didn't tell him about my foray into veterinary medicine. Gradually he got to thinking that I no longer had any interest in playing doctor.

Last week we had three days off. The temperature was perfect, so we decided to rent a Jeep to drive across the desert and go camping. Just as we were at the doorstep loading our water tank, tent and food into the car, a dark-skinned female neighbour came by. She didn't have her headscarf on and walked towards us confidently. Before I could even open my mouth, she said very brightly to José, 'Your wife is truly great. My tooth hasn't hurt ever since she helped me fix it.'

Hearing this, I hurriedly tried to change the subject. 'Hey, where are the sandwiches?' I started giggling to myself. 'Did we forget about them?'

José looked like he didn't know whether to laugh or cry. 'May I ask Your Excellency how long it's been since your career change to dentistry?'

I saw that it was no use pretending. I held my head up high, thought for a second, then told him, 'I started last month.'

'How many people's teeth have you worked on?' Now he was smiling too.

'Two women, one child. None of them wanted to go to the hospital. There was no helping it, so... Really, they were all fine after I fixed them up, able to bite into things again.' Everything I said was truthful.

'And what materials did you use to fix them up?'

'That, I can't tell you,' I said immediately.

'I won't go camping if you don't tell me.'

The rascal knew how to threaten me. Fine! I stepped back first and made sure to put enough distance between me and José. Then I said quietly, 'Won't come off, waterproof, very sticky, fragrantly scented, beautifully coloured. Can you guess what this nice thing is?'

'What?' he asked immediately, totally not using his brain.

'Nail! Polish!' I cried.

'Whaa— Nail polish for fixing people's teeth!' He was so shocked that his hair stood on end like a cartoon character. It was so cute. Seeing this, I laughed and ran to my safety zone. By the time he had snapped out of it and came chasing after me, this witch doctor had already fled the scene.

Child Bride

I first met Gueiga around this time last year. The eldest daughter of Hamdi, a police officer, she and her family live in a large house close to my own modest home. Back then Gueiga had a thick braid and wore long African print dresses. She walked barefoot and didn't wear a veil, nor did she cover up her body in fabric. She was often shouting after her goats outside my home, her voice crisp and lively. She was just a happy little girl.

Eventually she came to study with me. When I asked her how old she was, she said, 'You must ask Hamdi that. We Sahrawi women do not know how old we are.' She and her siblings didn't call Hamdi 'Father', they addressed him directly by name.

Hamdi told me that Gueiga was ten years old. 'You are probably around ten years old, too, right?' he asked me in turn. 'Gueiga gets along with you so well.' I didn't know how to answer this ridiculous question, so I just smiled awkwardly at him.

Half a year passed and I became close friends with Hamdi and his entire family. We had tea together almost every day.

One day I was drinking tea with just Hamdi and his wife, Tebrak. He suddenly spoke up. 'Our daughter will get married soon. Please inform her when you have a chance.'

I choked down some tea. 'You mean Gueiga?' I asked with great difficulty.

'Yes,' he said. 'The marriage will be ten days after Ramadan.' Ramadan, Islam's month of fasting, was soon to begin.

We drank another cup of tea in silence. In the end, I couldn't help but ask Hamdi, 'Don't you think Gueiga is too young? She's only ten years old.'

Hamdi strongly disagreed. 'Young? My wife was only eight when I married her.'

These were Sahrawi customs, I realised. I couldn't critique this matter from such a subjective point of view, so I shut my mouth.

'Please tell Gueiga for us,' implored Gueiga's mother once more. 'She still does not know.'

'Why don't you tell her yourselves?' I asked them out of curiosity.

'How can we speak of this so directly?' Hamdi replied with an air of righteousness. They really could be so antiquated sometimes, I thought.

After maths the next day, I asked Gueiga to stay behind to brew some tea over a charcoal fire. 'Gueiga, it's your turn now,' I said, handing her tea.

'What?' She seemed confused.

'Silly girl, you're going to get married,' I said bluntly.

She was clearly taken aback. Her face quickly became red. 'When?' she whispered.

'Ten days after Ramadan,' I said. 'Do you know who it might be?'

Shaking her head, she set her teacup down and left without a word. It was the first time I'd seen such worry on her face.

Some days later, I was buying groceries in town when I ran into Gueiga's older brother and another youth. 'Abeidy is a policeman in Hamdi's squad,' he said by way of introduction. 'He is my good friend, and also Gueiga's future husband.' When I heard he was Gueiga's fiancé, I purposely gave him a good look. Abeidy was tall and handsome, with a light complexion. The gentleness in his eyes and his polite manner of speaking made a very good first impression.

I went to find Gueiga once I got home. 'Relax!' I said to her. 'Your fiancé is Abeidy. He's young and handsome, not at all a rough fellow. Hamdi didn't pick just anyone for you.'

Hearing this, Gueiga shyly lowered her head. Though she was silent, I could see in her eyes that she had already accepted the reality of her marriage. It was Sahrawi tradition that parents would receive a huge bride price for their daughters who were married off. In the past, when there was no currency in the desert, the bride's family would demand a betrothal gift that included flocks of goats, camels, cloth, slaves, flour, sugar, tea leaves and so on. Now that they were a bit more civilised, they used banknotes to replace these items but kept a similar list of demands.

The day Gueiga's bride price arrived, José was invited to tea. I had to stay at home since I was a woman. Less than an hour into it, José came back and announced, 'That Abeidy gave Hamdi two hundred thousand pesetas! I never imagined Gueiga would be worth so much.'

'This is practically human trafficking!' I said disapprovingly. But somehow I was slightly jealous of Gueiga. I hadn't earned a single goat for my parents when I got married.

Gueiga's appearance changed within the month. Hamdi bought several large pieces of fabric for her, all in plain black and blue. The colours would bleed onto her skin because the material was dyed very poorly. When Gueiga wrapped herself in the dark cloth, her entire body would become blue. There was a whole different aura about her. Even though she still walked barefoot, she now wore anklets of silver and gold. She began coiling her hair up. The spices applied to her body gave off a pungent scent, intermingling with her strange odour from years of not bathing. All of this made her seem like a true Sahrawi woman.

On the last day of Ramadan, Hamdi performed the ritual of circumcision on his two small boys. Naturally, I was inclined to go and check it out. By then Gueiga was rarely seen out of the house. I went to her room and saw her there with just a soiled and tattered mat. The only new things were her clothes.

'What are you taking with you after you get married?' I asked her. 'No new stoves or pans?'

'I'm not going anywhere,' she said. 'Hamdi is keeping me here.'

Surprised, I asked, 'What about your husband?'

'He's moving here, too,' she said.

I was really envious. 'How long are you staying before moving out?' I asked.

'Traditionally, we can stay for six full years before we have to leave.'

No wonder Hamdi had demanded so much money for a betrothal gift. Turns out the son-in-law was to live with his bride's family after marriage.

The day before her marriage, as tradition dictated, Gueiga was supposed to leave home until the groom brought her back. I gave her a fake jade bracelet as a present, something she'd had her eyes on for a while. Gueiga's aunt, a very old Sahrawi woman, came by in the afternoon before she left home. Gueiga sat while her aunt began dressing her up. She let Gueiga's hair down and arranged it in over thirty small braids. Then she adorned the top of Gueiga's head with a small heap of fake hair, just like the imperial maids of ancient China. Every braid had a colourful bead woven into it. The top of her head also shimmered with fake jewels. No make-up was applied to the face.

Once her hair was well brushed, Gueiga's mother brought over some new clothes. Gueiga got into a pleated white dress, then wrapped her upper body in black fabric. Her already plump figure seemed even puffier now. 'So plump!' I sighed.

'Plump is pretty,' her aunt said. 'Plump is good.'

After she was all dressed, Gueiga sat serenely on the ground. Her face was really quite beautiful. Her head full of jewellery added radiance to this dim and gloomy chamber.

'Alright, let's go!' Gueiga's aunt and older cousin led her out the door. She was to stay with her aunt for the evening and return home tomorrow. A thought suddenly struck me: Gueiga hadn't bathed. Was there no need for such a thing even right before marriage?

On the day of the wedding, there were changes in Hamdi's home. The dirty straw mats had disappeared. The goats had been chased away. A freshly slaughtered camel hung by the doorstep. Red Arabian rugs were spread all over the main hall. The most curious thing was the goatskin drum set in a corner. It looked like it had to have been at least a hundred years old.

Dusk arrived. The sun was just dipping below the horizon. The vast desert was stained in blood red. Then the drumming began, a mournful and monotonous sound that travelled far into the distance. If I hadn't known it was a wedding, these mysterious rhythms might have been a bit frightening. I was walking to Hamdi's house in a sweater, imagining myself to be in one of those beautiful tales from *One Thousand and One Nights*.

The atmosphere took a downward turn as soon as I got indoors. There was a big group of Sahrawi men in the main room. Everyone was smoking. The air was absolutely unbreathable. Abeidy was also squeezed in among the crowd. I wouldn't have guessed that he was the groom if I hadn't met him before tonight. In the corner sat a woman who was dark as charcoal. She was the only woman who sat in the midst of this group of men. She wore a large black cape and threw her uncovered head back while banging ferociously on the drum. After a few dozen strikes, she stood up, shook her body and gave a high-pitched roar. This was a primal scream, recalling the war cries of the Native Americans. She was certainly the most distinctive person in the house.

'Who is that?' I asked Gueiga's brother.

'She is a slave on loan from my grandmother's house. She is famous for her drumming.'

'What a remarkable slave.' I clicked my tongue in praise.

Three older women came into the house. They began to sing along with the drum, a melody that sounded like crying, with no ups or downs. The men started to clap to this song. Because I was a woman, I had to watch everything from outside the window. The other young women were all crowded out there, faces completely hidden except for their large, beautiful eyes. After close to two hours, the sky had darkened but the drumbeat continued, as did the clapping and the song.

'How much longer will this go on?' I asked Gueiga's mother. 'It is early!' she said. 'You go home and sleep.'

Before I went back, I exhorted Gueiga's little sister to come and wake me in the morning when they were going to pick up the bride.

The desert had me shivering from cold when I was getting ready to return at three in the morning. Gueiga's brother and José were chatting and playing with José's camera. Gueiga's brother objected when I stepped out in my overcoat. 'She also wants to come?' I had to plead with him to take me. He acquiesced eventually. Women have no standing in these parts.

The street we live on was filled with Jeeps, both new and old. From the looks of it, Hamdi was a man of some prestige among his people. José and I got into one of the bridal Jeeps. Horns sounded incessantly from this row of vehicles as they drove in circles in the sand. With primal cries, the men sped off to the home of Gueiga's aunt.

Apparently the custom of old was to fire rifles into the air on camelback before retrieving the bride from her tent. Nowadays, the camels have been replaced by Jeeps. Car horns take the place of rifles. But the clamour and cacophony remain the same. What happened next angered me the most. Abeidy descended from the vehicle and, surrounded by a gaggle of youths, went to the room where Gueiga sat. Without greeting anyone, he grabbed Gueiga by the shoulders and forcibly dragged her out of the house. Everyone was laughing. Only Gueiga was struggling with her head lowered. Because she was plump, Abeidy's friends had to help him drag her. She started crying then. I couldn't tell if it was real or if she was faking it, but I was incredibly agitated seeing these people grab at her so boorishly. Despite my indignation, I bit my lower lip and watched to see how this farce would unfold.

By this time, Gueiga was already out the door. She suddenly reached a hand out to swipe at Abeidy's face. Several trails of blood appeared on his face from her scratching. Showing no sign of weakness, Abeidy twisted Gueiga's fingers and bent them backward. Everyone had quietened down. Only Gueiga's occasional cries resounded in the night.

As they fought, Gueiga was being dragged closer to the Jeep. I became extremely anxious. 'Silly girl,' I called out. 'Get in the car. You can't beat him.'

Gueiga's brother laughed. 'Don't worry, this is custom. If they marry without a struggle, people will laugh at them later. She is being a good girl by putting up this desperate fight.'

I sighed. 'If it has to be such a desperate fight, one might as well not get married.'

'She will cry more once she enters the bridal chamber later. Wait and see. It is very interesting.'

Interesting though it may have been, I didn't like this way of conducting a marriage.

By the time we returned to Gueiga's home, it was past five in the morning. Hamdi had already slipped away, but Gueiga's mother and younger siblings, as well as friends and relatives, all hadn't slept. We were invited to the main room to gather with Abeidy and his close friends. Tea and camel meat were served. Gueiga was sent to another little room to sit by herself.

After some snacking, the drumming began again. The male guests began to clap and moan. I was exhausted from lack of sleep, but I couldn't bear to leave now.

'Sanmao, go home and rest,' José said to me. 'I'll tell you what happens when I come back.' I thought about it for a second. The highlight hadn't yet come, so I decided against it.

The singing and clapping continued until nearly daybreak before I saw Abeidy stand up. The drumming stopped as soon as he rose. Everyone looked at him. His friends began to tease him.

When Abeidy entered Gueiga's room, I became very nervous. My heart was uneasy. I thought back to what Gueiga's brother had said to me: *She will cry more once she enters the bridal chamber later.* I felt that everyone waiting outside, myself included, was depraved. Strange that there are some things people won't change, with tradition as an excuse.

After Abeidy had pushed aside the curtain and entered, I sat in the main room, my head hung low, for a long time. It felt like centuries had passed when we finally heard Gueiga. 'Ah—' It sounded like a sob. Then there was silence.

I knew custom demanded that she cry out, but her cry was so pained, so real, so helpless and long. As I sat in silence, the rims of my eyes became moist. 'Think about it. She's just a ten-year-old child,' I said angrily to José. 'So cruel!' He looked up at the ceiling and said nothing. We were the only non-natives around that day.

Abeidy came out with a bloodstained piece of white cloth later. His friends started shouting with lewd excitement. From their perspective, the whole point of the first night of marriage was to openly use force and violence to take a little girl's virginity. That the ceremony had to conclude in such a way was deplorable and ridiculous. I got up and strode out without saying goodbye to anyone.

The marriage celebrations lasted a total of six days. During this time, guests would arrive at Hamdi's house to eat and drink tea every day at five in the afternoon. They would also sing songs and beat drums until late.

I decided not to go any more since their activities were the same each day. Hamdi's other daughter came to find me on the fifth day. 'Gueiga is looking for you,' she said. 'Why haven't you been coming?'

I had to oblige. I changed my clothes and went to visit Gueiga. During these six days of celebration, Gueiga had been isolated in her little room as usual. Without exception, the guests were not allowed to see her. Only the groom could come and go as he pleased. Since I was an outsider, I cast caution to the wind and went straight to Gueiga's room, pulling aside the curtain.

The room was murky, the air thick. Gueiga sat on a pile of rugs in the corner. She was very happy to see me and scrambled up to kiss my cheeks. 'Sanmao, don't leave,' she said.

'I won't. Let me get something for you to eat.'

I went out, grabbed a large piece of meat and handed it to her to gnaw on.

'Sanmao,' she began softly. 'Do you think I will have a baby soon?'

I didn't know how to answer. Her face, which used to be plump, had become so thin in five days that her eyes were sunken in. I felt a pang of sadness and anger as I stared at her.

'Can you give me medicine?' she asked in a low, urgent voice. 'Medicine so I won't have a baby?'

I still couldn't manage to shift my gaze from her ten-year-old face.

'OK, I'll give it to you. Don't worry. This will be our secret.' I patted her lightly on the hand. 'You can sleep now. The wedding is over.'

Night in the Wasteland

One day when José got home from work, he didn't come barging indoors like he normally did. Instead he stayed in the car, honking his horn to sound like *Sanmao, Sanmao*, so I set aside the calligraphy I was doing just for fun and pranced over to the window to see what was going on.

'Why aren't you coming in?' I asked him.

'I found out about a place that's got little fossilised turtles and shells. Want to go?'

I jumped with excitement and blurted out, 'Yes, let's!'

'Come on then!' José cried.

'Let me get changed,' I called out the window as I went to get ready. 'I'll also grab some snacks and a blanket.'

'Hurry up, will you! There's no need to bring anything. We'll be back in two or three hours.'

I'm an impatient person to begin with, and since José was pestering, I decided to drop everything and just go. I wore flip-flops and a long cloth dress that draped all the way down to my feet. On my way out, I grabbed the leather flask hanging from the door; it had a litre of red wine inside. This was the extent of my preparation.

'Alright, let's go!' I bounced up and down in the car seat, full of good cheer.

'There and back is about two hundred and forty kilometres,' José was saying to himself. 'Three hours driving, one hour gathering fossils and we should be home by ten, just in time for dinner.'

When I heard that it was such a distance, I couldn't help but look at the westerly sun. I thought about objecting. But ever since José got a car, his latent automobile infatuation complex has taken off big time. Furthermore, he has type O blood, meaning he doesn't change his mind easily. So even though I didn't feel it was quite right for us to be travelling this far around sunset, I didn't utter a word of protest.

We drove on the highway towards the southern edge of town for more than twenty kilometres. Then, upon reaching the checkpoint, there was no more road. We were about to enter the boundless desert.

The guard came and looked us over from the window. 'Ah, you guys again,' he said. 'You're going out at this hour?'

'Not very far,' José replied. 'Just about thirty kilometres out and back. She wants a cactus.' We sped off as soon as he said this.

'Why did you have to lie to him?' I reproached.

'Because he wouldn't have let us leave otherwise. Think about it. Would he let us drive so far at this time of day?'

'And what if something happens, God forbid?' I asked. 'The distance and direction you told him were all wrong. How would they find us?'

'They wouldn't come looking. How else did those hippies die?' He brought up another discomforting subject; we'd both heard about the recent tragic deaths of some hippies out in the desert.

It was almost six. Even though the sun was low in the sky, it was still piercingly bright all around. The wind was already howling up a bit of a chill in the air. Our car drove quickly over the sand, following the trail of tyre prints from someone before us. The smooth plane of desert, all sand and gravel, stretched out farther than the eye could see. A mirage appeared in front of us on the left, then two more on the right. They looked like lakes surrounded by little bushes.

All was silent except for the sound of wind. The deathly still landscape was like a grim and ferocious giant lying on its side. We were driving along its quietly outspread body.

'I feel like one day we'll end up dying in this wilderness,' I said with a sigh, looking out the window.

'Why's that?'

The car rattled as we flew onwards.

'We intrude upon the wilderness day in, day out, taking its fossils, digging up its plants, capturing its antelopes. We leave behind soda bottles, cardboard boxes and dirty things, all while we crush its body with our car tyres. The desert says it's not happy. It wants our lives as payback. Like this – *ooh, ooooh…*' I put my hands out as though throttling someone.

José roared with laughter. He loved it when I talked nonsense.

I decided to roll up the windows all the way because the temperature had already dropped quite a bit.

'The mountain maze is coming up,' said José.

I looked up at the far-off horizon. In the distance there were some little black points that gradually grew larger. It was the only mountain range within a few hundred kilometres. In actuality, it was a cluster of very tall piles of sand, spread out over twenty or thirty square kilometres of barren land.

These piles of sand were shaped by the wind, all curved and identical on the exterior. They were like a bunch of half-moons snatched from the heavens by an excavator and set in the Sahara. Even more curious was that these sand piles, each of them about a hundred metres high, seemed equidistant from one another. If one were to wander into this mountain range, it would be all too easy to lose your sense of direction and get lost. I'd named it the mountain maze. It was drawing closer and closer, until finally the first sand pile rose before us.

'We're going in there?' I asked softly.

'Yep, another fifteen kilometres to the right of here is where I hear there are fossils.'

'It's almost seven-thirty. The ghosts are about to come a-knocking.' I bit my lip, not knowing why I felt there was something off.

'What ghosts?' José refused to believe me. 'It's all super-stition.'

Not only was this guy bold and brash, he was also stubborn as a mule. So we finally drove into the mountain maze, weaving through those piles of sand. The sun was directly behind us; we were driving to the east.

The mountain maze didn't capture us this time. We were out in less than half an hour. Up ahead there were no more tyre prints at all. This area was unfamiliar to us. On top of that, we were driving in a regular car totally unsuited to the desert. Needless to say, I felt a bit spooked. José got out of the car to look around.

'Let's go back!' I had totally lost my spirit for fossil hunting.

'No.' José paid no heed to me. We started up the car with a shudder and went deeper into this foreign territory. After another few kilometres, a lowland appeared before us, its colour a dark coffee brown. A layer of light greyish lavender fog hung above it. Some tens of millions of years ago, this must have been a wide river.

'We can get out here,' José said. We glided gently downwards on a slope. José parked the car and got out to look around again. I also got out. Grabbing a handful of the ground beneath my feet, I saw that it was wet mud rather than sand. I stood there, perplexed.

'Sanmao, you drive and I'll run ahead. Stop when I give the signal.'

José sprinted ahead as soon as he said this. I turned the engine on and trailed him, maintaining a short distance.

'You alright?' he asked.

I stuck my head out the window to reply, 'No problem.'

He got farther and farther from me, then turned around and waved his two arms, telling me to drive on as he ran backwards. Suddenly I noticed that the ground behind José was bubbling. Something wasn't quite right. I slammed the brakes and yelled, 'Careful, careful! Stop...'

I opened the car door and ran towards him yelling. But José had already stepped into the quagmire. The wet mud was up to his knees in an instant. He was obviously startled. Looking back, he staggered a few more steps. Quickly the mud rose up to his thighs. He struggled a bit more, looking like he was going to fall over. I don't know how but he got farther and farther away from me the more he fought against it. There was now quite a distance between the two of us.

I stood with my mouth open, unable to speak, frozen in shock. I couldn't believe this was real, but the image before me was undeniably true! All of this had happened within the span of seconds. José could see that the quagmire was swallowing him up and desperately tried lifting his legs up. Just then I noticed that there was a protruding rock maybe two metres to his right. 'Go over there!' I cried urgently. 'There's a rock there.'

He also saw the rock and struggled to move towards it. The mud was up to his waist now. I watched helplessly from a distance. I was so anxious that my nerves felt as though they were about to fry. It was like being in a horrible nightmare.

When I saw him clutch on to that rock in the quagmire, it jolted me into action. I ran back to the car to look for something with which to reel him in. But there was nothing in there besides the flask of wine, two empty bottles and some copies of *United Daily News*. There was a toolbox inside the boot. Nothing else.

I went back to the edge of the quagmire to find José. He didn't utter a sound, looking at me in stupefaction. I scrambled wildly around the area, hoping to find a piece of rope on the ground, a few planks of wood, anything. But there was nothing in the vicinity except for sand and rocks. José was hugging the rock. His lower half was submerged in mud, but he wasn't sinking any further for now.

'José, I can't find anything to pull you out with,' I called to him. 'Hang in there.' There were about fifteen metres between us.

'Don't worry,' he said to comfort me. 'Don't worry.' Something in his voice had changed though.

All around there was nothing but the sound of wind, specks of sand flying in the hazy air. A huge quagmire in front, the mountain maze behind. I turned to look at the sun and saw that it was about to set. Spinning back around, I saw that José was also looking towards the sun.

The sky at dusk was usually a beautiful scene, but there was no way I could appreciate it in my current state. The wind came in cold gusts. I glanced at the flimsy clothes I was wearing, then at José stewing in a pit of mud, and then back at the setting sun – it looked like the gigantic red eye of a cyclops blinking shut. Temperatures here would drop to zero within a few hours. If José couldn't get out by then, he'd be frozen alive.

'Sanmao,' he called to me. 'Get in the car and fetch help.'

'I can't leave you here,' I said, suddenly becoming emotional.

I could certainly figure out directions to drive my way out of the mountain maze. But by the time I got from there to the checkpoint and found help, night would already have fallen. It would be next to impossible to go back through the mountain maze and find José in the dark of night. We'd have to wait until daybreak. And by then José would certainly be dead.

The sun was completely out of view now; temperatures were dropping rapidly. This was an inevitability in the desert night.

'Sanmao, get in the car,' José called, sounding angry. 'You'll freeze to death.' I was still squatting at the edge of the quagmire, thinking about how much colder José must have been than me. I was shivering so badly that I couldn't even speak.

José clung to that rock with half his body. Whenever he stopped moving, I stood up and said to him, 'José, José. You have to keep moving. Turn your body a little. Be brave…' When he heard this, he would stir for a moment. But it was too hard for him to move very much under the circumstances.

The sky had already darkened to a pigeon grey. Twilight was beginning to blur my vision, little by little. My mind was in turmoil. If I left him to find help, I'd risk not being able to come back and rescue him. It would be better to keep him company and freeze to death together.

Suddenly I saw headlights on the horizon. Startled, I jumped up. They were definitely headlights! Far, far away, but they were driving towards us.

'José!' I yelled. 'José, there's a car coming.' I went to honk the car horn, over and over again in a frenzy. I also flashed the headlights to attract attention. Then I climbed onto the roof, waving my arms, jumping and yelling like a madwoman.

Finally, they saw us. The car was driving over.

I came down from the roof and ran to them. I saw the car very clearly now. It was a Jeep used for driving long distances in the desert. There were lots of wooden trunks stuffed with tea leaves on top. Three Sahrawi men were in the car. They parked the car around thirty metres away, looking over at me from afar without approaching. Of course I understood why they might be suspicious of strangers in this wilderness. I hurried over to them just as they were getting out of the car. They should be able to see our predicament, as it wasn't completely dark yet.

I was out of breath by the time I reached them. 'Help, my husband fell into the quagmire,' I begged, full of hope. 'Please help pull him out.'

They ignored me and began discussing in their own language. 'It's a woman,' I heard them say.

'Hurry, please help!' I continued gasping for air. 'He's going to freeze to death!'

'We do not have rope,' said one of them.

I was stunned silent because the rejection in his voice was hard and unmistakable. 'You have turbans,' I tried to suggest. 'Three of them tied together should be long enough.' There were clearly thick ropes of hemp tying the trunks to the top of the car.

'How do you know we will rescue him? Strange.'

'I…' I wanted to persuade them, but I saw the glint in their eyes. They were looking me over with no good intentions. So

I changed course. 'Fine. I can't force you if you won't help. Forget it.'

I was about to turn around and go, leaving behind these lunatics in the wilderness. In a split second, one of the Sahrawi gave a signal with his head and another jumped behind me, grabbing my waist with his right arm, touching my chest with the other. I almost fainted from the shock. Instinctively I began screaming. I struggled like a wild beast in the clutches of this maniac, whose arm kept me in a steel grip. But it was absolutely no use. He pulled my body in and turned me around to face him, pressing his awful face closer to mine.

José could see everything that was happening from his vantage point. 'I'll kill you,' he cried with a stifled sob. He let go of the rock and tried to fight his way through the mud.

I grew anxious when I saw this and forgot about my own situation. 'José,' I called. 'Don't! Don't, I beg you...' Tears came to my eyes. Once I started crying, the three Sahrawi shifted their attention entirely to José. I faced the lunatic that held me. Mustering up all the force in my body, I raised my feet and kicked him in the abdomen. He was caught off guard and doubled over, howling in pain, setting me free in the process.

I turned and ran. Another one chased after me with long strides. I bent down, grabbed two handfuls of sand and flung them at his eyes. He covered his face with both hands. In the space afforded by these few seconds, I kicked off my flip-flops and bolted barefoot towards the car in mad desperation.

The three of them didn't run after me. They got into their Jeep and drove slowly towards where I was. It dawned on me that they had miscalculated one thing. They assumed only José knew how to drive and I wouldn't be able to get away no matter how much I ran. That's why they were pursuing me so leisurely.

I jumped into our car and started the engine, glancing at José, who was back next to the rock. I felt a throbbing pain in my heart as though someone had struck it with a whip.

'Go, Sanmao!' José screamed at me. 'Get out of here!'

I had no time to say anything to him. I stepped on the gas. The car shuddered to life. Before the Jeep could reach me, I sped up the hill and gunned it. The Jeep tried to block my passage. But when I drove my car straight at them like a kamikaze pilot, they immediately moved aside.

The accelerator was to the floor now, but I still couldn't escape the lights of the Jeep behind me. They had latched on to my car and wouldn't let me go. My heart almost leapt out of my chest. I was breathing so rapidly I thought I might suffocate. As I drove, I locked all four doors and reached down with my left hand to feel behind the car seat. I grabbed hold of the flick knife that José had hidden there.

The mountain maze was before me. Without a thought, I zoomed in. I swerved around one pile of sand. The Jeep followed. I darted in and out between the sandpiles like mad. Sometimes the Jeep would drop behind a bit. Other times it would be right up on top of me. No matter how erratically I drove, I couldn't escape them.

At this point I realised that if I didn't turn off my headlights, the Jeep would keep following me around and around. And if I ran out of gas, I would be dead meat.

With this in mind, I floored it with angry determination. Halfway around a hill, before the Jeep could catch up with me, I turned off the lights without slowing at all. I gripped the steering wheel firmly in my hands and made a sharp turn to the left. I veered off in a different direction, circling around to a hill that was behind the path of pursuit.

The curve of the hill cast a large shadow at night. I edged my car as close to the sandpile as possible, opened the passenger door and climbed out and moved a short distance away. I clutched the flick knife in my hand. How I wished our car were black, or even coffee brown or dark green. But it happened to be white.

I could see that the Jeep had lost me. They were ahead now, circling and looking all around for me. It hadn't occurred to them that I could be hiding. After circling a few times, they pressed on, picking up speed. I ran a few steps along the sand. Even though the Jeep was definitely gone, I worried they might still turn around. I climbed onto the hill to get a better view. At long last, the lights of the Jeep disappeared into the distance.

I slid down the hill and got back into the car. I realised I was covered in a cold sweat. Black circles bubbled up in my eyes. I thought I might vomit. Climbing back out of the car, I lay on the ground so the cold would wake me. I couldn't stay paralysed like this. José was still in that swamp.

A few minutes later, I managed to collect myself. Ursa Major shone brightly in the sky, a water dipper in the heavens. Below was Ursa Minor, its stars like guiding diamonds. It was easier to determine direction in the mountain maze at night than by day. If I headed west, I thought, I could get out of the maze. Then if I went north about 120 kilometres, I could reach the checkpoint. I could find help and bring people back here. But no matter how fast I could go, there was no way I would make it back tonight. And in that case, José... He would...

I covered my face with my hands, unable to think any further. I stood for a spell. There was nothing I could use to

mark my path but sand. But I had to mark the route somehow
so I could return early in the morning. My body was in severe
pain from the cold; I had to get back in the vehicle. Then,
almost by accident, I noticed the backseat of the car. It was
entirely detachable. I immediately opened up the toolbox
and took out the screwdriver so I could start dismantling the
seat. With great effort I was able to pull out the whole thing
using both hands. I dragged it out and threw it onto the sand.
This way it would be easier to spot tomorrow.

I got back into the car, turned on the headlights and
prepared to head to the checkpoint. I steeled my nerves and
told myself not to get too emotional. That it would be more
useful to find help than to drive back to see José. I wasn't
abandoning him.

The headlights shone on the large, black car seat that I'd
tossed to the side. The car engine was already running. But all
of a sudden I jumped as though a needle had pricked me. This
car seat was not only large, but flat, too – it probably wouldn't
sink. I got so excited that my whole body shook. I went down
to pick up the seat again, stuffing it into the back of the car.
Then I did a U-turn and drove back to the quagmire.

I drove slowly, following my own tyre tracks for fear of
losing the way. It still ended up taking me on a roundabout
path. Sometimes I couldn't spot the tyre prints at all. By the
time I reached the quagmire, I didn't dare drive too near.
I just shone the headlights onto it.

Just as before, the quagmire lay silent in the darkness. The
mud was completely still except for the occasional bubble
rising to the surface. I couldn't see José or the rock that
jutted out.

'José, José...' I pushed the car door open and ran along
the edge of the swamp, crying his name. But José really was

nowhere to be found. My whole body trembled. I screamed as I ran back and forth along the edges of the quagmire like a maniac.

José was dead. He must be dead. Terror reverberated through my heart. I was near-certain that the quagmire had swallowed him up. This sort of dread was enough to make a person go insane. I fled back into the car, supporting myself with the steering wheel, shaking like a fallen leaf in the wind.

I don't know how much time passed, but eventually I heard a very feeble voice calling out: 'Sanmao... Sanmao...' Bewildered, I raised my head to look. I couldn't see anything in the darkness. Turning the headlights back on, I edged the car forwards a little bit. There was the voice again. It was José calling me. I drove the car around for almost a minute until the headlights picked him out. He was still hanging on to that same rock. I'd parked in the wrong place and scared myself to death for nothing.

'José, hold on a moment. I'm coming to pull you up.'

He had both arms around the rock, his head resting on his wrists. He was completely still in the headlights.

I pulled the car seat out, half dragging and half carrying it down to the quagmire. When the mud reached my ankles, I hurled the big car seat in. It floated on the surface without sinking. 'The spare tyre!' I said to myself. I went and fetched the spare tyre from the boot of the car. At the edge of the quagmire, with one foot on the car seat, I tossed the spare tyre into the mud. I was one step closer to José.

Cold was prickling me like hundreds of tiny knives. The temperature probably wasn't at freezing yet, but I still felt like collapsing from the strain. No stopping now. There were too many things I had to do right away. No time to huddle inside the car. I used the jack to raise the right-hand side of the car and began removing the front wheel. *Faster, faster,* I kept urging myself. I had to get José out while I could still move my arms and legs.

Once I had dismantled the front wheel, I moved on to the back wheel. Under normal circumstances, it was hard enough for me to do these things quickly. But this time I got it all done within minutes.

I looked over at José. He had been completely still this entire time, stiffened in place. 'José, José.' I threw a palm-sized rock at him to wake him. He was already in a bad way. I grabbed one of the tyres I'd taken off and ran down towards him, jumping onto the floating car seat and then the spare tyre. I threw the tyre from my arms into the mud. Then I went back and did it again, so there were three tyres and a car seat floating in the quagmire.

I planted my feet widely on the last tyre. There was still a sizeable distance between me and José. He looked at me with great sorrow in his eyes.

'My clothes!' I suddenly remembered the long cloth dress that hung to my feet with its circle skirt. I hurried back to the car, took off all my clothes and used the flick knife to cut the dress into four wide strips. I knotted all the strips all together, then wrapped a pair of pliers in the material at the front. With this pile in my arms, I raced back along the tyres in the quagmire.

'José! Hey!' I called. 'I'm throwing something down. Catch it and hold on to it.' I wound the long strip of cloth around my hand and let it reach farther and farther. José grabbed on to it before it got all the way down to him. When his hand caught hold, I let out a breath. I crumpled on the tyre and began crying. I became aware of the cold again. I also became aware of hunger, now that my panic had subsided. After a few sobs, my attention returned to José and I started reeling him in. Once you let yourself go, though, it's difficult to regain your strength. No matter how hard I pulled, I couldn't budge José from the mud.

'Sanmao, tie the cloth to the tyre,' he said hoarsely. 'I'll pull myself up.'

I sat on the car tyre. José pulled himself forwards along the cloth strip, inch by inch. When I saw that he was near, I let go and tied it to the next closest tyre. From the looks of it, José was too weak to actually climb on to the tyres. He had been freezing for too long.

José collapsed to the ground as soon as he got out. I could still run, so I immediately went back to the car to get the flask of wine. This was a matter of life and death. I forced a few gulps of wine down his throat. As anxious as I was to get him inside, I had no choice but to leave him and go back to the mud to retrieve the tyres and the car seat.

'José, move your hands and feet,' I said while putting the tyres back on. 'José, you have to keep moving. Keep moving…' I kept looking back at him. He was crawling along the ground now, his face white as plaster and looking absolutely terrible.

'Let me help.' By the time he reached the car, I was securing the nut on the back tyre.

'Hurry up and get in the car!' I threw the spanner aside and climbed in myself.

I gave José another mouthful of wine and turned the heat in the car to high. I cut off his wet trousers with the flick knife and vigorously wiped his feet with the scraps of my clothing. Then I poured some wine on his chest and helped him get clean. It felt like a century had passed by the time the colour started coming back to his face. He opened his eyes for a moment and closed them again.

'José,' I called, patting him lightly on the face. 'José.'

Half an hour later, he was fully awake. He stared at me, eyes widened as if he'd seen a ghost. 'Y-you,' he stuttered. 'You…'

'Me? What about me?' His expression scared me out of my wits.

'You've suffered.' He locked me in a tearful embrace.

'What are you talking about? I haven't suffered!' Baffled, I wriggled my way out of his grip.

'Did those three guys get you?' he asked.

'No!' I said proudly. 'I got away. I got away a long time ago.'

'Then… How come you're naked? What happened to your clothes?'

Only then did I realise that I was in my underwear, covered in mud. José had obviously been frozen into a daze, too, as it took him this long to notice I wasn't wearing any clothes.

José lay next to me on the drive home. We would have to see a doctor for his legs right away. It looked like frostbite to me. Night had deepened. The mountain maze fell behind us like a bad dream. I was following Ursa Minor to the north.

'Sanmao, do you still want fossils?' José asked in a voice like a groan.

'Yes,' I said simply. 'And you?'

'Even more than you.'

'When are we coming back?'

'Tomorrow afternoon.'

The Desert Bathing Spectacle

One day around dusk, José had a sudden impulse to shave off his wild mane of hair. Upon hearing this, I immediately went into the kitchen to fetch the shears we use for gutting fish, thinking I would also tie a dishrag around his neck.

'Please sit still,' I said.

He started in fright. 'What are you doing?'

'Cutting your hair,' I said, grabbing a big tuft.

'Don't you get enough of a kick from cutting your own?' He took another step back.

'The town barber is no match for me. Let's save you the money. Come here!' I tried to nab him again.

José grabbed hold of his keys and fled. I set the shears down and chased after him. Five minutes later, we were sitting in that dirty, stuffy barbershop. José, the barber and I were all arguing over what to do with his hair, each of us unwilling to concede. The barber was very unhappy and scowled at me.

'Sanmao, can you just go outside?' José said impatiently.

'Give me some money and I'll go.'

I burrowed into José's pocket and found a blue banknote, then strode outside. The small road behind the barbershop led out of town. It was dirty and filled with piles of rubbish, flies buzzing about in swarms. A herd of skinny goats were foraging for things to eat.

I had never been to this area before. I walked past a decrepit house with no windows and a mound of withered thorny plants at the doorstep. Curious, I paused to take a closer look. There was a sign by the door that read: 'Hot Spring'. I was astounded. How could there be a spring inside this house atop a pile of rubbish? I decided to walk to the wooden door, which was ajar, and poke my head in.

Standing in the bright sun and looking into the dark interior, I could barely make anything out. I just heard an exclamation of surprise, someone yelling, 'Ah... ah...' along with people shouting in Arabic at each other. I turned and ran back a few steps, my head in a fog. What were the people in there doing? And why would they be so afraid of me?

Abruptly a middle-aged man in a long Sahrawi gown dashed outside. Seeing that I still hadn't run off, he rushed over as though he were about to grab me.

'What are you doing?' he questioned me angrily in Spanish. 'Why are you peeping at people taking baths?'

'Baths?' I was confounded.

'Shameless woman. Get out! Shoo, shoo...' He waved his hands about as though he were chasing away a chicken.

'Stop your shooing and wait a moment,' I yelled back at him. 'Hey, so what exactly are people doing inside there?' I walked back towards the house again.

'Baths. Taking. Baths. No more looking.' He shooed me once more.

'You can take baths here?' Curiosity welled in my heart.

'Yes!' The man was getting impatient.

'How does it work? How do you do it?' I was very excited. This was the first time I heard that the Sahrawi took baths, so I had to get to the bottom of it.

'You will know when you come bathe,' he said.

'I can take a bath here, too?' I asked, flattered.

'Women between eight in the morning and noon. Forty pesetas.'

'Many thanks, many thanks. I'll come back tomorrow.'

I immediately rushed back to the barbershop to tell José about this new discovery.

The next morning, I grabbed a big towel and trod through thick mounds of goat droppings back to the 'hot spring'. It stank the whole way. Truly turned my stomach, to be honest. Pushing open the door, I entered and saw a middle-aged Sahrawi woman who looked shrewd but aggressive. I assumed she was the proprietress.

'You want to take a bath? Pay first.'

I gave her forty pesetas, then looked at my surroundings. Apart from a pile of rusty buckets filled with water, there was nothing else in this room. The light was very dim. A naked woman came out to fetch a bucket before going back inside.

'How do you wash?' I was gawping left and right like a yokel.

'Come, come with me.' The proprietress grabbed me by the hand and escorted me to another room that was only about the size of three or four tatami mats. There were a few steel wires from which hung Sahrawi women's underwear, skirts, fabric for wrapping the body and so on. A pungent odour assaulted my nostrils. I stopped breathing.

'Here, take off your clothes,' commanded the proprietress.

Without making a sound, I took off all my clothes except for the bikini that I'd put on at home. I hung up the discarded clothes on the steel wire.

'Take it off!' urged the proprietress again.

'I'm done.' I gave her a dirty look.

'How can you wash while wearing this strange thing?' she asked, reaching out a hand to rudely grab at my flower-print bikini.

'How I wash is my business.' I pushed aside her hand and glared at her again.

'Fine. Now go out and get buckets.'

I obediently went to get two empty buckets.

'You can start washing through here.' She opened another door. We went deeper into the house, each segment connected to the next like a loaf of brioche. The hot spring finally appeared. It was the first time I'd seen water well up from the ground in the desert. I felt very emotional. Here it was in a deep well in the middle of a house. Quite a few women were drawing water and laughing amongst themselves. It was a lovely and charming scene. With a bucket in each hand, I stared like an idiot at the women. When they saw that I was wearing clothes, everyone stopped what they were doing.

We looked at each other with small smiles. These women didn't know too much Spanish. One of them came over, helped me fill the bucket with water and spoke to me in a very good-natured tone. 'Like this, like this.' Then she poured an entire bucket of water onto my head. As I hurriedly wiped my face, another bucket of water came down on me.

I ran away to a corner, thanking her profusely. I didn't dare ask for more guidance.

'Cold?' asked another woman. I nodded, extremely embarrassed. 'If you're cold, then go in.' They pulled open the next door. Who knew how many segments there were in this bread-loaf of a house? I was taken deeper into yet another room. A blast of heat hit my face. It was so foggy I couldn't see anything in here. I waited a few seconds, struggling to discern the four walls around me, and reached out a hand to feel my way around. I treaded cautiously until I felt somebody's leg beneath me. Bending down, I noticed for the first time that there were rows and rows of women sitting in this tiny room. On the opposite wall, a large tank bubbled with hot water. The fog was coming from there. It looked a lot like a Turkish bath.

Somebody opened the door for a few minutes. The air cooled down and I could finally see clearly again. Each of these women had a bucket or two by their side, all of them filled with cold well water. The temperature was so high here that the ground was steaming and hot to the touch. I couldn't keep my feet in one place. I had no idea how those women seated on the ground could tolerate it.

'Come sit here,' said a naked woman by the wall, moving aside to make space for me.

'I'm fine with standing. Thanks!' Glancing at the muddy ground, I honestly wouldn't have been able to sit even without the heat. I noticed all the women had little flat stones that they were dipping in water and scraping their bodies with. With every scrape, a black trail would appear in the thick grime. They didn't use any soap, nor much water. They scraped all over their bodies to loosen up the dirt before washing.

'Four years, I haven't bathed in four years,' one woman said to me cheerfully. 'I live in a *khaima*, in the desert far, far away...' I stopped breathing while she spoke to me. She lifted the bucket over her head and poured the water onto herself. Through the steam, I saw that the thick black water was slowly trickling onto my clean bare feet. My stomach churned. I stood still, biting my lower lip.

'Why aren't you washing? I'll lend you my stone to scrape with.' She kindly handed her stone to me.

'I'm not dirty. I bathed at home.'

'Why would you come here if you're not dirty? I wash once every three, four years.' She still looked pretty filthy even after washing. This room was very small and windowless and steam rose continuously from the tank. My heart was racing, sweat beading on my skin like raindrops. On top of that, there were so many people, the stench of their bodies intermingling. I felt like I might vomit. Moving over a bit, I leaned on the damp wall until I realised that it was coated in a thick layer of something slippery like snot. A good portion of my back was already drenched. I gritted my teeth and furiously wiped my back with my towel.

According to the aesthetics of the desert, plump women were considered the most beautiful, so average women would do anything they could to gain weight. Usually when women went out, besides wearing a long gown, they would wrap a large piece of fabric over their heads and bodies until they were tightly sealed. The more fashionable ones might throw on a pair of sunglasses. Then you really couldn't tell what they looked like any more. I was used to seeing women wrapped up like mummies. Seeing their huge naked bodies all of a sudden was both striking and frightening.

Talk about a bathhouse unmasked. I was like a slender stalk of dog's-tail grass growing next to a big fat dairy cow, completely eclipsed in comparison. One woman had scraped her body all over until black grime was everywhere. Before she could rinse off, one of her children started crying from the other room. Naked, she ran over and came back with a baby in her arms. She plopped down on the ground and began to breastfeed. The dirty water from her chin, neck, face and hair all trickled down to her chest, which her kid just drank in with the breastmilk.

I was stupefied at this horrifically filthy sight. My stomach fluttered again. I couldn't take it any more. I turned around and ran. Once I got to the outermost room, I gulped down the fresh air before going back to the steel wire to retrieve my clothes.

'They said you didn't bathe, just stood around staring. What is there to look at?' The boss lady seemed bemused in asking me.

'Just seeing how you bathe,' I replied with a smile.

Her eyes widened. 'You spent forty pesetas just to look?'

'Not too bad. It was worth it.'

'This place is for washing the outside of the body,' she added. 'You must wash inside, too.'

'Wash inside?' I didn't get what she meant by that. She made a colon-cleansing gesture with her hands. I was taken aback. 'Where do you do that? Please tell me.' I was so scared and excited, I buttoned my clothes up wrong.

'By the sea. You go see at Cabo Bojador. There are many *khaima*. Everyone goes to stay there in the spring and bathe for seven days.'

That night I told José about it as I was fixing supper. 'She said you have to wash inside, too, next to the sea at Bojador.'

'Are you sure you heard right?' José was also shocked.

'Yes, no doubt. She even made a gesture. I want to take a look.' I begged José. It wasn't too far to the Atlantic Coast from our small town of El Aaiún, less than four hundred kilometres round trip. We could go and come back in one day.

We'd heard before that there was a bay at Bojador. The nearly 1,000 kilometres of shoreline of the Spanish Sahara was almost completely rocky, with no beaches. We followed the tyre tracks of the cars before us, driving all the way without once getting lost. Once we reached the shore, we spent another hour driving along the rocky coast looking for Cabo Bojador.

'Look, down there,' José said. We parked the car next to a cliff. A few dozen metres below, the blue sea lapped gently at a semicircular bay. Countless white tents were set up all along the beach. There were men, women and children running about. Everyone looked serene and at ease.

'Who'd have known you could live like this in this crazy world?' I sighed with envy. It looked like paradise down there.

José went to survey the cliff and report back. 'We can't go down from here. I already looked around and didn't find any footholds. The people below must use a secret path.'

He came back to the car and got out a rope, tying it to the bumper. Then he placed a large rock behind the tyres so they were secured in place. Once the rope was fastened, he threw it down the face of the cliff.

'Let me show you. Don't throw your entire weight onto the rope. You have to get a firm foothold on the rock. The rope is just to stabilise you. Afraid?' I stood at the edge of the cliff listening to him explain, shivering in the wind. 'Are you scared?' he asked again.

'Very scared,' I said truthfully. 'Very.'

'Well, let me go first, if that's the case. You follow.' José slung his camera equipment over his shoulder and headed down. I took off my shoes and went barefoot after him. About halfway down, a strange bird began circling around me. I was afraid it would peck my eyes out so I hurried my way towards the bottom. In my distraction, I managed to reach the ground without too much trouble.

'Shh! Over here.' José was behind a large rock.

He told me not to make a sound. It turned out there were several completely naked Sahrawi women fetching seawater. These women were taking their buckets up the beach and pouring the water into a very large jar. At the bottom of the jar was a hose for the water to flow out. As one woman lay on the sand, another inserted the hose into the reclining woman's body like an enema, lifting the jar in her hands. The water flowed down the hose and into the recumbent woman's bowels. I shook José, pointing at the scene unfolding in the distance. I wanted him to ready his equipment, but he was too shocked to remember to take photos.

Once the full jar of water had been emptied, the woman at her side poured more seawater into the jar, continuing to pump it into the one who was lying down. The woman on the ground couldn't stop herself from moaning and groaning after three rounds of this. While getting filled with yet another bucket of water, she started screeching as though she were in great agony. We were scared shitless, watching from behind the rocks.

When the hose was finally pulled out, it was inserted into another woman's body for the next cleansing. Meanwhile, the woman who'd already been pumped full of water was getting even more water through the mouth. According to what the proprietress of the 'hot spring' had said, they had to do this three times a day for seven days before they finished. This was truly what you would call a spring cleaning. It was unbelievable that a person could accommodate so much water in her body.

A short while later, the woman who was full of water staggered to her feet and slowly made her way over in our direction. She squatted over the sand and began to excrete. All sorts of horrible stuff from her bowels came gushing forth. After excreting a pile, she moved back a few steps to excrete again while using her hands to cover up her waste with some sand. Just like that, excreting and burying at the same time, she repeated this ten or more times without stopping. When this squatting woman suddenly started to sing, I couldn't hold it in any longer and burst into laughter. It was a totally ridiculous sight and I couldn't help myself.

José jumped up to cover my mouth, but it was already too late. The naked woman had turned her head and spotted us behind the rocks. Her face contorted in surprise, mouth open. She dashed far away before she started to shriek. We stood up when we heard this. Then we saw many people running towards us from the cluster of tents. The woman was pointing a finger at us. The angry mob flew at us with brutal intention.

'Run, José!' I yelled and ran off. I wanted to laugh but I was too nervous. Looking behind me, I cried out, 'Don't forget to grab your camera!'

Once we scrambled to where our rope was dangling, José pushed me up with great effort. I don't know where I found the capability, but I made it to the top of the cliff in no time. José came up not long after. Although there was clearly no path leading to this precipice and our pursuers didn't follow us up the rope, they still managed to surface from some secret byway, giving us a real fright. We pushed aside the rock that was blocking our car tyre. There was no time to untie the rope. Just as soon as I threw myself into the car, we sped off like we had been shot out of a cannon.

More than a week later, I was still mourning the beautiful sandals I'd left at the cliff, but I didn't dare drive back there to look for them. When José came home from work, I heard him talking to a Sahrawi friend outside the window. 'I heard recently there is an Oriental woman who likes to watch everyone take baths,' the guy was sounding out José. 'People say your—'

'I've never heard of this,' José replied. 'My wife has never been to Cabo Bojador.'

My God, I thought when I heard this. This fool's about to give us away! I ran outside in a huff. 'I have! I know about the Oriental woman watching people bathe,' I said, face full of smiles. José looked astonished. 'Didn't you hear about the plane full of Japanese tourists that came last week? The Japanese love studying how others wash, especially Japanese women. They like to ask where people bathe...'

José pointed a finger at me, his mouth wide open. I shoved his hand back down. Upon hearing what I'd said, our Sahrawi friend had an epiphany. 'So it was a Japanese. I thought, I thought...' He looked at me, his face reddening.

'You thought it was me, right? I actually don't have any interests besides cooking and washing clothes. You got it wrong.'

'Sorry, I was mistaken,' he said, blushing again. 'Sorry.'

After this guy had walked off far into the distance, I stood there leaning against the doorframe, my eyes shut and a small smile on my face. 'No more daydreaming, Madame Butterfly.' José gave me a smack on the head out of the blue. 'Time to make dinner!'

Looking for Love

A tiny little grocery store opened up near our home about seven or eight months ago. With almost anything you could imagine available to purchase, life suddenly became much more convenient for us residents living some distance from town. No longer did I need to make a long journey under the blazing sun with my bags large and small.

I'd go to this store maybe four or five times a day. Sometimes in the middle of cooking I'd rush out to buy sugar or flour, always as a matter of utmost urgency, only to find that all my neighbours were in there shopping or the store didn't have any change. No matter what, whenever I went, I couldn't get in and out in ten seconds like I wanted. It wasn't great for someone as impatient as me.

After a week of this, I proposed to the young Sahrawi clerk that I keep a tab. Each night, I could record everything I'd bought during the day. I'd pay it off once I reached a thousand pesetas or so. The youth said that he'd have to ask his older brother before he could answer me. The next day he told me they'd be happy to let me keep an account. They didn't know how to write, so they gave me a large notebook and let me unilaterally record the accumulated products for which I owed them payment. It was from that point on that I got to know Salun.

Salun was usually alone in the store. His older brother had other business to attend to and only flitted by in the mornings and evenings. Whenever I went to settle my debts, Salun firmly rejected any need to double-check what I'd written. If I insisted as a courtesy, his face and ears would turn bright red and he'd start stammering. So I just let it go and didn't ask him to check my accounts any more.

Because he trusted me, I recorded my purchases meticulously. I didn't want to make a mistake and then have the blame placed on his shoulders. Though it wasn't his store, he seemed to take on a lot of responsibility. He wouldn't go into town even after closing up at night. Instead he always sat quietly by himself, gazing into the dark sky. Stiff and honest, he seemingly hadn't made any friends even after the store had been open for almost a month.

One afternoon, I went in to settle my account. I was ready to go after paying it off, but Salun kept his head lowered, fumbling with my notebook. The look on his face told me he hadn't forgotten to give it back to me; rather, he had something to say. I waited a few seconds. He remained silent, so I took the notebook from his hands and said, 'All set. Thanks, see you tomorrow!' I turned and made to leave.

He looked up abruptly. 'Señora Quero…' he began.

I stopped and waited for him to talk. Again he wouldn't speak. His face had already turned bright red.

'Is something the matter?' I asked him gently, so as not to deepen his anxiety.

'I want… I want to ask you to write an important letter.' He was too timid to look up at me as he spoke.

'Sure! For who?' I asked. This boy was really too shy.

'For my wife,' he said in a voice so small I almost couldn't hear it.

'You're married?' I was very surprised because Salun lived, ate and worked in this little shop. He had no parents, and his brother's family treated him with cold indifference. I never even suspected that he might have a wife. He nodded at last, nervous as though he'd revealed a most profound secret to me.

'And your wife? Where is she? Why isn't she living with you?' I knew what was in his heart. He was reluctant to speak, but longed for me to ask. He still didn't answer, glancing around for a moment to make sure nobody else was coming into the shop. Then he pulled out a colour photograph from under the counter and shoved it into my hands, lowering his head again.

This photograph, its edges already worn and frayed, showed an Arab woman in European clothes. Her features were dignified, her eyes large. But she had slathered a lot of colourful make-up onto a face that wasn't particularly youthful. She wore a revealing sleeveless blouse in a floral print, along with a very short and démodé apple-green miniskirt. Around her waist was a copper chain-belt. Below that her plump legs slid into a pair of extremely tall yellow high-heeled boots, shoelaces criss-crossed all the way up to her knees. A portion of her black hair had been swooped up like a bird's nest, while the rest fell on her shoulders. Cheap jewellery adorned her entire body, and she held a gleaming black fake leather handbag.

Looking at the picture alone was dazzling and overwhelming enough. If she were to appear in the flesh, powdery scent and all, it would certainly be even more astonishing.

I looked at Salun. He was earnestly waiting for me to react to the photo. I didn't have it in me to dash his hopes, but

I couldn't find the appropriate words to praise this artificial beauty. Instead I gingerly returned the photograph to the counter. 'Very chic. She's totally unlike the Sahrawi women around here.' I could only say this much and manage to avoid hurting him while salving my conscience.

Salun was very happy to hear me say this. 'She is very stylish and beautiful,' he said immediately. 'No girl around here can compare with her.'

'Where is she?' I asked with a smile.

'She is now in Monte Carlo.' He spoke of his wife as though she were a goddess.

'You've been to Monte Carlo?' I thought I had misheard him.

'No, we got married in Algeria last year,' he said.

'How come she didn't come back to the desert with you after getting married?'

His face dimmed as soon as he heard my question, the look of eagerness vanishing. 'Saida said I should go home first and, after few days, she and her brother would come to the Sahara together. But then, but then—'

'Then she never came.' I finished his sentence for him. He nodded and looked at the ground.

'How long has it been?' I asked.

'More than one year.'

'Why didn't you write to her sooner?'

'I…' He sounded like he had something stuck in his throat. 'Who could I tell…?' he sighed.

Why are you willing to tell some completely irrelevant person like me, then? I thought to myself. 'Let me see the address.' I decided I would help him out.

He showed me the address and, sure enough, it was Monte Carlo, Monaco, and not Algeria. 'Where did you get this address?' I asked him.

'I went to Algeria once to find my wife,' he mumbled. 'Three months ago.'

'Aiya, why didn't you mention it sooner? You're not speaking clearly. So you have tried to find her.'

'She was not there. Her brother said she left. He gave me this photo and address and told me to go home.'

Trekking such enormous distances, all for the sake of the vulgar woman in this photograph? I sighed and looked at Salun's honest and kindly face.

I suddenly thought of the customs here in the desert. 'Salun, let me ask you, how much of a bride price did you pay when you got married?'

'A lot.' He lowered his head again as if my question were touching on a sore spot.

'How much?' I pressed gently.

'More than three hundred thousand.'

I was stunned. 'There's no way you could have that much money,' I said dubiously. 'You're talking nonsense!'

'Yes, yes, my father left it to me when he passed away two years ago. You can ask my brother.' Salun defended himself firmly.

'Fine. Let me guess what happened next. You went to Algeria last year to buy goods to bring back and sell in the Sahara. But you ended up not buying anything. You married the woman in the photo, Saida, and the money went to her. Then you came back, and she still hasn't come. Am I right?'

A very simple story of a swindle.

'Yes, you guessed right! How did you know what happened?' He seemed almost a bit happy that I had guessed correctly.

'You really don't get it?' I widened my eyes, finding it extremely odd.

'I do not understand why she refuses to come here. So I must ask you to write this letter to her. Please tell her I, I...' He grew excited and held his head in his hands. 'I have nothing now,' he mumbled.

I quickly turned my gaze elsewhere. Seeing all the sentiments come pouring out of this stiff and honest fellow, I felt a great stirring in my heart. Since the very first time I met him, he seemed to radiate a kind of silent, lonely sorrow, like a character in an old Russian novel who has suffered tremendous misfortune.

'Alright, let's write a letter,' I said, pulling myself together. 'I have time right now.'

Upon hearing this, Salun quietly implored me, 'Please do not tell my older brother about writing this letter.'

'I won't say anything. Don't worry.' I opened up my notebook. 'OK. You speak, and I'll write. Go on...' I prompted him.

'Saida, my wife...' Salun seemed to tremble just spitting out these few words. He stopped.

'This won't do. I can only write in Spanish. How will she read the letter?' I lost my will to write again, knowing deep down that this female trickster wouldn't even getting around to reading this letter, let alone admit to being his wife.

'It is no problem. Please write.' Salun looked worried that I would refuse. 'She will find somebody to read the letter for her,' he implored. 'I beg of you...'

'Fine! Carry on.' I lowered my head and prepared to continue.

'Ever since we parted ways last year, I have never forgotten you. Once I went to Algeria to find you...'

I could see that Salun must feel great love for this woman, otherwise he wouldn't have been able to overcome his shyness. Here he was describing the passion buried deep in his heart in front of a total stranger.

'Done! Come sign.' I tore out the written letter from my notebook.

Salun knew how to write his own name in Arabic. He signed carefully and sighed. 'Now we just have to wait for her reply,' he said, full of hope.

I looked at him and didn't know how to respond. All I could do was keep silent.

'For the return address, can we put your mailbox number at the post office? Would it bother Señor José?'

'Don't worry. José won't mind. Let me write the return address for you.' I hadn't even thought of writing one in the first place.

'I will go and mail it myself right now.' Salun got a stamp from me, closed the front door of the shop and flew off into town.

From then on, Salun would start and stumble whenever he saw me come into the store. If I shook my head, a look of despair would immediately come over his face. At such an early stage, he was already suffering from the wait. How would he manage in the days to come? A month passed like this. Salun's wordless badgering was becoming a huge headache. I no longer went to buy groceries from his shop. I didn't know how to tell him, *No reply, no reply, no reply – forget it all and give up hope,* so I just didn't go to the store. He would still surreptitiously come to my window every day after closing up. He wouldn't knock, either, but simply wait for me to see him and tell him there was no reply. Only then would he murmur his thanks and slowly walk back to the shop, plopping himself down on the ground and gazing towards the sky. He would sit there for many hours on end.

After a long period of time, I opened my mailbox one day and found a few letters inside. There was also a notice from the post office asking me to come.

'What is it?' I asked the post office employee.

'Certified mail to your mailbox for a Salun somebody – Hamid. Is it your friend or did this get sent to the wrong place?'

'Ah!' I cried out, taking this letter from Monaco into my hands. All the hairs on my body stood on end. I snatched the letter and started walking home with quick steps.

I had completely misjudged this situation. She wasn't a trickster. She wrote back, certified mail, no less. Salun would be delighted beyond words.

'Read it, read it!' Salun urged, closing up the shop. He was trembling, his eyes glimmering like a madman's.

Opening the letter, I found that it was in French. I was very apologetic to Salun.

'It's in French…' I bit my finger.

Hearing this, Salun was beyond desperate. 'But it is still for me, right?' he asked quietly, as though he might wake from a beautiful dream if he spoke too loudly.

'It is for you. She says she loves you.' This was the only phrase I could recognise.

'Just guess, I beg you, what else does it say?' Salun had lost it.

'I don't know. Let's wait until José gets off work.' I walked home, Salun trailing stiffly behind me like a zombie. I had to invite him inside to sit and wait for José.

Sometimes José has to deal with difficult people on the job and comes home in a foul mood. I don't mind so much, having grown used to it. He came back particularly early that night. When he saw Salun, he nodded indifferently and went to change his shoes without saying a word. Salun held the letter in his hands, waiting for José to notice him. But José ignored him, going off into the bedroom. After a long spell, he emerged wearing shorts and headed towards the bathroom.

By this point, Salun was at his wits' end from the anxious wait. Suddenly, without making a peep, he fell to José's feet with the letter in his hands. It looked like he wanted to hug José's legs. I was startled to see all this happen from the kitchen. Salun had gone over the top. I was angry at myself for letting this madman cause a ruckus in our tiny home.

José had been lost in his own head until Salun fell to his knees before him and gave him a dreadful scare. 'What's going on?!' he yelled. 'What's the meaning of this? Sanmao, save me...'

I went over to pry Salun away. Getting both him and José to stay still was no easy feat. Already tired and disheartened, I couldn't wait to get rid of Salun so I could have some peace. José read the letter. He told Salun, 'Your wife says she also loves you. She can't come to the Sahara right now because she has no money. Please try to raise one hundred thousand pesetas and send it to her brother in Algeria. Her brother will use this money to buy a plane ticket so she can come to you and never leave your side again.'

'What?' I gasped. 'That's bullshit! She wants money again—'

Salun was completely unfazed. 'Saida said she will come?' he kept asking José, over and over again. 'She will really come?' His eyes were glazed over as if he were in the happiest of dreams. 'Money is no problem,' he muttered to himself. 'Easy to arrange, easy...'

'Forget it, Salun...' I could tell that he wouldn't snap out of it, despite my urgings.

'This, I give to you.' Overcome with joy, Salun took off the single silver ring that he wore and pressed it into José's palm.

'Salun, I can't take this. Keep it for yourself.' José slipped the ring back onto his finger in one movement.

'Thank you. You have both helped me very much.' And with this tremendous gratitude, Salun left.

'So what's the real deal with this wife of Salun's?' José asked, baffled. 'He's gone absolutely bonkers for her.'

'What wife? She's obviously a whore!' This fake flower deserved to be called out.

After receiving this letter, Salun left no stone unturned in finding extra work. By day he oversaw the shop, while at night he baked bread at a major bakery in town. With this backbreaking labour around the clock, he could only sleep from five to eight in the morning.

A fortnight of this quickly wore him down. He lost a lot of weight. His eyes were bloodshot, his hair dirty and unkempt, his clothes ragged. But he became much more talkative. When he spoke, he was full of hope for the future. Yet somehow I knew that he was still suffering deeply in his heart of hearts.

Not long after that, I realised that he had quit smoking.

'I must save every céntimo,' he said. 'Not smoking is no problem.'

'Salun, you've been working so hard day and night. How much have you saved?' I asked. It had been two months now, and he was already skin and bones.

'Ten thousand. I saved ten thousand in two months. I am almost there. Don't worry about me.' His speech was incoherent from long bouts of sleep deprivation, his nerves weakened to the extreme.

I kept on wondering what sort of sorcery Saida had used to get a man, with whom she had spent only three days, to fall in love with her like this, unable to forget the bliss that she bestowed upon him.

More time passed. Salun was still going crazy, half living and half dead. Could a person keep this up until he died?

One night, in his exhaustion, Salun put his hands on the red hot metal of the bakery oven. Both hands suffered serious burns. He still worked in the shop during the day; his brother wouldn't allow him to close up and rest.

I watched him at work, using both wrists to hold things for customers, rushing to and fro, getting one thing, knocking over another. When his older brother came in and looked on coldly, he grew even more nervous and scattered tomatoes all over the floor. While picking them up, he became distracted by the pain because his fingertips were swollen and filled with pus. Great big drops of sweat poured from him.

Poor Salun. When would he be able to free himself from this mad thirst for Saida? He seemed even more wretched than before.

Since burning his hands, Salun came over to my house each night so I could apply ointment before he went to work at the bakery. It was only in our home that he could indulge and reveal his innermost secrets. He had already completely forgotten about the setbacks Saida had dealt him before. If only he could save another peseta, he would draw that much closer to the happiness of his dreams.

One night when he came over as usual, we asked him to stay for dinner. He said it was inconvenient with his hands, so he might as well not eat.

'I will be fine soon. My hands are starting to scab up. Maybe I can bake bread tonight. Saida, she…' Once again he was back in that unchanging reverie. This time, José took pity and gently listened to Salun talk.

I had just brought out the cotton gauze to reapply ointment and dress his wounds. When I heard him bring up this tired old shtick again, a wave of disgust surged in my heart. 'Saida, Saida, Saida,' I said to Salun. 'All you do is talk about her. Either you really don't know or you're pretending you don't know that *Sa—i—da—is—a—whore.*'

The words came tumbling out of my mouth. There was no way to take them back. José lifted his head abruptly and watched Salun. The entire room froze over in dead silence.

I thought Salun might jump up and strangle me, but he didn't. What I said was like a big stick that had struck him down. He slowly turned his head to gaze at me, looking as though he wanted to say something. But no words came out. I stared back into his scrawny, pitiful face.

There was no anger in his face. He lifted the two hands that had been burned to a pulp, looking at one, then the other. Tears streamed from his eyes. Without saying a word, he leapt up and stormed out, running into the dark wilderness.

'Do you think he knows he's been cheated?' José asked me softly.

'He's known ever since the beginning. He just refused to snap out of it. He couldn't help himself, so who would help him?' I was certain about Salun's feelings.

'Saida bewitched him,' José said.

'Saida was able to bewitch him not just by fulfilling his lust. For Salun, her flesh and blood came to symbolise everything he lacks in life. What he wants is love, affection, family, warmth. When such a stiff and lonely young heart finds a bit of love, even the false kind, it's no surprise that he would try to hold on to it at all costs.'

José said nothing. He turned out the lights and sat in the dark.

We thought Salun wouldn't come back the next day, but he did show up. I changed the ointment on his hands and said, 'Alright! This shouldn't hurt any more when you bake bread tonight. Within a few days, the skin will have completely healed over.'

Salun was very calm and didn't speak much. As he was leaving, he seemed like he wanted to say something but couldn't. He suddenly spun around when he reached the door. 'Thank you!' he said.

I felt there was something strange going on. 'No need to thank me,' I replied. 'Don't go crazy again. Go on and get to work.' He gave me an odd smile. My heart prickled when I closed the door. Something was definitely wrong: Salun never smiled.

The next day, I was opening the door to take out the rubbish when I came face to face with two police officers.

'Are you Señora Quero?'

'Yes, I am.' *Salun's finally dead,* I told myself.

'There's a Salun Hamid…'

'He's our friend,' I said calmly.

'Do you know of his whereabouts?'

'His whereabouts?' I asked.

'Last night he fled after taking money from his brother's store, as well as the income from the bakery…'

'Oh…' I hadn't thought that Salun was capable of making this kind of decision.

'Has he said anything strange recently?' the policemen questioned me. 'Or did he say he was going somewhere?'

'No. If you knew Salun, you would know that he's a man of few words.'

After the police officers left, I closed the door and went to take a nap.

'How do you think Salun could bear leaving this desert?' José asked me during dinner that evening. 'These are the Sahrawi's roots.'

'Well, he can't come home now. They're looking for him everywhere.'

After dinner, we sat on the roof. There was no wind that night. José told me to light the lamp. Once it was lit, swarms of flying insects fluttered over, spinning incessantly around the light as though it were the one thing in life that they believed in. The two of us watched the flying insects.

'What are you thinking about?' José asked.

'I was thinking that moths must truly be happiest when they throw themselves into the flame.'

Nice Neighbours

On the surface, my Sahrawi neighbours all appear extremely dirty and drab. From their odours and unclean clothes, one might get the false impression that they're an impoverished and helpless bunch. In reality, not only does every family in the vicinity receive subsidies from the Spanish government, most people also have proper jobs. Some rent out their homes to the Europeans or tend to huge flocks of goats. Others have even opened up shops in town, a stable and considerable source of income. For these reasons, the locals often say that only the Sahrawi of economic means can live in El Aaiún.

Last year, during my first few months here, I often left town to go travelling in the deep desert because I wasn't yet married. Every time I came home, I returned totally empty-handed as though I'd been robbed blind. The poverty-stricken Sahrawi who lived in the desert were ready to pry the very stakes from my tent. Needless to say, everything I had on my person also disappeared.

Shortly after I started living on Avenida Rio de Oro, I heard that my neighbours were considered the wealthy people of the desert. I couldn't help but rejoice, imagining the myriad advantages of living alongside people who had money.

All the things that happened next were basically my fault.

The first time José and I were invited over to our neighbour's home for tea, we returned with goat droppings stuck to our shoes. Hamdi's little son had drooled over a large patch of my long skirt. The next day, I started teaching Hamdi's daughters how to mop the floors and hang their mats out to dry. Of course, it was me who supplied the bucket, soap powder, mop and water.

Since neighbours in these lands were so friendly with one another, my bucket and mop often made the rounds until sunset without ever reaching me. But this was no big deal because they were always returned to me in due course.

After living on Avenida Rio de Oro for a while, neighbours from near and far came to pay me a visit even though our house didn't have a doorplate. I didn't socialise much, apart from opening the door to give out medicine. I abide by the belief that 'a hedge between keeps friendships green'.

Eventually the door to our home was constantly opening and shutting. Whenever I opened the door, a crowd of women and children would rush in. And so it was that they got to see our way of life and daily amenities very clearly. Neither José nor I are stingy and we're relatively polite to others. Thus our neighbours gradually learned how to take full advantage of this weakness of ours.

Each day, from nine in the morning onwards, there would be an endless parade of children coming to our home to demand things.

'My older brother wants to borrow a lightbulb.'

'My mum needs an onion—'

'My dad wants a can of gas.'

'We need cotton—'

'Give me a hairdryer.'

'Let my sister borrow your iron.'

'I want nails and a little bit of wire.'

And all sorts of strange things. The worst was that we happened to have all of these objects in our home. We would feel guilty withholding them. But once we gave things away, we were almost certain to never get them back.

'These people are so annoying,' José often complained. 'Why don't they just go into town to buy what they need?' But when the next child came asking for something, there was no question we'd give it to them.

I don't know when it started happening, but our neighbours' kids started sticking their hands out to us to ask for money. They would surround us as soon as we left the house. 'Give me five pesetas!' they'd yell. 'Give me five pesetas!' Our landlord's children were among them, of course.

I absolutely refused to give out money. In spite of this, they persevered and came to nag me every single day. Eventually I told the landlord's children, 'Your father gets ten thousand pesetas from me every month for this crappy house. I might as well move if I have to give you another five pesetas each day.'

After this, they stopped asking. They demanded bubble gum instead, which I was more than happy to provide. I figured they no longer begged for money because they didn't want me to move away.

Labu, a young girl, came knocking one day. I opened the door to find the mound of a camel carcass lying on the ground, its blood dripping everywhere. It was quite a shock. 'My mum says to put this camel in your refrigerator.'

I turned my head and glanced at my shoebox-sized refrigerator. Sighing, I knelt down and said to her, 'Labu, tell your mum that if she gives me your big house to use as my needle box, then you can put this camel in my refrigerator.'

Immediately she asked, 'Where are your needles?'

That camel definitely didn't get refrigerated, but Labu's mother shot me dirty looks for almost a month. She said only one thing to me: 'You refused me and hurt my pride.' Every Sahrawi was very proud, it seemed. I was afraid to hurt them too often or decline to lend out my things.

Another day, a bunch of girls came to ask me for 'red potion', which was actually Mercurochrome, an antiseptic. I staunchly refused. 'Tell whoever cut themselves to come to me for the medicine,' I said. They insisted on taking it away with them nonetheless.

A few hours later, I heard the sound of drumming, so I ran out to see what was going on. Only then did I discover that the girls had smeared my Mercurochrome all over their faces and hands. They were currently wriggling on the public rooftop, dancing and singing with enormous glee. Seeing that the Mercurochrome had such a marvellous effect, there was no way I could get angry.

Even more frustrating was the neighbour who worked as a hospital assistant. He refused to eat with his hands like the rest of his family because he considered himself to be worldly. Every day, whenever it was mealtime, his son would come and knock on our door. 'My dad wants to eat. I'm here for the knife and fork.' Those were always his opening remarks.

Even though this kid never failed to return the knife and fork, I still got fed up. I decided I might as well just buy a set and give it to him, rather than have him come every day. Lo and behold, he was back on our doorstep two days later.

'Why are you back?' I asked him with a pout. 'What happened to the set I gave you?'

'My mum says she must put the knife and fork away because they are new. Now my dad wants to eat—'

'Not my problem if your dad wants to eat!' I yelled. The kid shrank into himself like a little bird. I couldn't bear it. I had no choice but to lend him the knife and fork. Eating is important business, after all.

Desert houses always have the ceiling partially open to the sky. Whether we were eating or sleeping, our neighbours' children were always able to look down into our home through the hole in its roof. Whenever fierce winds arose, sand rained down through it. Living in such an environment, José and I were forced to play the role of the quicksand river-dwelling monk in *Journey to the West*. We had no leeway to pick other parts.

José asked the landlord several times, but he wouldn't cover that part of the roof. So we bought our own materials. After working on it for three Sundays, José succeeded in laying a piece of yellow frosted glass as the ceiling there. Light could still shine down, making the room feel super clean and beautiful. I put the nine bonsai plants that I'd painstakingly raised beneath the new roof, a swathe of fresh greenery. My life improved tremendously because of this.

One afternoon, I was in the kitchen, deeply engrossed in a cake recipe and listening to music. Suddenly I heard what sounded like somebody walking across the glass ceiling. I stuck my head out to take a look and saw quite clearly the silhouette of a large goat above me. This horrible animal was making its way up our slanted roof as if it were a mountain slope. Grabbing a cleaver, I ran up the stairs that led to the rooftop. I hadn't even made it all the way up when I heard the sound of splintering, followed by an earth-shaking crash.

Wood and broken glass rained down. Of course, this goat also fell from the heavens and landed in our tiny home. In extreme agitation, I chased the goat out with a broom. Then, fuming, I looked up at the blue sky through the hole in the ceiling.

We didn't know who we could ask to pay for the hole in the ceiling, so we got materials to fix it up ourselves. 'How about making it from asbestos this time?' I asked José.

'No way, this house only has one window facing the street. We'd block out all the light if we used asbestos tiles.' José was miserable because he hated working on Sundays. We soon had a new ceiling in place, this time with a sheet of white translucent plastic. José also made a low wall, several feet high, to separate the neighbours' rooftop from ours. This wall was for keeping goats out, but it also kept the neighbours' daughters at bay. They often snatched the undergarments I'd hung out to dry on our roof. They weren't stealing because they'd throw the clothes back onto the roof after a few days, making it look as though the wind had blown them down.

Even though we had this new plastic roof, a total of four goats still managed to fall down into our home in half a year. We were completely fed up and told the neighbours when we next caught a goat that fell through the roof, we would kill it and eat it and certainly not return it to them. We asked them to please secure their goat pens properly.

Our neighbours were smart people. We clamoured; they didn't respond at all. They just hugged their goats close and smiled at us with narrowed eyes.

Even though the flying goat in peril was a recurring spectacle around here, José was never home to witness it. He never got a chance to experience what a stir this scene caused.

One Sunday around dusk, a flock of mad goats jumped over the wall and, believe it or not, got onto our ceiling again.

'José!' I cried. 'José! The goats are coming—'

José threw down his magazine and rushed into the living room. But it was already too late. A gigantic goat broke through the plastic sheet, dropping its entire weight onto José's head. The two of them lay moaning on the concrete floor. José crawled upright. Without a word, he got a piece of rope and tied the goat to a post. Then he went up to the roof to see which jerk had just released their flock.

There was nobody on the roof.

'Fine, we'll slaughter and eat it tomorrow,' José said through gritted teeth.

Once we got down from the roof and took another look at the goat, not only was this prisoner of war not bleating, it looked like it was smiling. I lowered my head to take a closer look – and my God! The nine bonsai plants, twenty-five leaves in all, that I had worked meticulously to cultivate over the past year, had been eaten clean away.

I was shocked and angry and heartbroken. I raised my hand, mustering all the force in my body, and gave the goat a good beating. 'Look, look!' I cried to José. Then I rushed into the bathroom and hugged a big towel as tears came pouring out of me. This was the first time that desert living had discouraged me to the point of tears.

Of course we didn't slaughter the goat.

Our relations with our neighbours continued onwards in harmony, still with all the borrowing, the door opening and closing continuously.

Once when I ran out of matches, I went to our landlord's next door to ask for some. 'I do not have any,' giggled the landlord's wife.

I went to the kitchen of another neighbour's house.

'I will give you three,' Khadija said to me with a stern expression. 'We do not have many ourselves.'

'This box of matches is the one I gave you last week. I've given you five boxes. How could you forget?' I was growing angry.

'Yes. Now there is only one box. How can I give it to you?' She seemed even unhappier.

'You hurt my pride,' I said to Khadija, taking a lesson from their own book.

I took three matches home, thinking to myself that it must not have been easy to be Albert Schweitzer.[1]

In the year and a half that we've lived here, José has become the neighbours' electrician, carpenter and plasterer. As for me, I've become a scribe, nurse, teacher and seamstress. These skills were all honed through helping our neighbours, anyhow.

Young Sahrawi women usually have pale skin and lovely features. In their daily lives, they have to keep their faces covered in front of their own people, but the veils come off when they're in our home. Around here there's a girl named Mina who looks sweet and pretty. She liked me, but she liked José even more. Whenever José was home, she would dress up very nicely and come over to hang out. She eventually decided our house was boring, so she found excuses to ask José to go to her house.

One day she dropped in on us yet again. 'José!' she called from outside the window. 'José!'

We were in the middle of eating. 'What do you want from José?' I demanded.

'Our door is broken,' she said. 'We need José to fix it.'

Upon hearing this, José set down his fork and made to stand up.

'You're not going anywhere. Keep eating.' I dumped the food from my plate onto his.

People around these parts can have four wives. I certainly didn't like the idea of four women sharing José's pay cheque.

Mina didn't budge from the window. José glanced at her again. 'Don't look again,' I snapped. 'Pretend she's a mirage.'

When this beautiful mirage finally got married, I was overjoyed and sent her a large bolt of fabric.

The water we use for washing and cleaning is managed by the municipal government. They send over one large bucket each day and that's it. So when we bathe, we can't wash our clothes. If we wash our clothes, then we can't do the dishes or mop the floor. To manage all these things, you have to keep careful track of how much water is left in the bucket on the roof. The bucket of water on the roof is very salty and can't be drunk. You have to buy drinking water separately from the store. Water is very precious around here.

Last week, to participate in a camel-racing competition in town, we rushed the few hundred kilometres home from a camping trip in the great desert. It was an incredibly windy day. My whole body was covered in sand and dust by the time I got home. I looked awful. As soon as I entered the front door, I ran to the bathroom to rinse off. I wanted to look nice because Televisión Española's desert correspondents had agreed to shoot me riding a camel for their newsreel. After I was all lathered up in soap, the water wouldn't come. I urged José to go and take a look at the bucket on the roof.

'It's empty,' José said. 'No water.'

'That's not possible! We haven't been home for two days so not a drop of water has been used.' I started getting worried.

Wrapping myself in a towel, I ran up to the roof in my bare feet. Like something out of a bad dream, the water bucket was indeed empty. I looked across at the neighbours' roof and saw a dozen or more empty flour sacks drying in the sun. It dawned on me then how the water must have all been eaten up.

Once I wiped the soap from my body with a towel, I went with José to the camel race.

That afternoon, all our boisterous Spanish friends were riding on the backs of camels, galloping their way through the race and looking magnificent. Only I stood beneath the sun watching others. '*Cobarde!*' the riders would taunt as they passed near me. '*Gallina!*'

There was no way I could tell them the reason I wasn't riding a camel was because I'd itch all over if I were to sweat too much. My skin would make soap bubbles.

Among our neighbours, the person I'm closest to is Gueiga. She's a warm, intelligent girl with a sharp mind. But Gueiga has a problem. Her way of thinking can be entirely different from ours, which is to say her conceptions of right and wrong often leave me stunned.

There was a night when José and I wanted to attend a cocktail party at the Hotel Nacional here. I ironed the black evening dress that I hadn't worn in a long time. I also put on a few slightly more expensive necklaces that I don't usually wear.

'What time is the cocktail party?' José asked.

'Eight.' I looked at the clock and saw that it was already quarter to.

It was only after I was dressed, had my earrings in and went to put on my shoes that I noticed my leather high heels were missing from the rack. I asked José and he said he hadn't moved them.

'Why don't you just wear whatever?' José hates waiting more than anything else. I looked at all the shoes lined up on the rack – tennis shoes, wooden slippers, flat sandals, cloth shoes, high boots – but not a single pair that would go with my long black gown. I was beginning to get really agitated. I looked again and… What the hell was this thing? How did it get here? What was it?

A pair of dirty black desert boots with pointed toes was resting on the rack. One glance and I knew they belonged to Gueiga. If her shoes were on my rack, then where could my shoes have gone?

I huffed over to Gueiga's house and grabbed her in my arms. 'Where are my shoes?' I asked angrily. 'Where are my shoes? Why did you steal them? Find them and give them back to me, you jerk!' I cried.

Gueiga leisurely went to look in the kitchen, beneath the mats, in the goat pen, behind a door. She looked everywhere but didn't find anything.

'My sister wore them out to play,' she answered me calmly. 'I do not have them now.'

'You'll pay for this tomorrow.' I gritted my teeth and walked home.

For the cocktail party that night, my only option was to change into a white cotton outfit and a pair of sandals. As I mingled with the bejewelled wives of José's superiors, the contrast was startling. One of José's co-workers even had the nerve to compliment me. 'You look great tonight, like a shepherdess. You're just missing a wooden stick.'

The next morning, Gueiga returned my high heels to me, already destroyed beyond recognition. I stared at her, then snatched the shoes.

'Hmph! You are mad, so mad, so I will get mad.' Gueiga's face was turning red with anger. 'Your shoes are in my home,' she continued. 'Aren't my shoes also in your home? I should be more mad than you.'

When I heard this absolutely absurd explanation, I couldn't help but guffaw. 'Gueiga, you should go to a mental hospital.' I pointed to her temple.

'What hospital?' She didn't understand.

'Forget it. Gueiga, let me ask you. Can you go around to all the neighbouring women and ask what, besides my toothbrush and husband, you're not interested in borrowing?'

She seemed to wake from a dream, hearing this. 'What does your toothbrush look like?' she asked immediately.

'Get out,' I cried in agitation. 'Get out.'

Gueiga kept speaking as she stepped backwards. 'I just want to look at your toothbrush. I do not want your husband. Really—'

After I shut the door, I could still hear Gueiga on the street talking loudly to another girl. 'See that? She hurt my pride.'

Thanks to these neighbours, my life in the desert was an unfailingly colourful experience. No longer did I know the taste of solitude.

Dilettante Fishermen

One Sunday, José had to work an extra shift and was gone all day. To kill time, I carefully counted up the money he had made since March. I wrote the sum on a clean white piece of paper and waited for him to return. When he got home that night, I put the paper in front of him and said, 'Look how much money we've made in half a year.'

He seemed very pleased when he glanced at my calculations. 'I didn't think it would be this much,' he said. 'Looks like it's worth suffering through this desert life after all!' In high spirits, he suggested we eat out since we weren't hurting for cash. I knew he wanted to take me to dine at the Hotel Nacional. We stepped out as soon as I changed my clothes. This was a rare occasion indeed.

'Let's start with *sopa de mariscos* and red wine, the good kind,' José told the waiter. 'I would like a steak, and the lady will have four orders of large prawns. For dessert, make it ice-cream cake. Four orders of that as well. Thanks!'

'Good thing I didn't eat today,' I whispered to José. 'Now we can have a real feast.'

The Hotel Nacional is run by the Spanish government. Its restaurant, decorated to look like an Arabic palace, has a nice local ambience and romantic lighting. There are never too many patrons. The air is fresh and fragrant, without a whiff of dust. Forks and knives are polished to a brilliant shine. All the tablecloths are immaculately ironed. Faint music streams in the background like a babbling brook. Whenever I'm there, I forget we're in the desert. It feels like returning to the good old days in Madrid.

Soon the dishes arrived on beautiful silver plates. A lush green salad complemented the row of fried prawns. Dark red wine filled our cups. 'The bird of happiness is with us!' I sighed with contentment, looking at our food.

'If you like, we can come here regularly in the future.' José was behaving very generously that night, as though he were a wealthy tycoon. After months of hard living, we had discovered there was one good thing about being in the desert: mundane pleasures were now sublime, filling our spirits with immense satisfaction. In other words, we valued our stomachs over our heads. Once dinner was over, we paid with two crisp green bills and strolled home happily. I felt truly blessed.

We ate at home the next night, of course. A round potato cake, a roll of white bread and a bottle of water sat on the table before us. 'Let me slice this up. You can eat two thirds of the potato and I'll take the rest.' While I was dividing our portions, I moved the bread roll to José's plate so it would look more full. 'It's really good. I put onions in it. Eat up!' I took a bite myself.

José wolfed down the potato cake in no time, then rose to go into the kitchen.

'There's no more,' I said quickly. 'That's all we have for tonight.'

'What's the deal?' he asked, looking at me with confusion.

'Take a look at this!' I handed him another paper with new calculations. 'This is how much money we've spent in half a year,' I said, slinging myself over his shoulder to explain. 'Yesterday I figured out how much we earned, and today I straightened out our expenses.'

'This much? We've spent this much?' he barked. 'We're broke!'

'Yes,' I nodded. 'See, I wrote it very clearly here.'

José snatched up the paper and began to read aloud my accounts. 'Tomatoes, sixty pesetas a kilo. Watermelon, two hundred and twenty. Pork, half a kilo for three hundred... Why did you buy such expensive groceries?' he grumbled, muttering to himself. 'We should be saving...' He stood as he read, voice growing louder and louder. 'Car maintenance, fifteen thousand. Petrol, twenty-four thousand—'

'Don't freak out! We've driven sixteen thousand kilometres in half a year. It all adds up.'

'So, we spent all the money we made,' José said. 'What a waste.' He looked so upset, his face was almost theatrical with despair.

'Look, it's not like we wasted anything. We haven't spent a single peseta on clothing in six months. Our money just disappeared from having friends over, taking photos, going on road trips, those sort of things.'

'Fine. From this day forward, no more hungry bachelors allowed over for dinner,' José announced with determination. 'Only black and white photography. And no more trips. I've lost count of the number of times we've criss-crossed this desert.'

In this sad little town, there's only one dirty and decrepit cinema. As for the streets, they are a far cry from what you might call festive. Most of our magazines and newspapers are totally out of date. We're able to get television two or three times a month on average. The people on screen look so ghostly, I don't dare watch it when I'm home alone. Water and power outages are commonplace. And when you want to go for a walk, there are the endless sandstorms to reckon with.

Life around here might be comfortable for the Sahrawi, but it often drives the Europeans to alcoholism, husbands and wives to conflict and single men to suicide. These are all tragedies that the desert forces out; only José and I seem to understand the art of living here. We manage to toil through hard days without too much trouble.

I listened calmly to José's plan to save money. 'Aren't you afraid we'll go nuts or kill ourselves after three months of such thrifty living?'

José laughed bitterly. 'True. If we don't get out of here for a holiday, we'll suffocate.'

'How about this? Instead of going inland to Algeria, let's go to the coast. Why don't we take advantage of that long stretch of shoreline?'

'We'd still need a ridiculous amount of petrol to drive to the sea and back.'

'Let's catch some fish then. We can dry and salt them. That would save on groceries and we'd make up for some of the petrol money, too.' I've always had a lot of energy when it comes to having fun. I wasn't about to get discouraged.

The next weekend, we packed our tent and went to explore the rocky coast. By night, we camped out on the cliffs. There were many advantages to a coastline without beaches. It was easier to rappel down the cliffs. When the tide receded, abalone stuck to the rocks and crabs in the crevices were revealed. There were octopuses in pools of water, spotted eels resembling snakes, disc-like electric fish and thousands of black shellfish growing directly on the rocks, which I recognised as mussels. There were also thick bands of kelp that we could dry and use to make soup. The scattered pieces of driftwood looked like modernist sculptures. I thought about taking home some speckled stones. I could stick them on cardboard to make art. This stretch of coast, preserved from human encroachment, was still primitive and abundant.

'These are the treasures of King Solomon!' I cried, hopping all over the slippery rocks. 'We hit the jackpot!' I was over-whelmed with glee.

'This pile of rocks is for you. Grab them quickly while the tide is still out.' José tossed me a bucket, a pair of work gloves and a knife. He was in his wetsuit, about to dive under to spear big fish.

Less than an hour later, my bucket was filled with mussels and abalone that we'd dug out, as well as sixteen big red crabs, each the size of a small washbasin. There was no room left in the bucket so I made a little prison with rocks, temporarily sealing them all in. I tied up an enormous bunch of kelp.

José came ashore with around ten pink fish strung around his waist.

'See, there are so many we can't even keep up.' This was the first time I discovered what it felt like to be a greedy person.

Seeing my large crabs, José went to grab almost another twenty grey and black little crabs. 'The little ones are called *nécoras*,' he said. 'They're tastier than the big ones.'

The tide was gradually coming in again. We retreated cliffside to scale and clean the fish. They filled up an entire bag. I took off my trousers, tied the legs into a knot and threw the crabs in there. We lashed the bucket to the rope and climbed up the cliff. That weekend was our first adventure, and we had plenty to show for it indeed.

On the way home, I kept urging José to speed up. 'Drive faster! Faster! Let's invite your co-workers from the bachelor quarters over for dinner.'

'Didn't you want to salt the fish?' José asked.

'Forget about it this first time. We'll treat everyone. They usually don't get to eat well.' José was very happy to hear this. Before we got home, we also picked up a case of beer and six bottles of wine for our guests.

The next few weekends in a row, all of José's co-workers wanted to come fishing with us. On our high of happiness, we thought we might as well make a dozen or so quiches and buy five cabbages and ten pounds of beef. We also added a mini fridge, a charcoal grill, five large buckets and six pairs of gloves, as well as a case of Coke and one of milk. With great strength and vigour, we set forth in multiple cars and ran wildly along the shore. By night we set up camp and had a barbecue, talking up a storm and having all the fun in the world. Unwittingly, the whole matter of saving money had been clean forgotten.

In our household, nobody manages the money. We keep cash inside a pocket of my Chinese down jacket. Whenever we need any, we just reach in and grab a bill. As for accounting, if we remember, we'll write it down on the nearest little piece of paper and toss it into a large sugar jar. After only a few trips to the sea, the pocket was empty, the jar full of little slips.

'All gone again, so quickly!' I muttered to myself, holding the jacket in my arms.

'Didn't we go to the sea in the first place to make salted fish and save on our groceries? But then there ended up being so many more expenses.' José scratched his head, befuddled.

'Friendship is priceless,' I said by way of comfort.

'Might as well sell the fish we catch next week.' José had made up his mind again.

'That's right! If you can eat fish, you can sell them! You're so smart.' I jumped up and patted José on the head. 'I hadn't even thought of that!'

'As long as we break even, I'm fine.' José wasn't a greedy person. I, on the other hand, had big ambitions and hoped to make a killing.

That Saturday at four in the morning, we got into our car and hit the road, teeth chattering from the cold. We drove headstrong through the dark of the desert, relying on our skilfulness, bravado and familiarity with the roads.

By eight, the sun had barely risen, but we'd already reached the high cliffs. We got out of the car. Behind us was the endless desert in all its mystery and tranquillity; before our eyes were the swashing waves of the sea beating on a stony shore. Not a thread of cloud hung in the azure sky. Flocks of seabirds flew around and around, sometimes letting out cries that underscored the desolation of the scene.

Flipping up my jacket collar, I raised my arms and craned my head into the wind, holding this posture without moving.

'What are you thinking about?' asked José.

'You first,' I parried.

'I'm thinking about the world in *Jonathan Livingston Seagull*.' José is a clear-headed, open-hearted person. The fact that he would be thinking about that book at this time, under these circumstances, was no surprise at all.

'And you?' he asked me again.

'I was thinking I'm madly in love with a handsome, lame-footed military officer. I'm currently walking with him through a beautiful glen, one bursting with heather. The wind is whipping my messy hair. He's gazing passionately at me – what romance, what suffering!' I sighed mournfully. I closed my eyes, hugged my arms and exhaled with satisfaction.

'Are you playing the lead in *Ryan's Daughter* today?' José asked.

'You guessed right. OK, time to get to work.'

I clapped my hands together and went to pull out the rope in preparation for rappelling down the cliffs. Everything seemed more interesting and lively after indulging in such crazy fantasies; this was my way of adjusting to a dull life.

'Sanmao, let's focus,' José said solemnly. 'You have to help me out.'

We stood by the rocks. José dived under the waves. Every time he speared a fish, he'd throw it into shallow water. I would hurry over to grab, scale and clean it, all while kneeling on the rocks. Once each one was clean, I would put it into a plastic bag. My hands were soon cut up and bleeding after scaling a few large ones. Soaking them in sea water was pretty painful.

José was bobbing in and out of the water, continuously throwing fish out. I worked furiously, laying out the cleaned fish in neat rows in the bag.

'Making money isn't that easy!' I said to myself, shaking my head, my knees growing swollen.

After a long time, José finally came ashore and I quickly gave him some milk to drink. He closed his eyes and lay back on the rocks, his face pale.

'How many?' he asked.

'Over thirty. They're so big. I'm sure we have sixty or seventy kilos.'

'No more, I'm exhausted.' He closed his eyes again.

'People like us should be called "dilettante fishermen",' I said, pouring more milk for José. 'In Paris back in the day, there were people who'd go to work during the week and then paint on Sundays. They called themselves dilettante painters. We're catching fish on the weekend, so we're dilettante fishermen. How about it?'

'So many tricks up your sleeve,' José said in spite of his uninterest. 'Coming up with a new name just for catching fish.'

After we were well rested, we transported the pile of fish up the cliff in three rounds. We put them in the car boot and covered them with a layer of crushed ice from the small fridge. Driving back through the desert beneath the glare of the sun was more labour on our part. Strangely, this time didn't feel as much fun as before. We were worn out and on our last legs. 'Please let me sleep for a bit before we sell fish,' I implored José as we approached town. 'Please! I'm exhausted!'

'Not possible,' José said. 'The fish will go off. Why don't you go home and rest? I'll sell.'

'If we're selling, then let's do it together,' I conceded. 'I'll just grin and bear it.'

As we were driving past the castle-like walls of the Hotel Nacional, I had a sudden stroke of inspiration and yelled, 'Stop!'

José stepped on the brakes. I got out of the car in my bare feet and poked my head through the hotel gate to look around. 'Hey, hey, psst...' I called out quietly to Antonio at the counter.

'Ah, Sanmao!' he greeted me loudly.

'Shh, don't be too loud. Where's the back door?' I asked softly.

'Back door? Why do you want to go in through the back?'

Before I had a chance to explain, the manager walked past. I hid behind a pillar in fright. When he stuck his head around and saw me, I fled swiftly to the car outside.

'I can't do it! I'm too awkward to make a sale.' I held my head in my hands, angry at myself.

'I'll go.' José threw open the car door and strode out. My dear José, he really has the bluster.

'Hey, you. Señor Manager.' He waved his hands at the manager, who came over. I hid behind José's back. 'We have fresh fish. Do you want to buy some?' José's tone was cool and calm, neither humble nor pushy. He didn't seem embarrassed at all, though I was pretty sure he was.

'What? You want to sell fish?' The manager looked at the scruffy clothes we were wearing. A look of distaste came over his face, as if we'd insulted him. 'Go through the side door to sell fish,' he said scornfully, pointing. 'You can discuss it with the people in charge of the kitchen…'

I shrank even further into myself and desperately tugged at José. 'See, he can't stand the sight of us,' I said. 'Let's go and sell elsewhere. We'll have to see this manager at future cocktail parties…'

'This manager's an idiot. Don't be afraid of him. Come on, let's go to the kitchen.'

All the kitchen staff surrounded us like they'd never seen anything like this before. 'How much per kilo?'

The two of us looked at each other and didn't know what to say. 'Um, fifty pesetas,' José offered as an opening price.

'Yes, fifty,' I reaffirmed quickly.

'Alright. Give me ten fish and let's weigh.' The person in charge was very polite.

We were extremely happy and flew back to our car to pick out ten big fish for him.

'You can take this slip to the accountant after the fifteenth to claim your money.'

'You don't pay cash?' we asked.

'We're a public office. Please bear with us!' The person in charge of buying fish shook hands with us. We got a statement showing that we would receive more than a thousand pesetas for this first batch of fish. I looked it over carefully before putting it safe and sound in my pocket.

'Alright, let's go to the Didi Hotel now,' José said.

The Didi Hotel has a grand reputation in the Sahara for providing free meals to labourers. By night it's a bar, with rooms for rent upstairs. The outside is painted peach pink. Inside the lights are green, and they play pop music all day long. There are always herds of Caucasian women dressed to the nines doing business inside. The labourers who come from Spain to fix the roads head to the Didi Hotel as soon as they receive their pay cheques. When they get drunk, they get thrown out. Their month's-worth of hard-earned income largely disappears into the pockets of these women.

When we got to the front of the hotel, I said to José, 'You go in. I'll wait outside.' After waiting for almost twenty minutes, he still hadn't reappeared. I carried a fish and went in after him. I reached the counter just as a very sexy 'didi' was touching José's face. He stood there like a real lemon. I strode over, glaring at the woman, and said loudly, 'Want to buy some fish? Five hundred a kilo.' I slammed the dead fish in my hand on the bar counter, where it landed with a thud.

'How can you just raise your prices willy-nilly? Your husband just said it was fifty a kilo.'

I gave her a dirty look, thinking to myself that I'd raise the price to 5,000 a kilo if she dared touch José's face again.

José pushed me back out of the hotel. 'You're causing trouble,' he said under his breath. 'I almost sold the entire lot to her.'

'Take it or leave it. Are you selling fish or selling your charms? I can't believe you let her touch your face.' I raised my hand to hit José. He knew he was in the wrong and covered his head, letting me swat at him.

In the midst of my fury, I rushed back into the hotel to grab the big fish I'd left on the bar.

The sun was high in the sky. We were hot and hungry and thirsty and tired and angry at each other. I wanted to throw out all of the fish, but I couldn't bring myself to say it.

'Do you remember Paco, the cook from the desert corps?' I asked José.

'You want to sell to the troops?'

'Yes.'

Without a word, José began driving towards the desert corps campsite. Before we got to the barracks, we saw Paco walking on the side of the road.

'Paco, do you want to buy fresh fish?' I called out to him, full of hope.

'Fish?' he asked. 'Where is it?'

'In our car. We have more than twenty.'

Paco stared at me and shook his head furiously. 'Sanmao, there are more than three thousand people at this camp. You think twenty fish would be enough?' He refused me in one fell swoop.

'Who knows? Why don't you take it and give it a try? Jesus fed more than five thousand people with five loaves of bread and two fish. What do you have to say about that?' I retorted.

'Take a lesson from me and go and sell them by the post office,' Paco advised. 'You'll find the most people there.' Of course, our prospective customers had always been Europeans. The Sahrawi don't eat fish.

So we ended up going to the stationery shop to buy a little blackboard and some chalk. We also borrowed a set of scales from the owner of the grocery store, whom we knew. On the board, I drew a jumping red fish and wrote: 'Fresh fish for sale, 50 ptas/kilo.'

We drove up to the front of the post office. It was five in the afternoon. All the parcels and letters flown in by airmail had just arrived. A huge crowd of people was checking their mailboxes, a lively scene indeed. We parked, put the blackboard in our car window and opened up the boot. By the time we had everything all set up, our faces were already pretty flushed. We sat on the pavement, barely able to look up at our potential customers.

Crowds of people kept passing, but nobody stopped to buy any fish. 'Sanmao, didn't you say we were dilettantes?' José said to me after sitting a while. 'Dilettantes don't need to rely on selling their leisurely pursuits to make a living!'

'You want to go home?' I was feeling pretty lacklustre about it myself.

Just then, one of José's colleagues walked by and saw us. He came over to say hello. 'Hey! Just chilling out?'

'No.' José stood up in embarrassment.

'We're selling fish.' I pointed to our car in the street.

This colleague was an old bachelor, a nice and sturdy fellow. He walked over to examine the blackboard and the open car boot and finally understood what was going on. He came back and pulled both of us into the street. 'If it's fish you're selling, you have to shout it out! You can't be so shy. Come, come, I'll help you.'

The co-worker casually grabbed a fish in his hands and raised his voice. 'Yoohoo, fresh fish for sale! Seventy-five a kilo! Yoohoo! Fish!' He had unexpectedly decided to raise the price himself.

When people heard his shouts, they began to gather around immediately. We were pleasantly surprised. The twenty or so fish were really no big deal. We sold them all in an instant.

We sat on the ground counting our money and found that we'd made over 3,000 pesetas. When we went to look for José's co-worker, he'd already walked off chuckling into the distance.

'José, we have to remember to thank him!' I said.

We were bone-tired when we got home. After showering, I went to the kitchen in my bathrobe and boiled a pot of water, throwing in some pasta.

'We're having that?' José asked unhappily.

'Let's keep it simple. I'm exhausted.' To be honest, I didn't even feel like eating.

'We've been toiling since early morning until now, and you're making me pasta? I won't eat it.' He was mad now, putting on clothes and getting ready to leave.

'Where are you going?' I yelled.

'Out to eat.' Looked like someone had suddenly become a blockhead. I had to change clothes and chase after him. As for eating out, of course there was only one place to go: the restaurant at the Hotel Nacional.

In the restaurant, I quietly nagged José. 'Only you could be so stupid. We're ordering the cheapest thing on the menu, got it?'

Right at that moment, we heard a clap and saw one of José's bosses coming over to us. 'What a coincidence,' he cried.

'I was just looking for someone to eat with. Let's all eat together.' He came and sat down without further ado.

'I hear they have fresh fish in the kitchen today,' he continued, speaking mostly to himself. 'How about it? Let's have three orders. It's not often you get this kind of fresh fish in the desert.' When you're used to being the boss, you forget to pay attention to those around you. Without asking us, he told the waiter, 'Lettuce salad, three orders of fish. Bring the wine first. We'll look at dessert later.'

The foreman in the restaurant was the same guy who bought the fish from us earlier in the day. When he passed our table and saw José and me eating the fish that we'd sold him for twelve times the price, his jaw dropped, aghast. He looked at us as if we were crazy.

When it was time to pay, we fought over the bill with José's boss. José ended up winning and put down our earnings from the fish we sold by the post office. We only got a little bit of change. Only then did I realise that, whether it was fifty or seventy-five a kilo, we had undersold. We were in the desert, after all.

The next day, we slept in very late. I got up to make coffee and do laundry. Lying in bed, José said to me, 'At least we still have that income from the Hotel Nacional to pick up. Otherwise, yesterday would have been a total disaster. We lost all our gas money. Let's not even talk about how hard we worked.'

'Speaking of income – that invoice…' I started shrieking and flew into the bathroom to shut off the washing machine. I dug out my trousers from all those bubbles and reached a hand into the pockets to feel. That statement had long since been soaked to shreds, a soft white pile. There was no way to put it back together.

'José, the last fish slipped away! Time to eat potato cake again.' I sat on the stone steps outside the bathroom, laughing and crying at the same time.

Seed of Death

Ramadan is about to come to an end. The past few evenings, I've been going up to the roof to gaze at the moon because the locals tell me the first night of the full moon is when Muslims break their fast and celebrate. My neighbours have been killing goats and camels in preparation for the feast. I'm also waiting for the local women to draw beautiful patterns in dark brown-red henna on my palms. This is a necessary adornment for women of these parts during the holiday. Since I'm a big believer in following local customs, I want to do as they do.

On Saturday, we didn't have any plans to go out into the desert, so José and I stayed home reading late into the night. We slept in until noon the next day. After getting up, we went into town to buy the out-of-date Spanish newspapers that had come in by airmail earlier in the morning. We had a simple meal for lunch. Once I washed the dishes, I came back into the living room.

José had his head buried in the newspaper. I lay on the floor listening to music. I was in a good mood because I'd slept so well. I was planning on going into town again that night to see a Charlie Chaplin silent film, *City Lights*. It was a bright and sunny day, no dust in the air. Beautiful music filled our small living room. This was the type of Sunday that made a person feel content and at ease.

Around two in the afternoon, some Sahrawi children were calling my name through the window. They wanted big bags for chopped meat, so I gave them each a few colourful plastic bags. After distributing the bags, I stood and gazed at the desert. Across the street there were a bunch of new houses going up. The stunning desert scenery was getting blocked off, day by day. It was heartbreaking.

A few moments later I noticed that two boys I recognised had started fighting nearby, a bicycle cast aside next to them. When I saw they were really going at it, I went over, hopped on their bike and rode in circles. This was really getting to be a brawl. I stopped riding and went over to try to break it up.

As I was getting off the bike, I spotted a Sahrawi-style hemp necklace on the ground. Naturally, I picked it up. 'Did you lose this?' I asked the two boys, holding it out to them.

When they saw what I had in my hand, they stopped fighting and jumped back quite a distance, a fearful expression on their faces. 'Not mine, not mine!' they said in unison, unwilling to even touch it.

Puzzled, I said to them, 'Fine. I'll put it on my doorstep. If someone comes looking for it, tell them the lost necklace is by my door.' With that I went back indoors to listen to music again.

Around 4 p.m., I opened the front door and saw that the street was totally deserted. The necklace was in the same place. I picked it up and examined it more closely. It was three objects strung together: a small cloth sack, a heart-shaped fruit pit and a piece of copper.

I'd long wanted a piece of copper like this, but I couldn't find it anywhere in town. I'd never seen anything like the cloth sack or pit before. I realised how soiled this string of objects must have been, probably not worth a peseta. Maybe somebody had thrown it out because they didn't want it any more. I decided I might as well take it myself.

I happily showed off the necklace to José when I got back in. 'Ugh,' he said. 'You just picked up someone's rubbish.' He went back to reading his newspaper.

I went into the kitchen and snipped the hemp string with a pair of scissors. The cloth sack had a weird smell that I didn't like, so I threw it in the bin. The pit also smelled bad, so out it went too. That left the rust-red piece of smooth copper, looking very much like a piece of bean curd. There was even beautiful white metal inlaid along its contours. It was quite different from the necklaces other people wore. I really liked it, so I scrubbed it clean with a cleansing powder. I dug out a thick piece of silk ribbon, strung the copper tablet on it and found that it fitted perfectly around my neck. It was a very modern look.

I ran back to show José. 'Looks great,' he said. 'It would go well with your low-cut black blouse. You should wear it!'

With my new necklace on, I returned to listening to music. After a while, I'd completely forgotten about it.

I started getting sleepy after listening to a few tapes. Something was not right. I'd only been up for a few hours. How was it that I felt so tired all over? I put the tape player on my chest because I was really groggy. This way I could change tapes without having to get up. The copper tablet around my neck just so happened to rest on the machine.

Within a few moments, the tape player suddenly started winding up like crazy. The music sped up and the rhythm was all off. It sounded angry. José jumped up and turned the tape player off, looking it over in confusion. 'It was fine earlier,' he mumbled to himself. 'Must be too much dust.'

We sprawled on the floor again to test it out. This time things got even worse. The whole tape got tangled up. We used a hairpin to extract the messed-up tape from inside. José went to get some tools to fix it.

While José was looking for his tools, I banged on the tape player with my hand. Whenever our electronics weren't working, I found that hitting them willy-nilly could usually solve the problem. No need to take things apart to fix them.

I had just started banging on it when my nose started itching and I sneezed. I used to have very serious allergies and would sneeze all the time. My sinuses were always acting up. But then a Spanish doctor helped me out a while ago and I haven't had problems since. When I started sneezing again this time, I muttered, 'Ha, it's back!' and went to get toilet paper. Based on previous experience, I'd have a runny nose any minute now.

The bathroom was mere steps away, but the sneezes continued to come. At the same time, my right eye began to feel uncomfortable. I looked in the mirror and saw that my eye was a bit red. I had to ignore it because my nose was starting to run.

After I'd sneezed more than twenty times, I got the feeling that something was wrong. Back in the day, I would never sneeze continuously like this. I still didn't pay it much mind, though, and went to get some medicine from the kitchen. But less than ten seconds after my initial flurry of sneezes was finished, I started sneezing up an even bigger storm all over again.

José stood nearby, looking confused. 'The doctor didn't cure you after all!' he said. I nodded, my hand over my nose, sneezing *achoo, achoo*. I couldn't even talk and felt absolutely mortified.

Once I had sneezed over a hundred times, I was a total mess from tears and snot. It was hard to stop for even a minute or two. I rushed to the window to breathe some fresh air. José went to get a cup of hot water from the kitchen and put in some tea leaves for me to drink.

I sat down in a chair and took a few sips of tea, wiping my nose and feeling the redness around my eye grow warm. When I went to look in the mirror again, my eye was already swollen. It had happened so fast, in less than twenty minutes. I thought it was weird, but didn't dwell on it because I needed to stop my sneezing first. The sneezes kept coming, a few times every minute. I held a wastepaper basket in my arms, wiping my nose and throwing the tissues in. By the time the next round of typhoon-like sneezes came over me, blood was coming out of my nose. I turned and said to José, 'This is no good. Now my nose is bleeding!'

I looked at José again and he suddenly shook before my eyes, like an image in a movie turning sideways. Then the walls around me and the ceiling began to spin. I lunged and grabbed hold of José. 'Is it an earthquake?' I yelled. 'I'm dizzy—'

'No!' he said. 'Quickly, lie down.' He came and held me.

I wasn't scared but confused, rather, about how I'd got into such a state in the span of half an hour. José dragged me to the bedroom. Everything was spinning around me. If I shut my eyes, I became dizzy as though the world had been turned upside down. After lying down for just a few minutes, my stomach began to feel strange. I struggled over to the bathroom, where I began to vomit loudly.

In the past, I used to throw up quite often, but not like this. It wasn't just my stomach churning, but an insane torture that felt like I was going to throw up all the organs in my body. After throwing up everything I'd eaten for lunch, I began vomiting clear liquid. After the clear liquid came yellow bile. After the bitter bile, there was nothing left to vomit. But I still couldn't keep myself from dry heaving loudly.

José grabbed me tightly from behind. I kept on retching, sneezing and bleeding from the nose until my strength was completely sapped and I could do nothing more but sit on the ground. He dragged me back to bed and wiped my face with a towel. 'Did you eat something unsanitary?' he asked worriedly. 'Is it food poisoning?'

'I don't have diarrhoea,' I answered him feebly. 'It's not from something I ate.' I shut my eyes to rest. Once I lay down for a bit, the symptoms seemed to go away, strangely enough. The force that had tossed my insides about like a wave had all but disappeared. I felt completely enervated and broke out into a cold sweat. But the room had stopped spinning. I was no longer sneezing, and the discomfort in my stomach had eased. 'I want to drink tea,' I said to José.

José jumped up to get some tea. I drank a mouthful and, within a few minutes, felt completely fine again. I sat up with my eyes wide open.

José felt my pulse, then pushed down hard on my stomach. 'Does it hurt?' he asked.

'It doesn't,' I said. 'I'm alright. How bizarre.' I made to get out of bed.

He looked at me, speechless. I really was better. 'You should still lie down,' he said. 'I'll make you a hot water bottle.'

'I'm fine, really,' I said. 'No need to do that.'

Suddenly José touched my face and said, 'Hey, when did your eye get so swollen?'

I reached a hand up to feel. My right eye was indeed very puffy. 'Let me look in the mirror!' I said. After just a few steps, I felt a spasm of pain in my stomach as though somebody had lashed me with a whip. I groaned and fell to the ground. I quickly returned to bed. Pain grabbed hold of me like a flash of lightning. My stomach felt as though somebody was twisting and wringing it from the inside. I shrank into myself and tried my hardest to fight it, but I couldn't help but start to moan. I endured it as best as I could. The pain kept growing worse. I began to lose control of myself, rolling back and forth in bed and crying out. Soon I was in such pain that my eyes clouded over and I could only hear myself screaming like a wild animal. José placed a hand on me to massage my stomach. I pushed him aside violently. 'Don't touch me!' I shrieked.

I sat up, then fell down again. Pain convulsed my abdomen without ceasing. Once I'd screamed myself hoarse, my chest and lungs began to hurt as well. My lungs were shuddering with every breath. By this point, I was like a rag doll being torn to pieces by some horrifying invisible force. The room had gone dark around me. I couldn't see anything. My mental faculties were all there, but my body was struggling ineffectively, a slave to the excruciating pain. I didn't have the energy to cry out any more and started to bite down on the pillows, clawing at the sheets, my whole body soaked in sweat.

José knelt by the bed, incredibly alarmed and close to tears. He kept on calling me by the Chinese nickname that my parents and sister had given me when I was young. 'Meimei! Meimei! Meimei...'

When I heard his voice, I froze. Everything around me was dark. There was the sound of something like a low explosion in my ears, or thunder rumbling closer and closer. The intense pain wouldn't let go of me for even a moment. I started screaming again. I heard myself crying out in Chinese, 'Mama! Papa! I'm going to die! Oh, it hurts…'

I couldn't think of anything else at that moment. All I could do was screech. All I could feel was the maddening pain of my organs being wrung out and ripped apart.

José picked me up in his arms and carried me out. He opened the front door and set me down. Then he ran over to open the car door and then put me inside. I knew I was outside, so I bit my lip to keep myself from crying out in pain. Bright light streamed in. I closed my eyes, discovering that I was terrified of it. 'Light, I don't want light,' I said to José, covering my eyes with my hands. 'Come shield me, quick.' When he ignored me, I screamed, 'José, the light is too bright.' He grabbed a towel from the backseat and threw it to me. I didn't know what was happening, but I was so scared that I immediately covered myself with the towel and hunched over on my knees.

There were certainly no doctors in the desert hospital on a Sunday. José couldn't find anyone to help. Without a word, he turned the car around and drove towards the barracks of the desert corps. When we got close and the guard saw what shape I was in, he immediately came to help. The two of them half-dragged, half-held me, carrying me into the medical room. The guard called for somebody to find the medical officer. I lay on the examination table, feeling like I was slowly getting better again. There was no more pounding in my ears, darkness in my eyes or pain in my stomach. When the medical officer charged in half an hour later, I was already sitting up. Besides feeling a bit weak, I was pretty much back to normal.

José described to the doctor the sickness that had so overwhelmed me in the afternoon. He listened to my heartbeat, felt my pulse, then looked at my tongue and knocked on my stomach. None of it hurt any more. My heart was just beating a little fast. He sighed, puzzled. 'She's fine,' he reassured José. 'There doesn't seem to be anything wrong with her.'

José seemed very discouraged and embarrassed, as though we'd played a trick on the medical officer. 'Look at her eye,' he said.

The medical officer pulled up my eyelid. 'There's pus,' he said. 'It's been inflamed for days, right?'

We strongly asserted otherwise, telling him it had become swollen within an hour. After further examination, the medical officer gave me an injection to reduce the swelling. He looked me over again and saw I wasn't joking.

'Maybe it's food poisoning,' he said finally.

'It's not,' I said. 'I don't have diarrhoea.'

'Maybe it's an allergy,' he tried again. 'You ate something that didn't agree with you.'

'I didn't break out in hives,' I countered. 'It wasn't a food allergy.'

The medical officer looked at me with great patience. 'Why don't you lie down,' he said. 'Call for me immediately if you vomit again or the pain comes back.' With that, he left the room.

It was a strange situation. An hour ago, I had come down with an illness like a woman possessed. But there were absolutely no symptoms when I was in the treatment room. Half an hour passed. José and the guard supported me all the way back to the car. 'If anything happens again, come back right away,' the guard said gently.

Sitting in the car, I felt very tired. 'Lean against me,' José told me. So I leaned on his shoulders and closed my eyes, the tablet around my neck dangling to his thigh.

The road home from the desert corps was a steep downward slope. José started the engine and slowly eased our way down. After only a few metres, I thought the car felt unexpectedly light. José wasn't even stepping on the gas, but the car felt as though there was somebody pushing it from behind, making us go faster and faster. José stamped hard on the brakes, but they didn't work. I saw him quickly pull the handbrake and shift into first gear. 'Sanmao, hold tight!' he said nervously. The car stalled and started careening down the slope. He stepped on the brakes again, but they were completely jammed.

The steep hill wasn't very high. Rationally speaking, there was no reason the car should be going so fast. But in the blink of an eye, we were speeding downhill as though we were afloat. 'Hold on to me tightly,' José said to me loudly. 'Don't be scared.' My eyes widened, seeing the road in front of José rush towards us. I wanted to cry out, but I couldn't because it felt like there was something blocking my throat. There was a ten-wheeler military truck coming straight at us. It seemed like we were going to crash right into it. It was only then that I let out a scream. With a great effort, José spun the steering wheel. Our car dived onto the side of the road, then continued to coast for a long time without stopping. José saw there was a mound of sand in front of us and steered us right into it. The car finally stopped. The two of us sat there amid a cloud of dust in the sand pile, our arms and legs ice cold, paralysed from the shock.

The people in the military truck got out right away and ran towards us. 'Are you OK? Everything OK?' they asked.

We could only nod, totally speechless. By the time they were digging us out with shovels, we were still sitting there limply as if hypnotised.

After a long time, José managed to say just one thing. 'It was the brakes,' he told the military officers.

A soldier told José to get out of the car so he could test it. He started the engine and tried out the brakes over and over again. Frighteningly enough, they were fine. José didn't believe it and tried it out himself. Turned out there was no issue. The thing that had just happened to us over the course of a few seconds felt like a bad dream, which vanished without a trace upon waking. Tongue-tied, we looked at the car, afraid to believe our own eyes.

When we thought back to it afterwards, we could never remember how the two of us managed to get back in the car and drive slowly home. That stretch of time disappeared from our memories, as though we were under a spell.

José helped me out of the car once we were home. 'How do you feel?' he asked.

'Completely worn out,' I said. 'But I'm not in pain any more.'

So José propped up my torso while my left hand held on to the car door. My body leaned against his. That little piece of copper bumped into him again. This was something I remembered later when I thought back on it. At the time, of course, I didn't notice something so small.

Because he was holding me up, José used his feet to kick the car door closed. I felt a dizzying pain. Four of my fingers had been slammed in the door. José hadn't noticed and was still trying to drag me towards our home. 'My h-hand,' I said. 'José, ah—'

He gave a yelp of surprise when he turned and saw what had happened. He let go of me and went to open the door.

My hand was freed, but my index finger and middle finger had been flattened. After a few seconds, warm blood began to flow, slowly soaking my palm.

'*Dios mío!* Did we commit some sin...' José quavered, taking my hand. He stood there trembling.

For some reason, I felt like I was about to use up the last ounce of strength I had left in my body. It wasn't that my hand hurt; I was just weak beyond belief. I desperately wanted to be left alone to sleep.

'My hand's fine,' I said to José. 'I want to lie down. Quick...'

Just then a neighbouring Sahrawi woman called out quietly from behind me. She hurried over and put a hand on my lower abdomen. José was still looking at my mangled hand when she said to him, 'She... Baby... is going to fall out.' I felt very far away, her voice reaching me from a distant place. I lifted my head and gazed weakly at José. His face was drifting this way and that like a reflection in rippling water.

José knelt down and held me tight. 'Go and get someone,' he said to the woman.

Hearing this, I used all my strength to utter just a few words. 'What is it? What's wrong with me?'

'Don't be afraid. You're bleeding a lot.' José's gentle voice wafted down to me.

I lowered my gaze. A river of blood was running down my legs and pooling thickly on the ground beneath. My skirt was already soaked. Blood continued to flow silently from my lower body.

'We have to find a doctor quickly.' José was shaking terribly.

I was very clear-headed at that moment, but felt like I could float away. I remember saying to José, 'We can't use our car.

We have to get someone else.' José scooped me up in his arms and carried me inside, kicking open the door. He put me on the bed. As soon as I lay down, I felt like my lower half had been split open. Blood poured out of me like a fountain.

I didn't feel any pain. A feathery sensation was slowly overtaking me; I wanted to fly out of my body.

Hamdi's wife Tebrak rushed into the room, followed by Hamdi in flowing trousers. 'Do not panic,' Hamdi said to José. 'She is having a miscarriage. My wife has experience.'

'It can't be a miscarriage,' José said. 'My wife is not pregnant.'

Hamdi reproached him angrily. 'Perhaps you did not know, or she did not tell you.'

'Whatever you say. I need your car to take her to the hospital. I'm positive she wasn't pregnant.'

The sound of their arguing came to me in waves, like iron chains slamming loudly against my weakened spirit. Life, at that moment, had no meaning to me. My only desire was for them to stop talking, to give me eternal peace. Even death would be less painful than the harm that their voices were inflicting on my flesh.

I heard Hamdi's wife talking loudly again. These sound waves were plucking and fiddling with me like I was a flimsy string. It was absolutely awful. I unconsciously raised my hands, wanting to cover my ears.

When my hands reached my messy long hair, Hamdi's wife cried out in alarm and immediately retreated to the door. She pointed at me and spoke sharply to Hamdi in their native language. Hamdi also took a few steps back. He said to José in a grave voice, 'The tablet around her neck. Who put it on her?'

'Let's get her to the hospital fast,' José said. 'We can talk about the tablet or whatever later.'

'Take it off,' Hamdi thundered. 'Take that thing off immediately.' José hesitated a moment.

'Hurry!' Hamdi yelled anxiously. 'Get it off. She will die,
you ignorant fools.'

With a shove from Hamdi, José came over and pulled on
the tablet. The silk ribbon broke; the tablet was in his hands.
Hamdi took off his shoe and smacked José's hand forcefully
with it. The tablet fell down next to the bed where I lay. His
wife kept talking rapidly.

'Think fast, who else did this tablet touch?' Hamdi asked José,
seemingly hysterical. 'What things? Quick. We do not have time.'

José started stammering, frightened by Hamdi and his
wife. 'It touched me,' he said. 'And the tape player. Besides
that – nothing else, I think.'

'Think harder!' Hamdi implored. 'Quick!'

'Really,' José said. 'There was nothing else.'

'May Allah preserve us,' Hamdi said in Arabic. 'It's fine
now,' he continued. 'Let's go out to talk.'

'She's bleeding...' José said worriedly. But he still followed
Hamdi out of the room.

I heard them close the door in the hallway and enter the
living room.

Strangely, my spirit seemed to revive. Buckets of cold sweat
were pouring out of me. I was breathing slowly and heavily.
My eyes felt very heavy and I couldn't open them. But my
body no longer felt adrift.

Everything around me felt amazingly peaceful and clear.
There was no sound whatsoever. All I felt was a comfortable
fatigue that was gradually submerging me. I was about to sink
into a deep slumber.

In a few short seconds, my highly sensitive spirit felt there
was something, a shapeless force, seeping into this little room.

I even thought I heard it making an almost imperceptibly slight hissing sound. Struggling to open my eyes, I saw only the ceiling. I shut my eyes again. But my sixth sense was telling me that a little river, a little snake, or something else long and thin had already crept in. It was flowing ceaselessly towards the tablet on the floor, entering calmly, slowly rising up and filling the entire room. An inexplicable sensation of cold and fear came over me. I opened my eyes again, but could not see what I felt.

After another ten seconds or so, a memory flashed in my mind like a sparked flame. Frozen in shock, I heard myself screaming. 'José... José... Ah, help...'

The door was closed. I thought I was screaming, but my voice was so hoarse. I yelled and yelled some more. I tried to move my body, but I had no energy. I saw the cup of tea on the nightstand by the bed and used all of my strength to grab hold of it, raise it and throw it down on the cement floor. The cup shattered loudly. I heard the door open. José rushed in.

I grabbed José. 'The coffee pot,' I said to him frantically. 'The coffee pot. When I was cleaning the tablet, I used the same cleansing powder to clean the coffee pot—'

José froze, then pushed me back into bed. Hamdi came in, sniffing left and right. José also smelled something. 'The gas...' they said at the same time.

We were off as soon as José got me out of bed. He and Hamdi dragged me all the way outside. José hurried back in to turn off the gas canister, then ran out. Hamdi dashed across the street to grab a handful of small stones. 'Hurry, use these rocks to seal the tablet,' he said, giving José a shove. 'Make them into a circle.'

José baulked. At Hamdi's urging, he ran back inside with the rocks.

That night we slept at a friend's house. We left the windows wide open at home to let the gas dissipate. We stared at each other, not knowing what to say, fear filling our hearts and minds completely.

Yesterday, around sunset, I lay on the couch in the living room, calmly listening to the sound of cars passing. I longed for José to be let off work early and come home. Not even the neighbours' children were gawking at the window like they usually did. I had been left in utter isolation.

Once José finished work, he came in with three of his Sahrawi colleagues.

'This is the deadliest and most powerful curse,' one of his colleagues explained to us. 'How unfortunate that you picked it up.'

'Is it a Muslim thing?' I asked them.

'We do not meddle with these things in Islam. It is witch-craft from Mauritania.'

'Don't all of you Sahrawi wear these pieces of copper?' José said.

'What we wear is something different,' his colleague said angrily. 'If it were the same, wouldn't we all be dead by now?'

'How do you tell the difference?' I pressed.

'Your tablet also came with a pit and a cloth sack, right? The copper also had a frame of white metal. Thankfully you threw away the other two things. Otherwise you would have died instantly.'

'A coincidence,' I asserted. 'I don't believe in these superstitions.'

Hearing me say this, the three locals appeared incredibly frightened. 'Don't say that!' they cried in unison.

'In this age of science, how can you believe in such strange things?' I continued.

The three of them glared at me. 'Did you ever have so many problems all at once, like what happened to you the day before yesterday?'

I thought carefully. Indeed, I'd had such experiences before. I have allergies. My eyes would often get swollen. I'd throw up. I frequently got dizzy. My stomach hurt. After intense exercise, I'd always bleed a little down there. I always managed to cut myself while chopping vegetables—

'Yes, nothing major. These little things happen to me quite often,' I admitted.

'The way this curse works is by exploiting your physical weaknesses,' one of the Sahrawi explained to me. 'It can transform little problems into a major evil power to take your life. You still think it's a coincidence that a spill from the coffee pot extinguished the gas flame?'

Silently, I raised my crushed left hand for all to see.

For the past few days, I've had one thought in my mind that I can't drive away, something that I've been pondering and pondering and pondering.

'I've been thinking that maybe, just maybe, I have a subconscious impulse to end my own life. So that's why I became so ill,' I say softly.

José seems shocked to hear these words come out of my mouth.

'What I— What I'm trying to say is that no matter how hard I try to get used to living in the desert, I've already reached the limit of my tolerance for this lifestyle and environment.'

'Sanmao, you—'

'I'm not denying the passion I feel for the desert. But, at the end of the day, I'm human. I also have moments of weakness—'

'I didn't know you had made coffee. When I was boiling water later, I didn't notice that the water had put out the flame. Are you telling me that I subconsciously want to kill the both of us, too?'

'We should talk about this with someone who understands psychology. We know too little about our own spiritual worlds.'

I don't know why, but these topics make people depressed. Humans are most afraid of themselves. I sigh and try to forget about it all.

The copper tablet was eventually collected from the floor by our bed by an imam, what the locals call a *santón*. He used a knife to cut out the metal between the two pieces. Inside the piece of copper, to our surprise, was an amulet with a drawing on it. Seeing it, I felt a wave of cold come over me, as though my whole body had been submerged in icy water.

The nightmare has passed. I haven't fully regained my health yet. Many friends have recommended that I get checked out. For me, though, I feel like there has already been an explanation for all of it. No need to bother a doctor.

Today is the day Muslims break their fast. Outside my window is a cloudless blue sky. A cool breeze is blowing in. The summer is already over. A beautiful autumn in the desert is about to begin.

A Ladder

When it comes to driving, I can't actually remember how I learned. For years I sat aside and watched attentively while others were behind the wheel. Later on, whenever there was an opportunity, I'd play around with the steering wheel myself. Eventually I picked it up quite naturally, just like that.

I'm a pretty bold person. Every time I get in someone's car, I politely ask, 'Will you let me drive? I'll be very careful.' Most people, faced with this humble request, are happy to oblige. Whether it's a big car or small, new or old, I always drive properly in order not to disappoint the goodwill of others. I've never had an accident.

Those who let me drive their cars always forget to ask one critically important question. Since they don't ask, I'm certainly in no rush to blab. So I surreptitiously drive on to wherever I please.

When José bought a car, I fell in love with it; it was the white stallion of my dreams. I often drove into town to run errands. Sometimes I'd also pick up my Prince Charming when he finished work. Because I drive so well, nobody ever asked about my driving licence. Unwittingly I even fell into the trap of self-deception, stubbornly deluding myself into thinking that I already had one.

On more than one occasion, José and his co-workers have discussed how obtaining a driving licence around here is more difficult than ascending to heaven. So-and-so's wife still hadn't passed the written test after fourteen attempts, they said. Meanwhile, there was a Sahrawi who had been taking the road test for two years. I calmly listened to these harrowing topics of conversation, my head lowered, not daring to let out a peep. Regardless, I still drove my car to and fro, day in, day out. As for ascending to heaven, I didn't feel like attempting to climb the ladder at the traffic bureau for the moment.

One day, I received a letter from my father. 'You should really get your driving licence during your free time in the desert,' he advised. 'Stop procrastinating.'

Whenever I get mail from home, José always asks, 'What news from your parents?'

My guard happened to be down that day. 'Dad says I should stop being lazy about my licence,' I blurted out.

Hearing this, José chuckled complacently. 'Alright, that is an order from Dad,' he said to me. 'I'm not the one forcing you. Let's see if you can weasel out of it this time.'

I thought about it for a moment. I had no qualms about self-deception, since it wasn't affecting anybody other than myself. But I wasn't willing to drive without a licence and deceive my father at the same time. He'd never asked about my driving, so it's not that I had been lying to him.

In Spain, you're required to attend driving school before you can get a licence. You can only take the test once the school registers you for it. So, even though I already knew how to drive, I would still have to pay this tuition. Despite the fact that we live in Africa, far from the Spanish mainland, we still obey Spanish law here because this land is Spanish territory.

The day after I agreed to attend a driving school, José borrowed a bunch of exercise booklets from his colleagues and gave them to me so I could read about traffic rules. I was really grumpy. 'I don't like to read,' I told him.

'You always have your nose buried in a book,' he retorted. 'What are you talking about?' He pointed at my bookshelf. 'Here you have astronomy, geography, demons and ghouls, spy romances, animals, philosophy, gardening, languages, cooking, manga, cinema, tailoring, even secret recipes in traditional Chinese medicine, magic tricks, hypnotism, dyeing clothes… All thrown together in one big mess. Are you telling me that you're going to get stumped by some traffic rules?'

I sighed and took the small stack of booklets from José.

This was different. I don't like to read things that other people assign me.

A few days later, I drove to the driving school with a bit of money to register for class.

The boss of this Sahara Driving School really seemed to take pride in his appearance. He had a few dozen blown-up colour photographs of himself in different outfits hanging in the office. He flashed and flitted about as though he were a movie star attending a premiere.

An unruly crowd of Sahrawi men were gathered at the counter. Business was booming. Learning how to drive is a very trendy thing in the desert. Huge cars are often parked right outside ragged and run-down tents. So many fathers sell their beautiful daughters in exchange for a car. For the

Sahrawi, the only way to demonstrate one's progress towards becoming civilised is to drive a car of one's own. Body odour, on the other hand, is a totally insignificant matter.

It was very difficult for me to wriggle my way to the counter through their heaps of fabric. Right after I said that I wanted to register, I noticed there were two Spanish traffic police just past the Sahrawi man to my right. In my fright, I squeezed my way back out and escaped into the background to gaze at the boss's glamour shots again.

From the reflection in the framed glass, I saw one of the police officers quickly making his way over to me. I played it cool and didn't even budge, focusing on counting the number of buttons on the boss's shirt. This policeman stood nearby and peered at me for quite some time. Finally, he opened his mouth. 'Señorita,' he said. 'I believe I recognise you!'

I had no choice but to turn around. 'I'm very sorry,' I said to him. 'I really don't know who you are.'

'I heard you say you want to register for this class,' he continued. 'Strange! I've seen you driving around town more than once. You really don't have a licence?'

Fearing the circumstances were unfavourable, I immediately switched to English. 'So sorry, I don't understand Spanish. What did you say?'

He was dumbfounded to hear that I didn't speak his language.

'*Licencia!*' he cried. '*Licencia!*'

'I don't understand.' I gave him an embarrassed and helpless look.

The police officer ran over to his colleague. He was pointing at me and saying, 'I saw her drive to the post office this morning with my own eyes. It's definitely her, no mistake about it. So it looks like she's only now learning how to drive. How much should we fine her?'

'She's not in a car now,' the other one said. 'How come you didn't catch her before?'

'I see her driving all day, all the time. I always thought she had a licence. Why would I stop her to check?'

While discussing the matter, they forgot all about me. I turned around and quickly squeezed back in amid the folds of fabric of the Sahrawi men.

I finished the paperwork quickly and paid the course fee. The girl at the information desk gave me the test date: I would be taking it in two weeks. With this all settled, I gathered the booklets on traffic rules and regulations that the school had given me and walked out the front door, totally at ease.

I opened the car door, got in and started the engine. I was just about to drive off when I looked in the rear-view mirror. Turned out those two police officers had been hiding around the corner, waiting to catch me. I immediately jumped out of the car in fright, then strode away quickly. I waited until José finished work to ask him to rescue our white stallion.

I was put into a driving class that started at half past noon. The driving school had its facilities in the desolate area just outside town, where they'd laid down some roads amid the sandpiles. My instructor and I sat in the stuffy car going in circles like little white mice.

The desert at noon was hotter than fifty degrees centigrade. Sweat soaked through my clothes, dripping into my eyes. Sand chafed my face so badly, it looked like I'd been slapped. The class was only fifteen minutes long, but intense thirst and scorching heat gnawed at me relentlessly like mad dogs. The instructor couldn't take the heat. Without even asking me, he took off his top and sat shirtless by my side.

After three days of this, I couldn't take the crazy heat any longer. I asked the instructor if I could change my time. 'You are pretty damn lucky,' he said. 'Another lady has a class at eleven at night. She can't learn a thing, it's so dark and cold. And you still want to change the damn time.' He banged on the scalding hot roof of the car as he said this, putting a small dent in it.

The instructor really wasn't a bad guy. But the prospect of baking in this oven, next to a guy who didn't want to wear clothes, for fifteen more classes wasn't massively appealing. Plus, he was the type that cursed every time he opened his mouth. It wasn't much fun.

I sighed. 'How about this?' I said to him. 'I'll sign off on all the hours you're supposed to be teaching me. I won't come any more and I'll take responsibility for the test.'

This seemed to be exactly what he wanted to hear. 'Fine!' he said. 'I'll give you a damn break. We are done. See you at the test.'

Before we parted ways, he treated me to a bottle of cold soda water to celebrate the completion of my driving classes.

José was really mad when he found out that my tuition fees had gone to the instructor for nothing and that I refused to go back. He forced me to take night classes. He said this class on traffic rules was expensive enough and I should get our money's worth.

So I went to take my first night class.

The class for Sahrawi people next door was a truly strange phenomenon. Everyone was reading aloud, memorising traffic rules line by line like they were speaking in tongues.

I had never seen so many intensely focused Sahrawi people before.

As for our class, which was conducted in Spanish, there were very few people and most were not interested in paying attention. My teacher was a very cultured middle-aged man, tall and lean with a small beard. He definitely didn't curse. This literary teacher was worlds apart from my previous militaristic instructor.

Once I got settled, the instructor politely came over and asked me to teach him about Chinese culture. I ended up giving him a lesson, even writing out and explaining many of our Chinese characters for him.

When I entered the classroom the next day, this literary teacher immediately opened a workbook. It was full of the Chinese characters for 'person' and 'sky'.

'How did I do?' he asked shyly. 'Do they look right?'

'You write better than me,' I said.

Quite pleased by this remark, he continued to grill me, asking about Confucius, asking about Lao Tzu. Luckily, this was my strong suit. I gave him very thorough answers, then asked if he knew of Zhuangzi. Wasn't Zhuangzi a butterfly? he asked.

The hour flew by. I wanted to hear him talk about traffic lights. 'Why, are you colour-blind?' he asked slyly.

By the time this intellectual released me from his 5,000-year history lesson, the day had grown pitch-black and ice cold. I made dinner in a rush once I got home to my poor starving José.

'Sanmao, do you know what the different lights mean on the backs of trucks?'

'Almost there,' I said. 'The teacher is very good.'

When José went to work during the day, I washed and ironed clothes, made the bed, swept the floors, dusted, cooked, knitted and generally kept busy all around. I didn't dare slack off when it came to the book of traffic rules, either, reciting them to myself constantly. It was like when I went to Sunday school as a kid. I firmly committed every single traffic rule to memory as though they were verses from the Bible.

Around that time, all my neighbours knew I was going to take the test. I shut my door tight so nobody could get in. The neighbouring women were writhing with jealousy. 'When are you going to finish taking the test?' they shouted every day. 'It is so inconvenient for us when you do not open the door!'

I held my ground and ignored them. It was time to get serious.

The day of my test was fast approaching. I certainly wasn't afraid to drive, but I had reservations about the written test. I'd been learning traffic rules while thinking about eggs and vegetables and wool, Confucius and Zhuangzi; I was a bit muddled, to say the least.

On Friday night, José picked up the book of traffic rules. 'Your written exam is three days from now,' he said. 'If you don't pass, then forget about the road test. I'm going to quiz you right now.'

José has always thought that I'm a genius and an idiot at the same time. He asked me a jumble of questions from all over the place, his tone insistent, his voice thunderous. I couldn't take in a single word he said.

'Slow down! I have no idea what you're even saying.'

He bombarded me with questions again, but I still couldn't respond.

Throwing the book aside in anger, he shot me a dirty look. 'You've gone to so many classes, but you still haven't learned anything. Stupid!'

I got pretty mad, too. I went to the kitchen and took a large swig of cooking wine to pull myself together. Once I had cleared my head, I threw the traffic rules back at José. I slowly recited the whole thing back to him, word for word. There were almost a hundred pages in the booklet, but I'd memorised them all.

José was dumbfounded.

'How do you like them apples?' I crowed, feeling pleased with myself. 'Thanks to my elementary school teacher, I can memorise anything.'

José still wasn't convinced. 'What if you get too nervous on Monday and can't understand Spanish again?' he asked. 'Wouldn't that be terrible?' This remark made me toss and turn all night. I got absolutely no sleep.

I really do have this problem with drawing a blank whenever I get nervous. It always comes back to me later, but in the heat of the moment my mind gets stuck in a rut.

You might say:

I could wait until this feeling
Becomes a hunted memory,
Only I am at that moment,
already wavering.[1]

I was insomniac until daybreak.

José was in a deep slumber, having toiled for an entire week. I didn't have it in my heart to wake him up. I got dressed, slipped out of the door and started up the car. I drove to the driving test centre far from town. Driving there without a licence was really asking for trouble, but if I walked there I'd arrive all dishevelled. Then I certainly wouldn't make a good impression and accomplish what I had set out to do.

I drove all the way to the front door of the office building. Of course nobody asked to see my licence. There probably aren't many stupidly brazen people in the world who would have done what I was doing.

I had just entered the office when somebody called out, 'Sanmao!'

I froze. 'How did you know my name?' I asked the man who had spoken.

'Your registration picture, look here! You're taking the test on Monday!'

'That's exactly why I'm here,' I said quickly. 'I want to meet the invigilator for the written test.'

'What's the matter? The invigilator is our colonel.'

'May I ask you to convey something to him?'

He noticed the odd look on my face and disappeared inside straight away. A short while later, he came out and said, 'Please come this way.'

The captain inside the office was a military officer with salt and pepper hair and an elegant bearing. After living in the desert for so long, encountering someone of such grace and style suddenly made me think of my father. It threw me off balance for a second.

He came over from his desk to shake my hand, then pulled out a chair and invited me to sit down. He also asked someone to bring us coffee.

'May I ask what's the matter? And you are…?'

'I'm Señora Quero…' I started to make my request. I was relying on him to resolve all the questions that had plagued me throughout that sleepless night.

'I see. So you want to take an oral exam on the traffic rules and recite the answers to me. Is that correct?'

'Yes. That's exactly it.'

'That's a good idea, but we have no precedent for doing this. Moreover, I see that your Spanish is excellent. You shouldn't have any problems.'

'I can't. I have problems. Let me set the precedent.'

He looked at me without saying anything.

'I heard that the Sahrawi are allowed to test orally. Why can't I?'

'If you want a licence just for driving in the Sahara Desert, then you can take an oral exam.'

'I want one that's good for anywhere.'

'Then you must take the written exam. No exceptions. The test is multiple choice. You don't have to write anything, just tick a box.'

'The multiple-choice questions are all ambiguous. I can't read clearly when I get nervous. I'm a foreigner.'

He sighed heavily. 'I'm sorry, we have to archive your exam,' he continued. 'There are no papers to file if you take an oral test. We wouldn't be able to account for it. I can't help you.'

'What do you mean you can't help me? I can make an audio recording for the archive. Señor Colonel, please use your brain...' My argumentative nature flared up.

He looked at me kindly. 'I say you relax and take the written test on Monday,' he said to me. 'I'm sure you'll pass. No need to be nervous.'

Seeing that he wouldn't budge, I decided not to force the matter. I thanked him and exited, cool and calm. When I got to the door, the colonel called out to me. 'Please wait,' he said. 'I'll ask two of my boys to take you home. This place is too out of the way.' I guess he called his subordinates his 'boys'.

I thanked him again and walked out. Two of his 'boys' were standing ramrod straight next to my car. When we saw each other, we all had quite a shock. They happened to be the police officers who had wanted to nab me for driving without a licence the other day. 'I really don't want to trouble you,' I said politely. 'If you could be so generous as to let me off this time, I'll go home myself.'

I was confident they wouldn't try to get me at that very moment.

So that's how I ended up driving home. José was still asleep when I got in.

All Sunday, I worked ceaselessly to memorise the manual. We ate nothing but bread with butter and sugar.

José refused to go to work on Monday morning. He said his time off was already approved and he could make up his hours the following Saturday. He wanted to accompany me to the test, which I didn't want at all.

We got to the testing site to find a dense mass of people crowded outside. There must have been a few hundred, including many Sahrawi. The written test and road test were all administered in the same place, directly across from the desert prison. The people in the prison weren't repeat offenders; those guys were all locked up with the police.

Most of these prisoners were doing time because they'd assaulted someone in a jealous spat over some bar hostess, or else they were labourers from the Canary Islands who'd got into drunken brawls with the Sahrawi. There weren't any real thugs or hooligans in the desert, probably because this place was too desolate. Even if gangsters were to come, they probably wouldn't manage to stir up much trouble.

As we waited to enter the test site, the convicts across the way watched us from the rooftop. Whenever a single Spanish woman went in, the boors would clap and yell, 'Hey! Baby, *belleza*, you damn well better do good on your test! Don't be afraid. Us old boys're here to support you, ya know… *Que sexy, buenorra!*'

Hearing these crude fellows call out so passionately, I couldn't help but smile.

'And you wanted to come here alone,' José said. 'If it weren't for me, they'd be calling *you* "baby", too.'

Actually, I quite enjoyed these crazies on the rooftop. At least, I'd never seen so many cheerful convicts before. Another one for the annals of spectacles past and present. There were more than two hundred people testing that day, both first-timers and repeats.

When the colonel and another gentleman opened up the doors to the test site, my heart started beating fast and unevenly. I also grew dizzy and felt like I wanted to vomit. My fingers were so cold I couldn't even bend them.

José gripped my hand tight so I couldn't chicken out and flee.

The people whose names were called all shuffled along, like lambs to the slaughter, and entered that frightening hole of a room. José gave me a gentle shove when the colonel called my name. I had to stand up and go.

'Good morning!' I whimpered, waving to the colonel.

He contemplated me for a moment. 'Please sit in the first row on the far right,' he said to me.

He wasn't telling anyone else where to sit, I thought. Why was he singling me out to crucify? It must have been because he didn't trust me.

It was dead quiet in the testing room. Each person's exam paper had already been distributed below their seat. Every exam was different, so it was no use sneaking a glance at your neighbour's test.

'Alright, let's begin. You have fifteen minutes.'

I pulled up the exam paper from beneath my chair. The writing on the paper looked like a swarm of ants. I couldn't read a single thing. I desperately tried to calm down, cool down, but it didn't work. The ants were all speaking languages I couldn't understand.

So I set down my pencil and paper and crossed my arms. José saw me sitting upright in my Zen pose from outside the window. He got so worked up, he looked like he was about to burst into the room and knock me awake with a big stick.

After sitting still for a bit, I looked at the paper again. Now I could read it.

I finally understood why I'd been chosen to be crucified. The questions on this exam paper were as follows:

You come to a red light while driving. You should:

a) Speed up and pass through.
b) Stop driving.
c) Honk your horn a lot.

You see pedestrians on a zebra crossing. You should:

a) Wave your hands to tell the pedestrians to walk faster.
b) Run over the crowd.
c) Stop driving.

There were two full pages of this, all the same, each a ridiculous joke of a test question. Reading through the exam,

I nearly choked trying to stifle my laughter. I breezed through in a flash.

The last question read:

While driving, you run into a group of Catholics parading the Virgin Mary around on the street. You should:

a) Applaud.
b) Stop driving.
c) Kneel down.

I chose 'Stop driving'. But then I realised the exam was issued by a Catholic country. They'd probably be happier if I answered 'Kneel down'.

With that I turned in my test after only eight minutes.

As I handed in the paper, the colonel gave me a small knowing smile. 'Thank you!' I said softly. 'Have a nice day!'

I wove my way through a large crowd of test takers who had their heads buried, working furiously, gnawing on pencils, erasing, trembling, knitting their brows. I quietly opened the door and slipped out.

José was still comforting me when the Sahrawi were up for their oral exams. 'Don't worry. This isn't such a big deal. If you don't pass, you can take the test again next weekend. Relax.'

I said nothing, keeping him in suspense.

At ten o'clock sharp, a gentleman took out a list to call the names of everyone who passed. He was calling out one name after another, but not mine. José instinctively put his hand on my shoulders.

I paid no heed at all.

Finally, when 'Sanmao' was called out, I shot a mischievous glance at José.

Even though I hadn't kept up my deception for long, José was unexpectedly delighted about this and gathered me up in his arms. He was a little too forceful and almost broke my ribs. The convicts on the roof began cheering and applauding at the sight of us. I gave them a peace sign and feigned an expression like Richard Nixon, who was in office at the time. That exam paper was my Watergate, for real. Next, I immediately went to take the on-site driving test.

All of the driving school's huge trucks and tiny compact cars were lined up in a row. The whole place was buzzing with excitement. The prisoners were roaring more vigorously than people at the horse races.

Out of more than two hundred people who had taken the written exam, there were only eighty-something left. The crowd of people who were there for the festivities alone was still pretty big. My militaristic instructor didn't go bare-chested this time. He was dressed very properly. 'Make sure you're not one of the first three to go,' he told me. 'Wait until others warm up the engines, then take your turn. That way you won't stall as easily.'

I nodded. I was confident about this whole thing. Nothing to feel nervous about.

'I'm not waiting any more,' I said after the second person finished. 'I'll take the test now.'

As soon as the light turned green in the test site, my car rattled and sped off like a wild horse. I shifted gears again and again, came to a stop, started up the engine, made a turn, reversed on a diagonal, reversed on another hard angle, drove up a ramp, then reversed in between two parked cars, sandwiching myself in the middle. Driving uphill, braking, starting up, going downhill, switching gears... I did everything even-handedly and methodically, impeccable in my execution. The end was in sight.

I heard the audience applauding me. Even the Sahrawi were yelling, 'The Chinese girl is really good!'

I was so absurdly happy, I lost it for a bit and quickly turned to glance at the main examiner in the tower. While doing this, I drove off the road and ploughed right into the sparkling waves of sand. I got agitated and my car stalled, coming to a halt right there.

The sound of applause turned into exclamations, then uproarious laughter. José was laughing the hardest of all. I couldn't help but start laughing myself. I jumped out of the car with half a mind to laugh myself to death, right then and there, so I could die like one of the Greek gods.

I'd been struggling for this all week, learning a lot in the process and reflecting honestly on myself. Now I had failed due to my own negligence; I would have to be more careful next time.

The next Monday, I went to take the test by myself. I wasn't in a hurry this time, waiting patiently until forty or fifty people had gone before I got into the car. All the manoeuvres they'd allotted four minutes to complete, I finished in two minutes and thirty-five seconds. I didn't make any mistakes.

When they were calling out the names of those who had passed, only sixteen were called out. I was the only woman among them.

'Sanmao drives as fast as a bullet,' the colonel teased. 'You'd be an excellent addition to the traffic police team.'

I was just about to walk home when I saw José coming to pick me up, his face beaming. He worked quite some distance away, but he'd come over in his lunch break.

'Congratulations!' he said as he approached.

'Hey, are you clairvoyant or something?'

'The convicts on the rooftop just told me.'

I really think that people in prison might not be worse than those who walk free. The truly bad seeds in this world are like the dragons that we Chinese like to talk about: they might be small or large, hidden or in plain sight. But you can't catch them, nor can you imprison them.

As I prepared lunch for José, I asked him to make another trip by himself to give the prisoners two cases of Coke and two cartons of cigarettes. They had been like a marching band cheering me on during my test. I didn't look down on them. It's not like my personal integrity is much greater than theirs.

I drove José back to work at noon, then returned to town. I parked surreptitiously before walking over to wait for my final road test. This ladder was getting more and more interesting, the higher I got. I was beginning to enjoy the whole process.

With midday temperatures at fifty degrees centigrade, the streets were deserted save for the short shadows of rows of buildings under the sun. The whole town felt dead; time here had frozen over. I was struck by how much this scenery looked like a print of a Surrealist painting. If only there had been a girl rolling a metal hoop, it would have been even more vivid.

The 'road test' began here, a place with absolutely no traffic.

Even though I knew that there was no way I'd run over a dog or crash into a tree, I still didn't want to be too imprudent.

Before starting the test, put on your indicator and look behind you. Keep to the right after starting. Don't drive on the yellow lines. Stop at intersections. Slow down for zebra crossings. Since there are no traffic lights in town, that was one less thing to worry about.

All sixteen of us finished testing pretty quickly. The colonel invited everyone to the driving test centre's canteen for some soda water. Among us there were eight Spaniards, seven Sahrawi and then me. The colonel immediately distributed temporary licences to those who had passed the test. The official licences would be mailed eventually from Spain.

Last week, I kept on telling myself that I had to climb to the top of this ladder before King Hassan II of Morocco came to the Spanish Sahara to drink tea. Now I'd climbed all the way, and the king still wasn't here.

The colonel gave out seven licences, including one for me.

Now that I had a licence, my mood and comportment while driving were totally different from before. It was like night and day.

One afternoon, I'd just parked my car and was about to walk off when those two police officers from before leapt in front of me. 'Ha!' they cried. 'We got you this time.' I took out my licence leisurely and raised it in the air in front of their faces.

They didn't even glance at it and started writing me a ticket.

'We're fining you two hundred and fifty pesetas.'

'What?' I couldn't believe my ears.

'You're parked in front of a bus stop. That's a fine!'

'There are no buses in town,' I cried. 'There have never been any.'

'There will be. The signs are already up.'

'You can't fine me on this basis. I won't take it. I refuse to pay.'

'No parking if there's a bus stop sign. Who cares if there's a bus?'

My mind becomes very clear whenever I get angry. Traffic rules flitted through my head, one by one. I pushed aside the officers, jumped in the car, and zipped forward a few metres away from the stop. I stopped the car, got out and shoved the ticket back at them. 'The traffic rules say that if you leave a spot within two minutes, it doesn't count as parking. I stopped for less than two minutes and then moved, so this isn't a violation.'

In this game of Cops and Robbers, those two had lost again. Let them throw the ticket out for a goat to chew on. I laughed victoriously and set out with my vegetable basket to the canteen at the desert corps. I wanted to see if I would have any luck today in buying fresh fruits and vegetables.

Day after day, a black sheep like myself, who never even grew up in the desert, strives to dispel the misery of these long, leisurely years with artfulness and pleasure.

O how fair though chilly this autumn![2]

Hearth and Home

I was the one who originally insisted on coming to the Sahara Desert, not José. But we then stayed here long-term because of José, not me. I've wandered through many countries in my lifetime. I've lived in highly developed societies. I'd seen through them, had enough of them. It's not that I wasn't inspired; my lifestyle had absorbed their influences in big and small ways. But I never had a place to settle down, a city where I could also leave my heart.

I don't remember when it was exactly, but one day I found myself absentmindedly flipping through an issue of *National Geographic*. It just so happened there was a feature on the Sahara. I only read it through once. I couldn't understand the feeling of homesickness that I had, inexplicable and yet so decisive, towards that vast and unfamiliar land, as if echoing from a past life.

After I returned to live in Spain, I realised there were 280,000 square metres of the Sahara that were Spanish territory. My desire to go only deepened, torturing me with nostalgia and longing.

This sentiment of mine became something of a joke among the people I knew. I often said I wanted to cross the desert, but nobody took me seriously. The friends who knew me better thought I wanted to go because of disillusionment or self-exile, a trip with no return… But this wasn't quite accurate either. Good thing that other people's judgement never bothered me in the least.

Eventually I organised myself and prepared to live in the desert for a year. Besides my father's encouragement, I had only one friend who didn't mock me or try to stop me, let alone drag me down. He quietly packed his things, went to the desert ahead of me and found work at a phosphate mining company. He settled down and waited for me to come to Africa all alone so he could take care of me. He knew I was a stubborn woman of singular will; I wouldn't change my mind.

When this person went to the desert and suffered in the name of love, I knew in my heart that I wanted to roam to the ends of the earth with him. This person was my husband José. All this is old news, already two years past.

After José went to the desert, I tied up all my loose ends. I didn't even say goodbye to anyone. Before getting on the plane, I left a letter and rent money for the three Spanish girls with whom I shared an apartment. When I stepped out, I was also closing the door on a familiar lifestyle, rushing towards the desert unknown.

Once the plane touched down in the makeshift airport of El Aaiún, I saw José for the first time in three months. That day he was wearing a khaki military-style shirt and very dirty jeans. He gave me a great big hug. His hands were extremely coarse, his hair and beard covered in yellowish dust. The wind had chafed and reddened his face; his lips were dry and cracked. In his eyes was a glimmer of hidden pain.

I felt an ache of astonishment, seeing how he'd undergone such a drastic transformation in such a short period of time. Only then did I think of the life I was about to face. This was my reality now, a major test rather than just an abstraction about which I had romantic and childish ideas.

My heart was beating fast. I had a hard time stifling my excitement. A lifetime's homesickness, and now I'd returned to this land. I didn't know how to feel any more.

Deep down inside, the Sahara Desert had been my dream lover for so long. I looked around at the boundless sand across which the wind wailed, the sky high above, the landscape majestic and calm. It was dusk. The setting sun stained the desert the red of fresh blood, a sorrowful beauty. The temperature felt like early winter. I'd expected a scorching sun, but instead found a swathe of poetic desolation.

José was silent. I looked at him.

'Now you're here in the embrace of your desert,' he said. I nodded, my throat constricted. 'Let's go, stranger!'

José had started calling me this years ago. It wasn't because Camus' novel was just getting popular, but rather that 'stranger' felt like a very accurate name for me. In this life, I'd always felt I wasn't a part of the world around me. I often needed to go off the tracks of a normal life and do things without explanation.

The airport was deserted. The few other passengers had long since gone. José hoisted my suitcase onto his shoulder. I strapped on my backpack, picked up my pillowcase and walked off with him.

There was quite a distance between the airport and the home that José had been renting for half a month already. We walked very slowly because my suitcase and backpack were extremely heavy. Occasionally a car would pass us on the road. We'd raise our arms and try to hitchhike, but no one stopped. After forty minutes of this, we turned and walked down a hill and onto another road. Finally we saw some signs of habitation.

'See there,' José said to me against the wind. 'This is the periphery of El Aaiún. Our home is down below.'

In the distance there were dozens of tents riddled with holes, as well as little bungalows made of iron. A few Arabian camels and herds of goats stood in the sand. This was the first time I'd seen the locals in the dark blue fabric they always like to wear. To me it was like walking into a fantasy, a whole new world.

The wind carried aloft the laughter of little girls playing a game. An indescribable vitality and joy can be found wherever humans exist. Even this barren and impoverished backwater was teeming with life, not a struggle for survival. For the residents of the desert, their births and deaths and everything in between were all part of a natural order. Looking out at the smoke ascending to the sky from their homes, I felt that these people were almost elegant in their serenity. Living carefree, in my understanding, is what a civilised spirit is all about.

Finally, in the waning light of day, we reached a long street with square houses made of concrete blocks scattered on either side. My eye was immediately drawn to the last tiny home at the end of this row, which had an oblong arched doorway. I knew instinctively that this was mine. Sure enough, José walked in that direction. Sweating profusely, he put my suitcase down on the doorstep. 'We're here,' he said. 'This is our home.'

Directly across from the house was a landfill. Farther ahead was a wave-shaped sand dune, and beyond that still was the vast sky. Behind the house was a high hill of stones and hard soil, not sand. I didn't see people in any of the neighbouring homes. There was only the ceaseless wind blowing violently through my hair and long skirt.

Once José opened the door, I let down the weighty backpack from my shoulders. A short, dim hallway emerged before my eyes. José picked me up from behind. 'Let me carry you into our first home,' he said. 'From today forward, you will be my wife.'

This was at once plain and profound. I had never been passionately in love with him. At the same time I felt incredibly lucky and at ease.

José took four large steps forwards and reached the end of the hall. I glanced around and saw a big square hole in the middle of the wall. The sky outside was pigeon grey. I struggled to my feet, threw down the pillowcase in my hands and went to examine the house further. There wasn't much to see. I could take it all in just standing by that hole in the wall. The larger room faced the street. I walked its width in four large steps, its length in five.

The other room wasn't big enough to fit anything besides a big bed. There was only a bit of space left at the doorway as wide as my wrist. The kitchen was about the size of four spread newspapers. Besides a cracked yellow sink, there was a cement block for a counter. In the bathroom, there was a flush toilet with no tank, a washbasin and the shocking sight of a white bathtub. It was a Dadaist work of art – if we didn't use it, it would just be a sculpture.

It occurred to me to check out where the stone staircase outside the kitchen and bathroom led to. 'No point,' said José. 'Upstairs is a shared rooftop. I'll show you tomorrow. I bought a doe a few days ago and put it in with the rest of the landlord's herd. We'll have fresh milk in the future.'

Upon hearing that we owned a goat, I felt an unexpected surge of glee. José worriedly asked about my first impression of the home. I heard myself give him a forced, nervous answer. 'It's great. I really like it. Really. Let's fix it up, little by little.'

Even as I was saying this, I was frantically sizing up the whole place. The cement floor was uneven; the wall was the dark grey of the concrete blocks and hadn't been whitewashed. The cement that had been used to seal up holes hung dry and naked.

I looked around, noticing the tiny bare lightbulb that hung from the ceiling. A dense swarm of flies clustered on the electric wire. The wind continued to howl through the hole in the corner of the wall on the left. When I turned on the tap, a few drops of a thick green liquid came out, but no water. The roof above our heads looked like it might collapse.

'How much is the rent?' I asked José.

'Ten thousand pesetas, not including utilities.'

'Is water expensive?'

'An oil drum full of water is ninety. Tomorrow I'm going to apply for water delivery from the city government.'

Speechless, I sat down on my suitcase in despair. 'Alright, let's go into town to buy a refrigerator and some groceries. We need to figure out our basic needs right away.' I grabbed my pillowcase and headed out the door with him again.

On the road we passed other homes, sandscapes, a cemetery and a petrol station. We didn't see the lights of the town until the sky was almost entirely dark.

'This is the bank. That's the city government. The courthouse is on the right. The post office is below that. There are quite a few shops. Our company's main office is that row of buildings. The one with the green light is the hotel. The building painted amber is the cinema—'

'Who lives in that row of tidy apartments? The big white homes with trees and a swimming pool. There's music coming through the white gauze curtains of that building. Is that also a hotel?'

'Those apartments are dorms for senior staff. The white house is the governor's home, so of course it has a garden. The music you hear is the Officers Club.'

'Aiya, there's a Muslim palace, José, look—'

'That's the four-star Hotel Nacional, not a palace. It's for government dignitaries.'

'Where do the Sahrawi live? I've seen so many of them.'

'They live in town, out of town, all over. We live in the Cemetery District. If you call a taxi in the future, that's the address you should give them.'

'There are taxis?'

'Yes, and they're all Mercedes Benzes. Once we buy our things, we'll take one home.'

We managed to buy a tiny refrigerator, a frozen chicken, a gas stove and a blanket all from the same store. 'I would have taken care of these things sooner, but I was afraid you wouldn't like what I bought,' José said sheepishly. 'So now you can have your pick.'

But what was there to choose? There was only one fridge in the store. All the gas stoves were the same. I lost all vigour thinking about the gloomy home we were renting. When it was time to pay, I opened up the pillowcase. 'We're not married yet,' I said. 'So let me pay for some of this.' This was an old habit of ours, splitting things evenly.

José didn't realise what I had been toting around this whole time. He freaked out when he got a closer look. He clutched the pillowcase close, dug around in his own pockets and paid the entire bill.

When we got outside, he said to me quietly, 'Where did you get so much money? How could you store it all in this pillowcase and not say a peep?'

'It's from my dad. I brought it all with me.'

José sulked silently. I stood in the wind, staring at him.

'I think... I don't think you'll get used to desert living for the long haul. Once you're done travelling, I'll quit my job and we can leave together.'

'Why? Have I complained? Why do you want to quit?'

José patted the pillowcase and gave me a strained smile. 'You came to the Sahara because you're stubborn about your romantic ideas. You'll get tired of this place soon enough. With all that money, you won't be living like others do here.'

'The money isn't mine, it's my father's. I'm not using it.'

'Alright then. Tomorrow morning, we'll deposit it in the bank. You... From now on, we'll live on my salary alone. We'll make do, at any rate.'

I almost became angry, hearing his words. We'd known each other for so long. He knew I'd travelled alone through many places. But in his eyes, because of this bit of money, I was ultimately just a shallow and useless woman. I wanted to say something back to him but kept my mouth shut. I would prove my potential in our days to come. Right now it would be a waste of breath.

That first Friday night, I took a Mercedes Benz sedan home to the Cemetery District. I spent my first night in the desert bundled in a sleeping bag. José was wrapped in a thin blanket. It was close to freezing. We slept on a piece of tent canvas over the cement floor, shivering until daylight.

Saturday morning, we went to the courthouse to apply for our marriage certificate and also bought a stupidly expensive mattress. As for a bed frame, that wasn't worth dreaming about.

While José was applying for our water service at the city government, I bought five of the large straw mats that the Sahrawi use, a pot, four plates, and a fork and spoon for each of us. As for knives, we had eleven ready-mades between the two of us, all of which could be used for cooking, so I didn't get any more. I also bought a bucket, a broom, a brush, clothes pegs, soap, cooking oil, rice, sugar, vinegar…

Everything was so dishearteningly expensive. With the small stack of bills that José gave me, I couldn't bring myself to buy any more than this.

My father's money was stored in an account with the central bank. We wouldn't be able to touch it for half a year, with the interest rate at 0.46 per cent.

We went to pay the landlord a visit when we got home around noon. He seemed a very generous Sahrawi man and we all left with good first impressions of each other. We borrowed half a bucket of water from him. José went to the roof to scrub out the dirty parts of the bucket while I cooked. Once the rice was done, I dumped it out and used the same pot to cook half a chicken.

We ate on the straw mats. 'Did you add salt to the rice?' José asked.

'No, I used the water we borrowed from the landlord.'

It dawned on us then that El Aaiún drew its brackish water from a deep well. There was no fresh water. José ate lunch at work on most days, so naturally this had never occurred to him.

Even though we'd bought a few things for the home, it still looked like just a couple of mats on the floor. We spent the entire weekend cleaning up. Sahrawi children began to poke their heads in through that hole of a window, screeching up a storm.

On Sunday night, José had to leave to go to the phosphate mine. I asked if he would be home the following afternoon. He said he would. His workplace was nearly a hundred kilometres round trip from our rented home.

The man of the house was only around on weekends. Usually José rushed home after work and then took a shuttle bus back to the dorms when it got super late. During the day, I went into town on my own. Our Sahrawi neighbours would come by in the afternoons if it wasn't too hot.

It took forever to get all the documents together for our marriage. Thanks to a retired commander of the Legión Española, I often tagged along for a ride on the big trucks that sold water, venturing out within a radius of a few hundred kilometres. At night I would pitch my own tent and sleep near the nomadic herders. No one dared touch me since I was under the commander's care. I always brought along white sugar, nylon thread, medicine, cigarettes and so on to give to the locals, who had nothing.

Only by going deep into the desert, taking in the beautiful sight of wild antelope running in flocks at sunrise and sunset, was I able to forget the hardship and ennui of my reality.

I spent two months this way, often leaving town to travel on my own.

Once the announcement of our marriage was posted in the local courthouse of our former Madrid residence, I knew I would be settled down for real very soon.

Home suddenly became a place that I couldn't bear to leave.

Every time I wanted to milk our goat, it would scramble all over and try to ram me with its horns. I had to buy a lot of grass and wheat for it to eat. Our landlord still wasn't very happy with us borrowing his goat pen.

Sometimes, if I got there slightly too late, the landlord's wife would have squeezed out all the goat's milk already. I really wanted to love and protect this goat, but it refused to acknowledge me or José. I ended up donating it to the landlord, rather than force the matter further.

Right before we got married, José was taking on others' night shifts in order to make more money. There was no way for us to see each other regularly with this round-the-clock schedule. Without him at home, I had to attend to many menial tasks on my own.

Besides the Sahrawi, there was also a Spanish family that lived nearby. The wife was a bold and robust woman from the Canary Islands. She asked me to accompany her every time she went to buy fresh water. On our way there, it was easy to keep up with her because our water tanks were empty. After buying ten litres of fresh water, I'd always tell her to go on ahead.

'How are you so useless?' she teased loudly. 'Have you never carried water before in your life?'

'I... It's too heavy. You go ahead – don't wait for me.'

Beneath the burning sun, both hands gripping the handles on the water tank, I'd walk four or five steps and then stop, panting, before going on for another ten. Stopping and starting, soaked all over with sweat, my spine would spasm with pain, my face and ears growing red, my pace slowing. My home was still a tiny black speck in the far distance, seemingly always out of reach no matter how far I walked. As soon as I got home with the water, I'd immediately lie on the straw mats to ease the pain in my back.

Sometimes when the gas was used up, I didn't have the energy to take the empty drum into town to exchange. You had to walk into town first to hail a taxi. I was too lazy for this. So I often borrowed our neighbours' charcoal stove and squatted outside, fanning the flames, choking while my eyes teared up from the smoke.

It was at times like these when I felt glad that my mother wasn't a clairvoyant. Otherwise, her beautiful cheeks would be drenched for the sake of her beloved daughter – *Oh, my daughter, precious pearl, apple of my eye!* She would no doubt dissolve into tears.

But I didn't lose heart. Gaining life experience is always invaluable.

Before we got married, whenever José was working overtime, I'd sit on the straw mats listening to the wind howl outside as if wailing with complaints. We had no books or newspapers at home, no television or radio. We ate on the ground. When it was time to sleep, we went into a different room and lay on a mattress on the ground.

The walls were hot to the touch during the day and frigid by night. As for electricity, we had it when we were lucky. Most of the time we weren't. At dusk, I'd gaze through the square hole at the grey sand, fine as powder, sneaking in and spilling everywhere. When it was dark outside, I lit white candles and waited to see what shapes their tears might drip into.

There were no drawers or closets in this home. We kept our clothes in suitcases. Shoes and odds and ends were kept in a big box. To write, we had to find a board to put on our knees. The cold grey-black walls made us feel even chillier at night.

Sometimes José would catch the night shuttle to work. As soon as he shut the door with a clang, my tears would start to flow without rhyme or reason. If I went up to the roof, I could still see his silhouette. Then I'd rush back down and run out to chase after him. I would run until I caught up with him. Out of breath and wheezing, I would walk by his side, head hung low.

'Can't you stay? I beg of you. There's no electricity today. I'm so lonely.' I would implore him, leaning into the wind, hands shoved in my pockets.

José always felt really bad when I did this. His eyes would be rimmed in red. 'Sanmao, I'm filling in for someone's morning shift. I have to be there by six. If I stayed here, how could I make it on time? I don't have a bus pass for the morning, either.'

'You don't need to make more. We have money in the bank. Don't work so hard.'

'Someday we'll ask your father to borrow the money in the bank to buy a little house. I'm making extra for your living expenses. We just have to endure it a bit longer. After we get married, I won't work extra shifts any more.'

'Will you come back tomorrow?'

'I'll definitely be back in the afternoon. You should go to the hardware store tomorrow morning and find out how much wood costs. Once I'm off work, I'll get cracking on building a table for you.'

He hugged me tightly before giving me a push towards home. I ran slowly in that direction while glancing back at him. In the distance, beneath the stars, José was waving at me.

Sometimes one of José's colleagues who had a family of his own would drive over at night to pay me a visit. 'Sanmao, why don't you come over for dinner and TV? We can bring you back later. Don't stay here all cooped up by yourself.'

Knowing there was a touch of pity in their good intentions, I would proudly refuse. I was like a wounded animal during that time, taking offence at the tiniest of things. I was so low in spirits I'd often weep. The Sahara Desert was stunning, yet living here required an unfathomable determination to adapt. It wasn't that I was tired of the desert; I was just running into little frustrations while acclimatising to it all.

The next day, I went into town with the slip of paper that José had written for me to investigate prices at the huge hardware store. It took quite a while before the assistants had time for me. After endless calculations, they finally told me it would cost more than 25,000 pesetas. They didn't even have everything in stock. I thanked them and walked out, thinking I would check for mail at the post office. The money we'd set aside for making furniture wouldn't even be enough to cover a few boards.

While walking through the plaza outside the store, I noticed they'd thrown out a pile of long wooden boxes used for shipping. The planks were huge and nailed together. It seemed like nobody wanted them. I rushed back to the store. 'Can I have the empty wooden cases outside for free?' I asked. I blushed deeply with embarrassment saying this. I'd never had to beg anyone for a few pieces of wood before.

The proprietor was very polite. 'Sure, sure, take whatever you'd like.'

'I want five of them,' I said. 'Is that too many?'

'How many people are in your family?' asked the boss.

I told him, thinking it was rather beside the point. Once he agreed, I went immediately to the square where the Sahrawi liked to gather and hired two donkey carts. We hoisted up five of the empty wooden cases onto the carts. It occurred to me that I needed more tools, so I bought a saw, a hammer, a tape measure and a couple of kilos of nails in different sizes, as well as a pulley, some rope and coarse sandpaper.

On the way back, I trailed behind the donkey carts, whistling all the while. I'd changed. Like José, after three months of desert living, the former me had already disappeared. Now, even a few wooden boxes could fill me with glee.

Once I was home, I couldn't fit the boxes through the front door. I didn't feel comfortable leaving them outside, worried that the neighbours would come and snatch my treasures away. For the rest of the day, I opened the door every five minutes to check if the boxes were still there. I remained anxious until sunset when I finally saw José's silhouette emerge on the horizon.

I went up to the roof and started waving my arms to signal to him. He understood and started running. When he reached the doorstep, his eyes widened at the wooden boxes that blocked the window.

'Where did you get this amazing wood?' He ran his hands all over them.

'I asked for it,' I told him from my seat on the low ledge of the roof. 'It's not dark yet. Let's make a pulley system so we can get them up here.'

That evening, we ate four boiled eggs and endured the bone-chilling cold to finish our pulley. The wooden cases were hauled up to the rooftop. We removed the nails and pried apart the boxes. José's hand was bleeding from the work. I wrapped my arms around a box and pushed my feet against the wall to help him remove each and every thick board.

'I was thinking, why do we even need to make furniture? Why can't we be like the Sahrawi and just sit on mats all day?'

'Because we're not them.'

'But why can't I change?' I pondered this while holding three planks in my arms. 'I'm asking you.'

'Why don't they eat pork?' José smiled.

'That's a matter of religion, not lifestyle.'

'Why don't you like to eat camel? Are Christians forbidden from eating camel?'

'In my religion, camels are for threading through the eyes of needles, not anything else.'

'So we need furniture in order not to live sad lives.'

This was a poor explanation, but I had made up my mind about wanting furniture. Even if it made me feel ashamed.

José couldn't come home the next day. We'd used up all of his salary. He was taking on extra shifts like mad so we could live more stably in the future. The day after, he still couldn't return. His colleague even had to drive over to tell me.

The thick planks were stacked up twice as tall as me on the roof. One morning, after returning from town, I noticed that the pile had diminished. Our neighbour had taken some to fence in the goat pen.

There was no way I could stand guard on the roof all the time. My only option was to go to the landfill across from us and pick up a few empty cans, puncture holes in them and hang them from the corners of the boards. If somebody came to steal these treasures, the cans would make a noise so I could catch them at it. Even so, I was tricked by the wind multiple times. Whenever the wind blew, the cans would rustle.

One afternoon, I was organising the boxes of books that we'd had shipped in by sea when I stumbled upon a few pictures of myself. In one photo, I was wearing a long gown, a fur coat and dangly earrings. My hair was in an updo. I had just come out of a performance of *Rigoletto* at the Berlin State Opera. Another photo showed a bunch of friends and me out on a winter's night in Madrid, all dressed up. We had gone into a hotel in an old part of town to dance and sing and drink red wine. I was very pretty in the picture, long glossy hair resting on my shoulders, a smile on my lips...

I flipped through the past, one photo at a time. Then I threw the whole stack down and collapsed on the floor in a heap. I felt like I was a spirit looking back at the world of the living; my heart filled with despair and helplessness.

No time to look back. The empty cans on the roof were rustling again. I had to go and protect my wood. For now, nothing was more important to me than that.

I wanted a taste of many different lives, sophisticated or simple, highbrow or low. Only then would this journey be worthwhile. (Although perhaps a life plain as porridge would never be an option for me.)

Nothing special here. How many others have been as lucky as me to see 'the setting sun on the Yellow River, a plume of smoke rising up into the evening sky of the Great Desert' in this life?[1] (Although there was no Yellow River here, nor does the smoke rise straight up.) Then I thought:

On an old road, in the autumn wind, a scrawny horse keeps trudging
The sun, slanting, to the west, setting –

Heart-torn, lovelorn, the wanderer, to the verge of the sky
a-roaming.[2]

This was more to my tune. (Even though I had no scrawny
horse, just a lean camel.)

Friday was the day of the week I looked forward to most
because José would come home and stay until Sunday
night. José wasn't particularly romantic and, in the desert,
my sentimental nature was hardly flourishing either. What
occupied our minds the most was how to improve our home
and overcome both material and psychological miseries.

I used to be quite stupid, boiling rice and preparing
vegetables one after the other since there was only one pot.
Then I came to my senses. I put uncooked rice in with the
meat and vegetables and made it all together into a veggie rice
medley. Much simpler this way.

That Friday night, José sketched out all sorts of furniture
diagrams by candlelight and asked me to pick one. I chose
the simplest. On Saturday morning, we put on our heavy
sweaters and set to work.

'First, let's cut it to size. You sit on the wood so I can saw.'

José worked unceasingly; I wrote numbers on all the freshly
sawn wood.

Hours flew by. The sun rose high above us. I put a wet
towel on José's head and rubbed sunscreen on his bare back.
His hands became blistered from the work. I couldn't help
much, but I could at least sit on the wooden planks. I also
brought him cold water to drink and shooed away any goats
or small children who came by.

The sun poured down like molten iron. I'd been outside
so long that the ground and sky seemed to spin slowly. José

didn't speak at all, like Sisyphus pushing his huge rock. I was enormously proud to have a husband like this. Before I'd seen only his neatly printed documents and love letters. Now I was getting to know a whole new side to him.

José lay on the ground after we ate our veggie medley. He was already asleep by the time I came in from the kitchen. I couldn't bear to wake him, so I crept up to the roof and moved down the planks he'd sawn up, separating them into piles for our table, bookshelf, wardrobe and coffee table. It was sunset by the time he awoke. He leapt to his feet. 'Why didn't you wake me up?' he asked angrily.

I lowered my head and said nothing. Silence is a woman's greatest virtue. No point in arguing that he was sapped of strength, that I had wanted him to rest. José is as hard-headed as they come. But he worked until eleven and lo and behold, we had a table.

The next day was the Sabbath. We should have been resting, but José couldn't sit still with the work unfinished, so he was hammering away up on the roof. 'Give me more rice now and I won't need to eat later tonight. Still have to build the wardrobe against the wall. This one is complicated and will take some time.'

While eating, José looked up suddenly as if remembering something and smiled at me. 'Do you know what these wooden boxes used to hold? Martín the truck driver told me the other day.'

'Maybe freezers? They're so big.'

José couldn't stop chuckling after I said this. 'Do you really want to know?'

'Could it have been for machinery?'

'For coffins,' he said slowly. 'The hardware store bought fifteen coffins from Spain.'

The grand epiphany made me think back to the boss at the hardware store, who had kindly asked how many people were in my family. So this was what he was getting at.

'Are you telling me that the two of us living people are building furniture from coffin boxes? For our home in the Cemetery District...? How do you feel about this?'

'It's all the same to me.' José wiped his mouth, stood up and went back to the roof to continue working.

This piece of unexpected news got me very excited. It wasn't all the same to me; I loved my new table even more.

A few days later, the courthouse contacted us to let us know we could get married. After we tied the knot, we took a detour to José's office to ask for his early shift bus pass, marriage subsidy, rent allowance, tax break, my health insurance...

By the time we got married officially, our home had a bookshelf, a table and a long hanging wardrobe in the bedroom. There was a small coffee table under the cooking station where we put our bottles of oil and sugar. We also had colourful striped curtains made of desert linen.

When guests came over, they had to sit on mats. We didn't buy a metal bed frame. The walls were still made of concrete blocks. We didn't bother to plaster them, so of course we couldn't whitewash them.

José's company agreed to grant us 20,000 pesetas as a furniture subsidy after our marriage. His salary increased by more than 7,000 pesetas. His taxes were decreased. The rent allowance was 6,500 per month and he also got two weeks off for marriage leave. So it turned out there were significant economic gains to be had from signing our names on a slip of paper. Because of this, I decided not to be an iconoclast any more. There was some good in marriage, after all. Friends volunteered to take on José's shifts and so we ended up having an entire month to ourselves.

'The first order of business is taking you to see the phosphate rocks.'

Riding in the company Jeep, we followed the path of the conveyor belt from the quarry's excavation area until we reached the causeway where the phosphate was loaded for export. This was where José worked.

'Oh my God! This is like a James Bond flick! You're Double-Oh-Seven and I'm the evil Oriental woman in the movie—'

'Pretty impressive, no?' José said.

'Who set up this massive project?'

'A German company called Krupp,' José muttered under his breath.

'Spanish people probably couldn't build something so magnificent.'

'Sanmao, could you be a darling and shut your mouth?'

For our honeymoon we hired a guide and rented a Jeep to drive westward. We went into Algeria from Al Mahbes, then turned around and went back into the Spanish Sahara, passing Semara to enter Mauritania. We drove all the way to the border of Senegal before doubling back on another route, heading back up to Villa Cisneros in the Spanish-controlled desert. We finally went back to El Aaiún after all this.

Crossing the Sahara this time, we both fell deeply in love with the land, so much so that we felt we could never again leave this desolation without flowers.

By the time we got back to our home sweet home, there was only one week of our holiday left. We started fixing up our hovel like mad. We asked our landlord to patch up our walls, but he refused. We went into town to enquire about other homes for rent, but everything was too expensive.

José made some calculations one evening, and the next day he went to buy lime and cement. He also borrowed a ladder and some tools and set to work himself.

We worked day and night, eating plain white bread with milk and multivitamins to sustain our physical strength. Toiling without pause after such long and arduous travels, we quickly became very thin, our eyes large and shining, our steps uneven.

'José, I'll have time enough to rest soon. You have to go back to work next week. Why don't you take a break for a few days?'

Standing on the ladder, José didn't even bother to look at me.

'Really, there's no need for us to be so thrifty. Besides, I... I have money in the bank.'

'Don't you know that masons in these parts are paid by the hour? Plus, my handiwork is just as good as theirs.'

'You jerk, do you just want to save until we're old so we can let our children waste our money?'

'If we have a child one day, he'll have to get a part-time job when he turns twelve. I won't give him any money.'

'So how are you going to spend your money in the future?' I asked softly from beneath the ladder.

'Taking care of my parents in their old age. And once we leave the desert and settle down, we'll bring your parents over.'

My eyes welled up hearing him talk about my parents, who were separated from us by innumerable mountains and seas. 'My mother and father are understanding when it comes to us, but they're quite proud deep down. My father, in particular, would never agree to live overseas—'

'Who cares if he agrees or disagrees? You just go home and kidnap him. It'll be a long while before they can escape back to Taiwan.'

So I had no choice but to focus on mixing lime and cement for the castle in the sky of my husband, this exemplary son-in-law. Occasionally little wet chunks would fly from the ladder and land on my head or nose.

'Hurry up and learn Chinese, José.'

'Can't learn. I refuse.'

José could do nearly anything, but languages weren't his forte. He still couldn't speak French after learning for nearly ten years. Forget about Chinese. I wouldn't force him.

By the last day of our honeymoon, the house had been thoroughly whitewashed inside and out. We really stood out in the Cemetery District, like a crane among chickens. Even without a house number posted, there was really no need to apply for one at the municipal government.

In July, we received an extra month's salary. Our marriage subsidy and rent allowance were fully paid out. After work, José ran home by way of steep slopes and shortcuts. As soon as he was through the door, he began pulling out wads of cash from every pocket, throwing them into a huge green pile on the floor. The sight of it wasn't a big deal to me, but for José, who was still wet behind the ears, it was his first time making such a huge amount of money. 'Look, look, now we can buy a foam mat and a blanket and some sheets, a pillow, we can eat out, we can buy a bucket for water storage, get some new pots, a tent...'

We two money worshippers knelt on the ground in front of the banknotes in reverence. After we counted it all, I cheerfully set aside 8,000 pesetas.

'What's this for?'

'New clothes for you. Your trousers are faded, your shirt collars are ruined and your socks have holes in them. You also need a decent pair of shoes.'

'I don't want anything. Let's fix up the home first, then you can fix me up. Who needs new clothes in the desert?' And he insisted on continuing to wear his ragged shoes to work.

I stacked concrete blocks on the right-hand side of our bedroom and put coffin boards on top. Then I bought two thick sponge mats, placing one of them upright against the wall, the other horizontal on the boards. I covered the whole thing with a colourful striped cloth to match the window curtains and sewed it up tightly from the back. It was now a proper sofa. The dark colours were exceptionally beautiful and bright against the snowy white walls.

As for the table, I threw a white cloth over it along with a fine bamboo curtain that my mother had sent. My loving mother had gone so far as to send me the lampshade made of Chinese cotton and paper that I'd wanted. I also received a clay tea set, while my beloved friend Lin Funan sent me a big bundle of contemporary prints and Mr Ping airmailed me a large trunk full of books. Whenever my father encountered any bizarre posters on the way home from work, he'd also buy them for me. My older sister contributed clothes, while my younger brothers were the snazziest of all, sending a kimono-like bathrobe for José. When he wore it, he looked like Toshiro Mifune – one of my very favourite actors.

Once we hung up my mother's cotton paper lantern alongside the flamboyant calligraphy of Lin Hwai-min's Cloud Gate Dance Theatre, its black background with white characters emblazoned on the wall, our home began to boast an ineffable ambience and mood.

This was just the kind of home that could inspire you to strive for better.

While José was at work, I stained the bookshelf a dark brown with some kind of varnish, I'm not quite sure what it's called in Chinese. The shelf immediately seemed much sturdier than before.

I often self-analysed. It is truly difficult to extricate oneself from the station in life into which one is born. My home, if a Sahrawi were to look at it, was filled with things I did not need, but I, on the other hand, couldn't free myself from these shackles. I needed to make everything within these four walls as complex as before. Slowly, I made my way back to the past me, which essentially means I was once more awhirl with sentimentality.

Whenever José went off to work, I would go to the landfill across from our home to pick up scraps. I brought back and cleaned up an old car tyre. Setting it on the mat, I stuffed a red cloth cushion inside so it became like a bird's nest. Everyone vied for this seat in the house.

I retrieved a large glass bottle of deep green and stuck a bloom of wild thorns in it, lending it a feeling of poetic bitterness. I bought a small can of paint to slather Native American-inspired patterns and colours onto various bottles. A camel skull had long been set on the bookshelf. I nagged José to make a lantern out of some iron sheets and glass. I found a nearly putrid sheepskin and, taking a lesson from the Sahrawi, salted it and dyed it with potassium alum. It also became a cushion.

Christmas came. We left the desert for Madrid to visit José's parents and returned with all of José's books from grade school upwards. Our little home in the desert had a scholarly whiff from that day forward.

I found the desert to be truly charming. On the other hand, the desert didn't care a jot for me.

Poor civilised peoples of the world! No getting rid of all our useless belongings.

'This home is still lacking plants,' I said to José one evening. 'No greenery whatsoever.'

'It's not just plants we're lacking. We'll never be satisfied.'

'No, so that's why we have to scavenge where we can.'

That night, we crept over the low wall outside the governor's house and desperately uprooted some of his flowers with our bare hands.

'Quick, put them in the plastic bag. Hurry and get that climbing vine, too.'

'God, how did this root grow so damn deep?'

'We also need some soil. Throw in some clods.'

'This should be enough!' José whispered. 'We have three plants already.'

'I just want one more,' I said, still digging. 'Just one more and we'll be all set.'

Suddenly I noticed that the guard in front of the governor's house was making his way over. Startled out of my wits, I shoved the big plastic bag against José's chest. 'Hold me!' I ordered. 'Hold me tight. Kiss me hard. The wolf is coming. Quickly!'

José grabbed hold of me, pressing those poor flowers between us.

Sure enough, the guard came closer in quick strides, ammunition rattling against his chest. 'What's going on here? Two of you sneaking about?'

'I... We...'

'Get out of here. This is no place for you two to speak sweet nothings.'

We held each other tight and walked towards the low wall. God, it would be great if we could make it out without losing the flowers we'd stolen.

'Hey, go out through the front!' the guard barked. 'Quick!'

So we slowly escaped, holding each other. I even gave a slight bow to the guard. When I told this story to the old commander of the Legión Española, he had himself a good long laugh.

I still wasn't fully content with our home. A place without music was like a Chinese landscape painting without a stream or waterfall. To save money for a tape player, I went on foot to buy vegetables at the Legión Española's faraway canteen. I felt extremely awkward the first time I went. I wasn't like the other wives, who barrelled their way through snatching up goods. I waited in line in an orderly fashion. It took me four hours to buy a basket of vegetables, but the price was one third of what it would be at a typical grocery store.

Eventually I was going there all the time. The soldiers saw how well-mannered I was and felt aggrieved on my behalf. They even gave me a bit of preferential treatment. As soon as I approached the counter, before I even managed to squeeze my way in there, they would openly call out to me over the swarm of big fat rude women: 'What'll it be today?'

I'd hand them my grocery list and, after a while, they'd have it all ready in a box around the back. I'd pay up and head out to call a taxi. Before the car even pulled up, there'd be a strapping fellow in soldier's garb carrying the box and putting it in the car for me. I'd be home in less than half an hour. There were all sorts of military personnel stationed here, but I only cared for the Legión Española. (These were the desert corps I mentioned before.)

They were very masculine and hard-working, respectful of certain women who deserved respect. They knew how to wage war, but they also knew elegance. Every Sunday at dusk, the Legión Española's orchestra would perform in the municipal government plaza, playing classics like *The Magic Flute*, *Night on Bald Mountain* and *Boléro*, all the way up to a finale with *The Merry Widow*.

I saved for a tape player and cassettes by going to the soldiers' canteen. A television and washing machine, on the other hand, never held any appeal for me.

We started saving again. Our next major purchase was going to be a car. Nowadays you can buy one on credit, but José didn't want to be a modern man. He needed to pay it off all at once. So I had no choice but to keep walking and wait to revisit this matter in a few months.

The only shortcut I could take going into town was through two Sahrawi graveyards. Their burial method entails wrapping the body in cloth and setting it in a sandpit, then covering it with an assortment of rocks.

One day, I was weaving past these rock piles as usual, careful not to step on the bodies in eternal slumber and disturb their peace, when I noticed an extremely old Sahrawi man sitting nearby. Curious to see what he was doing, I made my way over and discovered that he was carving stone.

Heavens! At his feet were piled nearly twenty statuettes made of stone. There were busts, birds, children, spreadeagled nude women with half of a baby coming out of their private parts. In addition, he'd sculpted all sorts of animals, antelope, camels… I nearly fainted from the shock. 'Great artist, do you sell these things?' I asked, kneeling down.

I reached out to pick up a face. I couldn't believe my eyes, moved by the rough, natural look of his work. I needed to have it right away.

The old man looked up at me, dazed. Something about his expression made him seem a little crazy. I picked up three of his sculptures and gave him 1,000 pesetas. I made off in a rush towards home, having forgotten all about my errand in town. Suddenly he cried out hoarsely, stumbling after me. I held the stones close, unwilling to surrender them.

Once he caught up with me, he started dragging me back.

'Is it not enough?' I asked frantically. 'I don't have any more cash on me, but I can get you some...'

He couldn't speak. He just bent down, put two more bird statuettes into my hands and let me go on my way.

I didn't have lunch that day. I lay about on the ground playing with the artwork of this great nameless man. Words can't express the emotions that were stirring in my heart.

When my Sahrawi neighbours found out I'd spent 1,000 pesetas on these things, they laughed themselves to the brink of death. They thought I was an idiot. I thought it was just a matter of different cultural levels, which made it impossible for us to communicate. To me, these were priceless treasures!

José gave me 2,000 pesetas the next day. I went to the cemetery but didn't find the old man there. The scorching sun lit up the empty graveyard. Apart from the yellow sand and piles of rocks, there was nothing there. It was as if a spirit had given the five sculptures to me as a memento. I was overwhelmed with gratitude.

José patched up the big square hole in our roof not long after.

To our home, we added a sheepskin drum, a sheepskin water bag, leather bellows, a hookah, a colourful bedspread handwoven by the people of the desert and oddly shaped rocks formed by sandstorms – the locals call them desert roses.

The magazines we ordered began arriving one after the other. Apart from Spanish and Chinese publications, we didn't neglect to include *National Geographic*, of course.

One year later, and our home had become a real palace of the arts.

Whenever our single friends had spare holiday, they had no qualms about coming out all this distance to hang out with us for a whole day. For these people without family, I always found a way to serve them lots of fresh fruit and vegetables and whip up sweet and sour ribs. As such, José made some beloved friends who were steadfast in their loyalty and devotion to us.

Our friends didn't just eat and run. Whenever somebody's mother sent *jamón* and sausage from faraway Spain, they'd always make sure José had some to bring home to me after work. They were all very kind-hearted people.

One weekend, José unexpectedly came home with a bundle of precious and valuable bird of paradise plants. I took the flowers into my arms very slowly, afraid that the stunning red birds would fly back to paradise if my movements were too rough.

'Manolín sent these to you.'

They were a gift more valuable than gold.

Every weekend after, there were more and more birds of paradise blooming and burning themselves in a corner against the wall. José was given them all to bring back home.

By and large, José's books were about the wilderness, the ocean and astronomy. He didn't like investigating questions about human nature. He would still read books about this, but he always said that life shouldn't be analysed by appearances.

So he showed great care with the birds of paradise, changing their water, adding aspirin, cutting the stalks that were gradually rotting. As for Manolín's intentions, he didn't worry too much about him. Once the burning firebirds entered our home, Manolín refused to come over any more.

While José went off to work in the mines one day, I went to the office to dial Manolín on a local extension. I told him I wanted to meet him alone. When he came, I gave him a cold soda water and looked at him very seriously. 'Just say it! You'll feel much better.'

'I... I... You still don't get it?' He held his head in his hands, looking extremely depressed.

'I had a feeling before. Now I see. Manolín, my good friend, lift your head up!'

'I'm not attempting anything. I'm not holding on to the faintest hope. Please don't blame me.'

'No more flowers, alright? I can't take it any more.'

'Fine. I'll go. Please understand. I apologise most sincerely to you, and also José. I—'

'Pico,' (I called him by his surname), 'you didn't trespass on me. You gave a woman great praise and encouragement. There's no need for you to ask for my forgiveness—'

'I won't trouble you any more. Goodbye.' His voice was so quiet it sounded like silent tears.

José didn't know that Manolín had come over by himself.

A week later, he came home from work with a big cardboard box of books. 'Manolín sure is strange,' he said. 'He just quit out of the blue. They wanted to keep him on until the end of the month, but he refused. He wanted us to have all these books.'

I picked up a book at random and, lo and behold, found it was called *En Asia se muere bajo las estrellas*.

I felt a sudden pang of loss in my heart.

After this, whenever our single friends came over, I always became very conscious of my words and deeds. The housewife holed up in the kitchen took the place of the main actor of the past, who had been all too eager to squeeze in and chat up a storm in their midst.

Our home was now comfortably appointed, clean and pleasant. The free girls' school I ran went on a long holiday.

I had been teaching the local women for nearly a year, but they weren't focused when it came to learning numbers. They didn't care about hygiene, either, or understanding finances. Every day when they came, they would want to try on my clothes and shoes, or my lipstick, eyebrow pencil and hand lotion, or else they'd just pile onto my bed. I'd bought a bed frame by this point, which was such a novelty for these women who slept on mats on the floor.

My orderly house was thrown into massive disarray whenever they came. They couldn't read, but they knew more about Jacqueline Kennedy Onassis and other famous people than even I did. They also recognised Bruce Lee and were very familiar with the sexiest Spanish actors and actresses. When they found a photo they liked in a magazine, they'd simply rip it out. They'd wrap themselves up with my clothes on underneath and walk off without telling me, only to return the pieces all dishevelled several days later, with the buttons cut off.

When they came, the house became the set of a disaster movie that they directed and starred in themselves. No need to write a script. A thriller for your viewing pleasure. After José bought a television, I didn't open the door for them no matter how hard they knocked or how much they cursed us. The television, when we had electricity, was our most direct link to the great big outside world. But I still wasn't particularly interested in watching it.

I handwashed our bedsheets innumerable times before José brought back a tiny washing machine. I still wasn't satisfied. I wanted a white car, like the one in the colour ads.

I got to know many of the European housewives in town back then.

I was never one for calling upon others much, but I hit it off with the middle-aged wife of one of José's supervisors. She offered to teach me how to mend clothes. I grudgingly paid her a visit every once in a while in the apartments reserved for senior staff.

One day, I brought her a dress to ask for her help with its sleeves, which were giving me trouble. She happened to have a bevy of ladies in her home at the time.

At first they were all polite to me because I had higher academic qualifications than them. (What philistines. What can an education tell you about a person? What use is a degree?) But then one of those airheads asked me, 'Where do you live? We'll come and visit you next time.'

'José is entry level staff,' I replied very casually. 'Not a director. We don't have assigned housing.'

'We can still come and find you! You can teach us English. What street do you live on?'

'I live outside of town in the Cemetery District,' I said.

An awkward hush fell upon the room.

The good-hearted wife of José's supervisor seemed protective of me. 'Her home is really stylishly decorated,' she said to them. 'I never thought that she could transform a house rented from a Sahrawi into something so beautiful, like in a magazine.'

'Never been there, haha,' said another one of the housewives. 'I'd be afraid of catching a disease.'

I have pretty healthy self-esteem, but their words still hit a sore spot. 'In my view, coming to the desert and not having to face any material hardship is your own loss,' I said slowly. 'An experience you're missing out on.'

'Desert? Forget about it. You can't even tell this is the desert, living in these kinds of apartments. Oh, you! It's too bad you don't move into town. Rubbing shoulders with those Sahrawi, tsk tsk…'

When I said goodbye and left, the supervisor's wife came after me. 'Come back again!' she said softly. 'You must come!'

I smiled and nodded, then went downstairs and headed swiftly to my sweet white home. I resolved to never move into town.

This land became a hotbed of turmoil when Morocco and Mauritania both laid claim to the Western Sahara. Reporters from all over arrived with their heaps of photographic equipment.

They all stayed in the Hotel Nacional, a place that I didn't frequent for obvious reasons. By then we'd bought a car (my white stallion) and had even less of a reason to stick around town during our time off.

It just so happened that we were driving back to town one day and, more than fifty kilometres out, saw someone waving on the road. We pulled over immediately to see what had happened. It turned out this person's car had completely sunk into soft sand and he needed assistance.

We had experience with this sort of thing. We immediately pulled out an old rug and used our hands to help this foreigner dig four trenches around the tyres. Then we put the rug under his front tyres and told him to step on the gas while we pushed from behind. With the rug in place, the tyres wouldn't sink even if the sand were softer than it already was.

It still took us almost an hour to get his car completely out and onto solid ground again.

The man was a reporter from a news agency. He insisted on taking us out to eat at the Hotel Nacional. We were absolutely exhausted, though, and as soon as we got him off our back we went home. By the next day, we'd forgotten all about it.

Less than two weeks later, I was at home by myself when I heard someone by the window. 'No question, it's got to be this house. Let's try.'

I opened the door to find the man whose car we had helped push. In his arms was a big bundle wrapped in cellophane – birds of paradise, what else. He had a friend with him, whom he introduced as his colleague.

'May we come in?' he asked very politely.

'Please come in.'

First I put his flowers in the kitchen, then poured some cold soda water for them. I walked slowly since I was carrying a tray. Just then I heard this foreigner telling the other one in English, 'Heavens! Are we in the Sahara? My God! My God!'

When I walked into the small room, they leapt to their feet from the sofa and took the tray.

'Don't trouble yourself. Please sit.'

They were looking all around, unable to keep their hands off the stone sculptures I'd bought in the cemetery, tutting their praise as if in a trance. One of them gave a gentle push to the rusted steel spokes of the little bicycle I hung in the corner, the wheel tracing an arc.

'I had to add a little bit of pop art to this life in the desert,' I said to him with a smile, stopping the wheel with my hand.

'God! This is the most enchanting desert household I've ever seen.'

'Salvaged waste.' I beamed with pride.

They sat down on the sofa again.

'Watch out! You're sitting on coffin boards.'

They jumped up theatrically and gently lifted the cloth cover back to take a look.

'There's no mummy inside. Don't be afraid.'

In the end, they nagged me for a long time about buying one of my statuettes. I sighed heavily and gave them one of the stone birds, which had a touch of pink from the stone's natural colouring.

'How much?'

'No need. For someone who knows how to appreciate it, it's priceless. For someone who doesn't get it, it's worthless.'

'We... We want to give you something as a token.'

'Didn't you give me these birds of paradise? I think our exchange is complete.'

They thanked me profusely on their way out.

A few weeks later, we were waiting to catch a movie in town when another foreigner came over and extended his hand to us. Baffled, we didn't know what to do but shake hands with him.

'I heard from a reporter at another news agency that you two have the most beautiful home in the desert. I'm not mistaking you for someone else, am I?'

'No, you're not. I'm the only Chinese person around these parts.'

'I hope... if... if it's not too presumptuous, I'd like to come and see your home so I can have a point of reference.'

'You are...?' José asked.

'I'm from Holland, but I am here at the behest of the Spanish government. I've come to this land to build homes for the Sahrawi on contract. We're constructing a residential area. I was wondering if I could—'

'Certainly,' José said. 'You are welcome any time.'

'May I take photos?'

'Yes, no need to worry about these little details.'

'Can we include your wife in the photographs?'

'I'm just an ordinary person,' I jumped in. 'Don't go to the trouble.'

He came over the next day and took many photographs, asking what the house looked like when I first moved in. I showed him a roll of film from the month after we first moved in.

When he left, he told me, 'Please tell your husband for me that you two have built a beautiful Rome.'

'Rome wasn't built in a day,' I answered.

Humans are really strange. When no one validates you, you often can't perceive your own value.

For a while, I revelled in this desert castle.

One day our landlord came round. He rarely comes and sits in our home. But he came, sat, got up and looked about with big lumbering movements. Then he said, 'I told you long ago that you are renting the greatest home in the Sahara. Now you understand!'

'May I ask if something is the matter?' I asked him directly.

'You cannot find a house of this quality for my original asking price anywhere else. I want to raise the rent.'

I wanted to tell him, 'You're a pig.'

But I didn't say anything. I got out our lease and nonchalantly threw it down before him. 'You raise our rent and I'll report you tomorrow,' I said to him.

'You— You— You Spanish are bullying us Sahrawi.' He was actually angrier than I was.

'You are not a good Muslim. Even if you pray every day, your god will not look after you. Now get out of my house.'

'You insult my religion just for raising the rent a little—' he cried.

'You're insulting your own religion. Please leave.'

'I— I— You damn—'

I shut my castle gate and raised my drawbridge, ignoring his curses in the street outside. I put on a cassette tape. Dvořák's *New World Symphony* filled the house.

I walked over to the round cushion-seat made from a tyre and sat down gently, as if I were a king.

My Great Mother-in-Law

My wedding to José wasn't a hugely romantic affair involving elopement and whatnot. We'd simply walked to the courthouse and registered. But even though we accomplished what we set out to do, neither set of parents was able to attend.

On my side of the family, I could talk to my parents about any topic, thanks to the openness and sympathy with which they treated their children. I'd received my family's approval before the wedding. Afterwards, I just sent them a telegram to let them know the date. My father and mother had long been concerned about me. Even though the abruptness of my marriage might seem unfilial or disrespectful, how could my parents not, after laying eyes upon the ideal son-in-law that their wandering daughter had chosen, feel joy and sorrow entwined? They warmly accepted José into the family.

My father even exhorted me again with words like those our Heavenly Father had once conveyed to this mortal realm: 'He is my beloved son and you must hear and obey him.'

On José's side of the family, I don't know how my parents-in-law got to be so unlucky, but none of the four daughters or one son who were married had discussed it with them ahead of time. (They have two more sons and one daughter who are unmarried, so perhaps there's hope yet.)

Among these darling children, there were some who'd announced their marriage one day in advance (like José). Others had written letters after getting married (like the oldest sister in America). And then there were those who sat obediently before their parents in Madrid, all while they were secretly getting an overseas proxy marriage in Colombia (the second oldest sister).

These siblings had all found their way into beautiful, blissful marriages, but still they chose to do this funny and inconsiderate thing to their parents. They gave no sign of it at home, but outside the house all eight of them would keep watch and help each other out, working together, sixteen hands lifting up the sky. They kept their parents completely in the dark. By the time their parents wanted to get up in arms, the rice was already cooked – alas, too late.

It might be that their family environment had been too strict, conservative or authoritarian, and this was why such tragicomic situations had emerged. (More proof it's not just traditional Chinese culture that places emphasis on how you raise your children. The Western world is also full of strange practices!)

Anyway, ever since I got married, my husband's surname has adorned my ID, so I totally stopped paying any attention to my own family. (Not actually true.)

Regarding my mother-in-law, I'm very much aware that heaven is high and the emperor is far away, so I can get away with not paying attention. But in order to clear our filial debts, I write to her once a week to pay our respects, reporting details of our daily lives and diets. If only my humble apologies could curry favour with my mother-in-law, I'd consider this, too, a belated happiness.

In this mortal realm, men might seem sombre or cruel on the surface. But deep down their spirits are benevolent, their hearts open and minds frail. One need only make a small gesture to dupe them into good faith.

A good son necessarily comes from a good father. My father-in-law soon started writing to me. The love he had for me was the same as he had for José.

Because this writer happens to be a woman, the same sex as the mother-in-law, I not only know her as I know myself, I also know how to read between the lines. Accepting that I am but a lowly creature, I realised, too, that she couldn't be much more clever than me – unless my divination skills had failed me and I was in for a surprise, and she was either like the bodhisattva Guanyin (whether or not Guanyin is actually a woman, I still don't know), or else she was like Holy Mother Mary (definitely a woman and, what's more, a virgin). Anyway, in either case, I was bound to receive her goodness and mercy.

A pity my mother-in-law wasn't either of these two types of women.

Half a year of married life passed. I had been writing diligently to my mother-in-law, but nary a word she returned. I wasn't about to get discouraged, intently focused as I was on stealing her heart. This project would take some time yet. (I hereby give myself the title 'Great Pirate of the Seven Seas', certainly a ne'er-do-well.)

To all the daughters-in-law reading this, know that if you had a hand in setting up your own marriage, like Eve deciding to feed Adam the forbidden fruit herself, then your situation is similar to mine. I urge you to treat your mother-in-law well. Do not, by any means, overlook this.

If you are still Eve, but your mother-in-law created you from your husband's ribcage and presented you to him, then don't read any further to avoid wasting your precious time. (But, a word of caution, don't forget the tale of *Southeast Fly the Peacocks*.[1])

It's said that the couple who ate the forbidden fruit knew they were in the wrong. Long ago they exiled themselves to the end of the world to become shepherds and live together as man and wife. This kind of life, sometimes marked by dispute and conflict, other times by love and tenderness, is a dull existence that easily gets frittered away.

In my letters to my parents, I included photos of myself with a tousled mane, reciting to myself – *wild hair like fragrant grass / growing each day you're farther away*.[2] The photos of our home looked dismal and bleak as the underworld. The true happiness within was boundless as heaven.

Being far from the emperor, my old mother-in-law, gave me leeway to misbehave at home, doing as I pleased, indulgent and complacent to the point of forgetting my very form.

Fine. Don't forget now about a certain Mister Bai from days of yore who spoke these words:

Lush grass on the plains,
in one year, withers and thrives once each.
Wildfire does not burn it completely;
when spring winds blow, it lives again. [3]

Winter came. The master of this lush land, old boss José, suddenly spoke up. 'It's almost Christmas. We have to go home to see Mother.'

Hearing this, tears of excitement overcame me. I seized he who spoke and urgently asked, 'Which mother? Yours or mine?'

Answer: 'Ours.' (Such diplomatic language. Not clever at all.)

It's at this point that you know the period of thriving for the grass on your plains has passed. Withering time has come! (Whither the withering.)

Don't bother getting appendicitis, colic, stomach bleeding, bronchitis, back spasms or a broken leg or any of these desperate measures in early December. I myself have tried all of these. By the time it's 20 December, you'll still be lugging your little suitcase onto the plane, your man holding a knife to your back. Warriors must pay the price.

Having grown up in a family of lawyers, I'd seen and absorbed every kind of criminal behaviour that our society can produce. On top of that, my own parents are truly honest citizens of the highest order. They often warned me that I'd have to first respect and restrain myself in order to manage my affairs in the outside world, put myself in others' shoes, think of others' circumstances and feelings. Only then could I be a good citizen of the world… (This is always the first step to a legal settlement, they say.)

So after I got married, I often reflected on and evaluated myself carefully, counting the ways in which I'd done wrong as a daughter-in-law of the Quero family. What a disaster, keeping these accounts. Whether civil or criminal matters, I had committed all sorts of heinous crimes, more than just those that provoke a simple rebuke.

For example, in my mother-in-law's eyes, I'd been involved in illicit sexual relations, robbery, fraud, embezzlement, trafficking, abuse, damage, hindrance and so on and so on – all sorts of unforgivable offences. Once I had this self-awareness, I realised I was caught in dire circumstances.

Let me tell you. Don't be afraid. No matter what bad deeds you've committed, you might as well toughen up. Your guilty conscience will be your own little secret. Don't let your mother-in-law see through you.

Alright, so, the more you think about it, the more clear-headed you become. You realise that your mother-in-law must hate you from the bottom of her heart. Don't second-guess your all too trustworthy powers of thought. You can't be wrong. She hates you. She is your number one imaginary enemy. On the plane en route to her home, you should be forming an initial mental image: the imaginary enemy has been born. Don't be too naive. She might be the CIA, and it just so happens you've joined the FBI. Don't take this lightly, thinking she's still family no matter what. Even if you're both part of a set-up, maybe there's some kind of conspiracy or bet you don't know about.

When you get off the plane in Madrid, there will be no one offering flowers to a criminal like yourself, even though you'd given them advance notice of your arrival. (Lucky you if there are no plain-clothes officers waiting to arrest you. Already a great fortune bestowed upon you. You should go and buy a lottery ticket.)

At the airport, I'll say I'm thirsty and want to go and sit in a cafe for a little while. After dawdling over three soda waters, I drag my feet all the way to a taxi. (Too bad there isn't any E. coli in the soda water to give me acute enteritis so I can get hospitalised and not have to deal with anyone!)

Finally, both my legs trembling, I'm standing outside the gate at my mother-in-law's beautiful apartment. I put down my suitcase and say to José nervously, 'Ring the doorbell! Say I'm here.'

The son certainly won't pay any attention to your crazy talk. He takes out the keys from his pocket and opens the door himself. (The return of a prodigal son is more precious than gold!)

Your husband strides into a hallway with no end. 'Papá, Mamá,' he calls. 'We're home.' Even if I were more bold, I wouldn't be able to step over that threshold. My face is frozen into a smile. I stand outside the door, counting backwards by the second. Seven, six, five, four, three, two, one...

Then I see the end of the hallway. A large number of troops appear out of the blue. Father leads the way, followed by Mother. Little Sister squeals and squeezes. The Brothers come with arms wide open. (All with big beards.)

I know the hour has come. My fate, my luck, I accept it all and fly towards them. Originally I thought I would throw myself into Father's arms to be safe. Didn't think Mother would grab me first in a tight embrace, taking me in from all angles, face lit up.

The imaginary enemy is mighty indeed, with many a clever trick. Need to be on the defence. Thus the Quero family's new daughter-in-law is dragged indoors.

'Father, Mother, I've done something I feel terribly sorry about. Please forgive me.' (Note that you should say 'I' and not 'we'. Their son has escaped blame. Innocent, he remains.)

If your mother-in-law is Chinese, you must be even more shrewd. Get down on both knees as soon as you enter. Kowtow like a mortar and pestle grinding garlic. Don't worry. You won't be asked to stand and freeze for three hundred days.[4] If your mother-in-law's spiritual practice runs deep, she'll pull you up herself. It will be a struggle to call out 'Mother' to your imaginary enemy. Don't be so unwilling. There's still 'Mama' – this is the true term of endearment. You mustn't ignore the power of diplomatic language. Would you rather call her Señora Quero? (Then you lose in the first round. A stupid person, you are!)

I enter the in-laws' home and look around me, finding this household to be neat and tidy, bright and spacious. The bathroom is spotless, the balcony filled with abundant flowers and plants. Every bedroom is immaculately made up, the kitchen cutlery spick and span. Father is a retiree with a clean and elegant style. Eldest Brother and Second Brother wear well-ironed trousers. Little Sister is cordial and courteous. I take in all of these achievements and quietly mark them to Mother's credit. The imaginary enemy has just risen another level in her martial prowess. Take a deep breath. Prepare to take on a heavyweight battle with your featherweight self. (Mother is your enemy. You must sleep on brushwood and taste gall. Do not forget this – do not!)

Alright. In your own home, or your Mama's home, you can sleep until one in the afternoon; you can serve your husband soy sauce and water for a meal; you can forego doing the laundry for a whole week. You can also pull your husband's hair, kick his legs, open his chequebook on a whim and so on and so on. You can do all sorts of bad things as you please; there won't be any retribution.

Now, as luck would have it, you've been forced to take up residence in your enemy's home. (She has a grudge against you. She won't tell you this. You'll have to confirm your suspicions and carefully find proof.)

You were the first to do harm. Now don't be careless when it comes to your defence. There are all kinds of ways to trap the authorities.

If your imaginary enemy is a stupid person, she'll toss a large vase at you as soon as you enter the door. You'll be a bloody mess. That'll play right into your hands. You can run out the door and escape – *he who fights and runs away may live to fight another day* – but the original sin will still be on you. If you have a conscience, then there is no need to report her for injuring you – if you think otherwise, your knowledge of this world is truly laughable indeed!

Unfortunately, my imaginary enemy is completely unlike this. She's taking the high road, not hitting or yelling. This is even more frightening. I see that she's crossed way more bridges than I've ever walked roads. I'll have to think carefully back to *The Art of War, Romance of the Three Kingdoms, Water Margin, Dream of the Red Chamber, Journey to the West...* These great books can provide you with some ideas. *Tome of the Filial Daughter* and *Master Zhu's Maxims for the Home* might have the opposite effect, but flip through them when you have the need. One can learn much from historical precedence on the art of dealing with mothers-in-law.

During my stay at my mother-in-law's house, I never forget that the person I am facing harbours immense hatred for me. Don't relax your imagination. Keep this firmly in mind. (I've got some brains yet, heh heh!)

As a guest in your mother-in-law's house, don't let yourself be a defenceless city. Even as a guest, do not forget: you are still the daughter-in-law.

In the morning, when you hear Mother getting out of bed and going to shower, you must immediately get up, too. After putting on clothes and make-up and freshening up, don't let the enemy snatch up the dishrag and broom. Best to strike pre-emptively and grab the goods. You must complete the chores of household cleaning to absolute perfection. (Don't let the enemy catch any little mistakes!)

So, in my mother-in-law's house, I display warmth and affection to my all my in-laws. But my true essence is often revealed to José. When I'm alone in the bathroom, I warn myself frequently and quietly: *Don't scold José, he belongs to her now, if you scold him, she'll hit you.* This is no secret. Even children understand this logic.

Alright. Maybe you'll listen to me and not scold your husband in front of his mother to avoid a beating. If you've listened too closely, you'll think, *Fine, I'll be very sweet to her son. I love him too, after all! Maybe this way I can make peace with the imaginary enemy.*

You're a product of the times. May I please ask how you plan to express your so-called sweetness? Have you ever thought that the sight of you lying in natural repose, watching television next to your husband, is already offensive to your mother-in-law's sense of decency?

Furthermore, have you seen your mother-in-law eating cake while sitting on your father-in-law's knees? Of course not, right? So, of course, I wouldn't go and sit in José's lap in front of my mother-in-law. And I most certainly would not kiss him. That would be a capital offence.

Don't even bother watching television. When movies come on in the afternoon, you can go straight to the kitchen and take on those greasy pots and pans and knives and forks and cups. This would be best. Should you emerge from the kitchen after long hours of toil, you'll find your father-in-law asleep, the siblings out, mother-in-law talking to her beloved son in the TV room. You walk in awkwardly, sit down silently. Your mother-in-law doesn't so much as glance at you. Quietly, you move closer to your husband, wanting to join the conversation. But he suddenly seems annoyed by you. After this small evasion, if you're sensitive, you'll realise that you have leprosy!

Don't get too upset. Sandwiching your beloved husband between you and the enemy will really make him suffer.

You should walk away. No matter how evil-hearted you are, sometimes you must be fair and reasonable. (Occasional moments like this won't hurt your vitality.)

Even though you don't have anybody to talk to, you must pay attention. Maybe you get up at seven in the morning to follow after the enemy, tidying up, making beds, buying groceries, chopping and cleaning in the kitchen, serving lunch, bringing out plates, then washing the whole big batch of pots and pans. Maybe you're getting used to being the Second Little Sister of the house. You'll get tired and want to take a nap like your father-in-law, but wouldn't that be too dangerous if your enemy has her eyes open and you have them shut? I implore you not to be tempted by small gains. Go to the back balcony instead, take down the dry clothes. Find the ironing board and iron the pretty Little Sister's jeans in the kitchen. She's dating boys and studying at the same time. Don't give her more work to do.

The imaginary enemy is your most dangerous enemy. Whether she sees good or ill in your marriage, she has a major influence on all of it. (Is there a son in this world who doesn't love his mother?) She has a mother–son love complex. Your husband (and my husband is the same) has an Oedipus complex. This is a naturally occurring principle of the world. If you refuse to understand and want man to conquer nature, then please go and ask the great master psychologist Freud. The consequences are sure to be disastrous. Even though I've practised a little hypnotism myself, there is no treatment for this malady.

Maybe after you finish the ironing it's already sunset and lights are coming on all around. You've lived in the desert for so long. Perhaps you might enjoy diving into the bustle of the city, frolicking with all its splendid men and women, watching neon lights flicker and tasting once more the sorrows and joys of civilisation.

You can give it a shot. Ask, 'Can I go out for a walk with José?'

Mother might answer, 'Didn't you already go out this morning? Where else are you off to?'

Don't get pouty and talk back. *This morning was to buy groceries with you. It doesn't count.* By all means, you mustn't go crazy, slip on your coat and escape for an all-nighter because you didn't get permission.

Respect the enemy. Reduce your conflicts as much as possible. This is the key factor to keep you from stumbling. At the end of the day, you're still a featherweight scarecrow.

Christmas finally arrives. Three days before, Mother calculated how many people would be coming over: Father, Mother, five daughters, three sons, four sons-in-law, one daughter-in-law, two family friends, Uncle and Auntie, cousins, Eldest Bro's foreign girlfriend, Little Sister's French teacher, fourteen thrashing, shrieking, flailing grandchildren… Altogether a blissful family of thirty-seven.

It's the newcomer's turn to make Christmas dinner this year. We want sweet and sour pork and chop suey and Kung Pao chicken…

Everybody at the family meeting raises their hand with a great cheer to pass this motion. My heart thuds so hard, it almost bursts out of my chest. I glance at José, whose head is buried in a detective novel. He might as well have plugs in his ears. He might as well be blind.

Only in this moment do you realise that your beloved husband is like Jesus's disciple Peter and will thrice deny you before the rooster crows.

On 23 December, you get up early and take three baskets and a small trailer to buy enough food for a battalion. You poke your head around to see what Mother's doing. She's kneeling on the ground, scrubbing away at an enormous array of special silverware. You turn to go and find Little Sister. She's always with her boyfriend in the morning and going to class in the afternoon.

Under the pretence of changing into boots, you creep into the bedroom. You raise your head to glance at your beloved husband. (Still curled up in bed.)

'Can you come help carry groceries?'

Right at that moment, Mother walks in and your husband's name becomes Peter. He answers loudly, 'Go by yourself. Men don't go to the market.' (The second denial of Peter.)

Don't hate him for it. How he can be your slave in front of his mother's face?

You start striding towards the vegetable market alone, unable to keep your hands in your pockets as you usually do, the empty baskets jostling uncomfortably against you. But, let me tell you, no matter how awkward you feel, you must keep your head high and back straight. This way, a certain warm and salty liquid will flow down into your stomach rather than ruin your beautiful eye make-up.

So, the fact of the matter is, maybe you've lost, but this round of bets isn't over yet. Until you reach the end, you won't know who's won. A critical point – don't lose heart!

It's Christmas Eve. You wake up early in the morning. Mother is already away getting her hair done. Father is taking a walk, as usual. Little Sis is meeting her boyfriend, Eldest Bro has gone sledging. Second Bro is God knows where. José is meeting his former classmate. The house is totally deserted.

The other good folks won't be back until they drag their sons and daughters home for family merriment in the evening. Hmm, you think. What a great opportunity. If you don't abscond now, then when? I'll go to the department store and buy myself some nice new clothes in a stroke of vanity.

No need to run. You're forgetting that you are the mainstay of this evening. Christmas dinner for thirty-seven, and they want you to make it happen with two large saucepans. You roar with laughter. How often do you get such an amazing opportunity to show off your authority to your imaginary enemy? You are not the weak one. You aren't any less capable than her. This is the perfect chance to kill your mother-in-law's spirit and boost your own prestige. If you don't attack now, then when?

Don't think you can't summon the strength to cut through these mountains of meat. Don't let that broken ankle from four months ago get in your way either. Use great wisdom and tell yourself: weakness of the flesh is temporary, triumph of the spirit is forever...

To raise another example, perhaps your physical strength is already like 'the boundless forest shedding its leaves shower by shower.' But your will happens to be 'the endless river rolling its waves hour after hour.'[5]

If you want to be annoying and ask yourself repeatedly, *Why me, why do I have to?* then you, scarecrow, are truly a hollow bag of straw. Why? For your own good. *But I don't want to eat that much meat.* Let me tell you again. You're just making this much and you won't have to eat it all yourself. The benefits are yet to come.

Every man for himself, and the devil take the hindmost. Christmas is just once a year. When you return to your own home in the desert, you'll have to revert to something completely different and show more love and respect to your good husband. You won't lose anything in this business!

(Remember *Dream of the Red Chamber*. Who married Jia Baoyu in the end? Don't take after Miss Lin any more. She's lovable and sympathetic but ultimately ends up nowhere good!)

Silent night, holy night. The great feast finally reaches the table, one course after another. Thirty-six people gathered together, eating in boundless happiness. As someone new, you've been forgotten, of course. What's so bad about that? For once the imaginary enemy isn't studying you with great urgency. You also don't need to track her every move. Perfect time to relax your nerves. Sprinkle soy sauce, white sugar and garlic everywhere. Doesn't it feel like going back to those happy times of home-made mischief?

Only when they open the champagne in the antechamber do you manage to squeeze into the crowd. You wipe the grease from your hands and take a big gulp from José's cup. He won't notice you're there next to him, of course. (Don't worry. The Bible says Peter had to deny thrice. His conscience came back after the roosters crowed and he left, covering his sobs. At the time, Jesus only looked at him with love and affection and didn't say a word of accusation. So you shouldn't curse either. José will go out and cry, naturally. It is not that he will not come around; the hour has not arrived.)

After looking all over the place, dear Father nabs the new daughter-in-law from her corner by the wall, hugging and kissing her. In front of everyone, he cries, 'Long live the cook! Long may she live!'

Don't get carried away and start declaring this yourself. Mother has been toiling her entire life and Father hasn't given her a single word of praise. Today he praises you because he is showing his humanity, but also as a stratagem. You better back away wisely, clean up the plates and dishes and return to the kitchen to make yourself scarce. Don't get giddy with the rest of them and go dancing around the living room. Mother is still cleaning the table and chairs. She's also tired. You have even more reason to see this through all the way. Don't let her snatch away both credit and labour at this hour. (Don't forget that an Aries girl like yourself is predatory by nature.)

To deal with your heavyweight imaginary enemy, you must kill her with kindness. Don't dash your eggs on a rock.

Silent night! Let me sleep peacefully for once! This scarecrow is so exhausted, her hay is coming loose one sheaf at a time. You close your eyes, counting sheep one by one in the ice-cold dishwater. O beloved and cherished desert, how I want to go home to you soon!

People disperse as the music ends. I wipe my hands and come out to say goodbye to the married older sisters.

'You two must come over to see our new swimming pool,' says the husband of one of José's sisters. 'José said he can come tomorrow with Mamá and Papá.' (A swimming pool in the winter?)

'Tomorrow? I... I made plans with a few friends,' I reply quickly. 'We used to be room-mates. I have to see them.'

'This won't do,' another sister interjects. 'This won't do at all. You won't even come once to their home? Why don't you make some calls and drop your other plans?'

'Alright, that's enough. We'll take turns. The whole lot of us can see them on separate days. We want to learn how to cook Chinese food.'

'I... José, aren't we going back to the desert on the twenty-sixth?'

'Ha! This old dog has already helped you pull off the perfect deception. José has a really bad cold. The doctor's note is here. Heh heh, you two can bask in your freedom until January the sixth.'

You know that Uncle and Auntie have traditional values regarding contact between men and women. If you fall into the pool, he won't rescue you. You turn quickly to look for José, your eyes crying out *Help!*

The horror of split personalities. Peter refuses to look at you again. (The roosters are almost about to crow. You've already denied thrice. Why aren't you leaving to go and sob? Oh, Peter!)

The imaginary enemy smiles sweetly at you. Don't go out and sob in Peter's place. You have to reciprocate and beam back at her.

After so much talking and struggling, you're weary. You can no longer struggle. It's time for peace talks. No more bashing your head against the wall.

This large family keeps eleven modern cars of all different colours in its garage. But on all the home visits to come, you still tag along with José, threading above ground and underground like city rats. Every day you undercut the restaurants of your countrymen. Today it's catering for Second Sister's family. Tomorrow, a buffet for Auntie's family. Your copy of *Yuanshan's Cookery* is almost worn to pieces.

Maybe you return to the home of your imaginary enemy by night, amid the ice and snow. You look at your two hands, so coarse now, and have an urge to pinch your husband to death. You throw yourself at him, preparing to attack. (Don't forget to lock the door to your bedroom first.) But your José's movements are quicker than yours. 'What are you doing?' he hisses.

'I'm going crazy. Ever since I got to your home, I've lost myself and I've lost you. All I have is a bunch of enemies that

I've dreamed up. I struggle and struggle, I'm going crazy from exhaustion...'

'They all love you so much, even more than I'd imagined. And you're still not happy? Don't you see how they eat your gruel every day and don't ever complain? Now you want to repay them in this way. What a thoughtless woman you are.'

Fine. You don't need to be like the wife in *Mad Woman*. Turn out the lights, take a Valium, set your alarm. Cover up these few dry hay-stalks of yours and go to sleep. In your dreams, there will be a river of tears on which you can float all the way home to the desert.

(Peter, Peter, don't forget. You'll be taking down the cruelly crucified later.)

Only a few days after Christmas does the imaginary enemy go out and buy a gift for you. You won't lose to her. She's been using the large, colourful bedspread you brought her from the desert for a while now. (Ha! You had the forethought to strike pre-emptively.)

The holy object she presents you with happens to be a thick volume entitled *Encyclopedia of Spanish Recipes for Every Season*.

Don't forget your foreign etiquette. After you open the present in front of her, you must immediately gasp in amazement and appreciation and cluck your thanks. Your enemy will smile sweetly and say, 'Come and thank Mother with a kiss.' Don't hesitate. Go and give her a firm kiss on the cheek. (Good thing you don't wear lipstick. You won't leave a bloodstain mark.)

'You should learn how to cook some Western cuisine. José is too skinny. You must feed him food from his homeland on a proper schedule.' (Food of the homeland, for us, means camel meat.)

The new year passes. The beautiful coming Sunday happens to be 6 January. Don't be too naive and ruffle your feathers against the birdcage before you're entirely out of it. The imaginary enemy is neither old nor deaf.

Seeing the imaginary enemy grow sadder with every passing day, I wish I could turn invisible. I don't want her to see me; I'd rather not open up this abduction case again for her to settle accounts.

Long ago, her son could have chosen not to leave the nest at such a young age. It was me, Jonathan Livingston Seagull, who abducted him and brought him to this land beyond time, gravely injuring the old bird's heart.

I committed the original sin. How can I blame her for hating me?

In the dead of night, I surreptitiously get out of bed and open my leather bag. I count my secret savings. More than 10,000 pesetas left.

When you get up bright and early the next morning, you see Mother taking beef out of the freezer to defrost for lunch.

I go over and put my arms around her waist, hugging her from behind. 'Mother,' I say to her. 'Since we've been home, you've been working hard for too long. Why not let your son take you out for seafood today? Father, the Brothers, Little Sis, we'll invite the whole family for dinner. How about it?' You can't be insincere when you say this. The imaginary enemy is such a meticulous person. Could you really fool her with your tone of voice and expression?

So let me teach you a method. You don't even need to put up any pretence of consideration for her. Don't you have a vivid imagination? If you don't use your natural-born talent now, then when? Close your eyes, resolve yourself, and imagine Mother is the Mama you haven't seen in a very long time. Focus all your energy on imagining this, from outside to in. You'll find that your heart will immediately soften; you'll love her and speak with sincerity. As for the 'real Mama' who has always occupied your heart, you'll have to temporarily shut her into another part of your heart and not let her out.

With this little bit of magic, you'll be able to conquer the imaginary enemy.

Mother and Father aren't terribly rich, but they do have some olive trees in Andalusia to the south. They aren't poor people, just thrifty by nature. They rarely go out to eat. On the occasion that their son invites them to dine at a restaurant, they will happily agree to it.

Little Sis, Little Bro and Second Bro all meet at the restaurant. We two couples, Mother holding on to José, Father propped up by daughter-in-law, make a beautiful portrait of family harmony and parentage.

Mother is of noble bearing, Father a true gentleman. José's handsomeness is a force of nature. Only the daughter-in-law looks ashen after cooking that banquet for thirty-six guests. Long has her visage been unable to return to the beauty of a rose.

Everyone gobbles up lobster, prawns, shrimp, clams, salmon. This is no Snake Alley. This is the most famous seafood restaurant in all of Madrid!

Your deep-rooted bad habits flare up again, along with your vanity. The new clothes you'd dreamed of in the desert, you think silently to yourself, are all on the table now. These people are eating your clothes, a button here, a zipper there. A piece of red cloth, a sleeve. Now they're eating a belt.

Don't be heartbroken. Don't get anxious. You're Eve, the first person in the world. Are you worse at maths than an elementary school student? Think about it. Your mother-in-law was pregnant with your good man for nine months. She gave him flesh and blood, life itself. In the course of twenty-odd years, how much money has she spent on his studies, his literacy, juvenile court, illnesses, clothing, food, shopping, haircuts, the labours of raising a child? How many baskets of olives has Father sold?

You take another look at José. Such a good young man, yours for the price of this table of seafood. Are you losing in this transaction, or are you in fact turning a profit?

You resolve yourself again, thinking about how your own parents held you up. They raised you as the pearl of their palms, the apple of their eye. You turn it over and over in your mind. Aren't other parents the same, putting blood, sweat and tears into raising their sweet babies?

Hot tears nearly burst from your eyes with this revelation. You can't take care of your own parents, but wouldn't it be repayment all the same to put a few more prawns on the plates of José's father and mother? (It is unfair, but don't think any more of it. Otherwise, you'll stop yourself again.)

If only José could understand his wife's intention. If only he could be enlightened. We could sacrifice our bodies for parents on both sides, and still it would not be enough! (In this world, men sacrifice themselves for women, and women for men. You'd have to light a lantern and scour the land to find dutiful children who would sacrifice themselves for their parents. Don't bother looking. You won't find them.)

It's time to go. Pack your suitcases. Little Sis watches nearby, reluctant to part. With a sense of siblinghood, imagine she's your own flesh and blood little sister. Wouldn't you want to give her some pretty clothes? Give them to her, a young girl in the first throes of love. Mother and Father have strict rules in the house. She has few decent clothes. She has to change boyfriends frequently, instead of changing clothes.

This isn't just sibling love. This is leaving the door open for the future. Maybe one day, Sanmao's star will perish in the western sky, leaving behind future nieces and nephews, and pretty Little Sister will have to take in orphans so José can look for happiness again. Arrangements are needed in advance; one can't simply clutch Buddha's feet in a moment of need.

The moment of departure has finally come. Your heart rate speeds up to 150 again. Father is cheerful. He goes out to take his walk as usual, rain or shine, without bothering to bid farewell.

Mother's facial expression is frigid as a snowy mountain. As for me, this criminal character who entered the Quero family home with a guilty heart, I leave the Quero family home with a guilty heart. I feel conflicted, self-conscious, remorseful. I can't lift my head up. I bend down to put on socks, almost like I'm kneeling before the imaginary enemy. Little Sis has braved the rain to call a taxi. (Everyone with a car has gone to work. No one to drive us.) When Little Sis comes back up, yelling, 'Come, the car is here', my nerves are so worked up that I just want to burst right out that door so I can avoid the enemy's emotional agitation or a sudden explosive confrontation.

Hearing that the car is here, this mother-in-law can't take it any more. She desperately hurls herself at me like an arrow. I stand there unmoving, preparing myself to receive a torrent of slaps. (I'll give you my left cheek to slap, then my right cheek to slap. I make up my mind not to retaliate. Would a hero fight back?)

Closing my eyes, gritting my teeth, I wait for the enemy to attack. Who knew the enemy would instead hug me tight to her bosom, sobbing and trembling. 'My child!' she says.

'You must come back home soon! Life in the desert is too hard. Your home is here. Mamá misunderstood you before. She loves you now.' (Reader, look close. The enemy has finally called herself 'Mamá' rather than 'Mother'.)

I've made the imaginary enemy cry. I'm the one who has been on the defensive from beginning to end. I never attacked her. Why is she crying then?

Little Sis and José pry Mother's arms from around me. 'Mamá, don't make a fuss,' they call. 'The car downstairs can't wait any longer. Let go.'

Only then do I manage to struggle my way out of Mother's bosom.

Amid this autumnal atmosphere, a warm spring rain unexpectedly falls, slowly wetting my face.

Now let's go back to see what else the aforementioned Mister Bai has to say (he's still not done). Sanmao has gone to her mother-in-law's house, and now he speaks for the mother-in-law:

Afar, fragrance occupies ancient roads;
A fine jade-green stretches to a ruined city.
Once more I see off a nobleman;
The lush grasses full of the emotion of departure.[6]

I finally killed my imaginary enemy.

My dear mother-in-law Venus was gradually born in the call of a clarion.

Stealing Souls

I own a camera that's really not too shabby. Of course what I call 'not shabby' is in comparison to the little toy-like boxes that most other people have. I didn't often use this camera when I lived in Madrid because it attracted a lot of attention whenever I had it strapped to me. In the desert, I'm not exactly the type of person that commands attention. Moreover, in this sparsely populated land, you rarely see people to begin with. Standing amid the sand, using a hand to block the sunlight, you might feel overjoyed just to see a black speck of a person on the horizon.

When I first got to the desert, my greatest ambition was to use my camera to record the lives and customs of the nomads in this desolate region. Thinking back, I felt passionate about this other culture because of the extreme differences between us; in this distance I found a kind of spiritual beauty and emotion.

The time I spent plunging deep into the great desert was mostly before I got married. When I first arrived in this vast and mysterious land, I used all the communication skills possible to get to know every side of it. Most valuable to me was seeing how people could derive the same joys from life, the same loves and hates as people anywhere else, even while living in this desert where not a single blade of grass can grow.

Taking pictures was a completely necessary part of my life in the desert. My financial circumstances at the time meant I couldn't really afford much on my travels through the great sands, let alone rent a car. Nor did I have the capacity to spend too much money on the relative luxury of photography, even though to me it was such an important and worthy investment.

My photographic equipment was limited to a camera, a tripod, a telephoto lens, a wide-angle lens and a couple of filters. I bought a few rolls of film with a high ISO. The rest were the most basic black and white or colour film. I didn't bother with a flash since I knew I wouldn't use it much.

Before I came to the desert, I would occasionally get one or two good shots out of every few hundred photos or so. I did buy and read through some photography manuals back in Madrid just as I was preparing to move. What I learned on paper, I felt, was knowledge that had not yet been tested. With this openness and earnestness, I came to northern Africa.

The first time I was driven into the actual desert, I clutched my camera in hand, marvelling at every single thing and wanting to photograph it all. Mirages that looked like dreams or illusions, like ghosts. Continuous dunes, smooth and tender as the female form. Wild sandstorms pouring down like rain. The burned and dry land. Cactuses with arms outstretched, calling to the heavens. Riverbeds that had dried up millions of years ago. Black mountain ranges. The vast sky, a blue so deep as to appear frozen. A wilderness covered in rocks… These images set my mind awhirl and ablaze with their riches.

On these incessantly bumpy journeys, my deep awe for the land often made me completely forget about my own toils.

How I hated my limited means at the time. If only I'd sensibly set out to learn photography much earlier, I could have melded each vision to which I bore witness together with the emotions I felt. I could have created a record of them, an invaluable memento of my life's journey!

Although I didn't have much money for photography and the flaying desert wind would surely damage my camera, I did my best under those circumstances and still shot a bunch of what could be considered documentary exercises.

As for the natives of this desert, I felt a kind of ineffable love for everything about them, whether it was their gait, the way they ate, the colours and styles of their clothes, their gestures, language, marriages or religious faith. What's more, I enjoyed examining them up close because it satisfied the endless curiosity I had.

It would be impossible to depend on the power of one person alone to capture the world's largest desert on film, particularly at the standard I was hoping to achieve. I thought it through after I had made several trips. I would have to start by focusing on just a few things, rather than overestimating and overworking myself on a comprehensive and enormous project.

'Let's take photos of people!' I said to José. 'I like people.'

José didn't come with me when I travelled with the convoys distributing water in the desert. Through a friend's introduction, I hit the road with a trustworthy Sahrawi fellow named Bashir and his assistant. This journey would start at the Atlantic coast and go all the way up to the Algerian border, then back down again. We would drive well over 2,000 kilometres in one go. At every nomadic campsite, Bashir's water trucks always arrived on time with a few dozen oil drums full of water for sale.

Physically speaking, it was truly a struggle, just plain misery, to ride in this open-top run-down vehicle with no glass to block the wind, the sun beating unceasingly down on us. But since José had allowed me go, I had to repay his confidences by keeping it together while travelling, always returning home safely to town within a few days. The first time I went into the desert, I didn't take anything with me except for a backpack and a tent. I had no means of bringing the things that the nomads wanted. Accordingly, I found it hard to win anyone's friendship.

The next time I went, I knew the importance of being a witch doctor. I brought a medicine chest with me. It also became clear to me that there were women who loved to doll themselves up and children who loved to eat, even at the ends of the earth. So I bought many glass-bead necklaces, cheap rings, even a big pile of shiny keys, durable fishing line, white sugar, powdered milk and candy.

Entering the desert with these things in hand, I felt a sense of deep shame about trading material goods for friendship. But I realised that I was only wishing that they would come to trust me and allow me to get to know them. What I wanted in exchange was their friendship and goodwill, and for them to see that I cared about them. It was one step closer to asking them to accept this girl from another land, who might as well be an alien.

Although we think of the tents of nomadic peoples as being clustered, they're actually spread out over quite a distance. Only small numbers of camels and goats gather in herds, munching on the sad little leaves of withered trees for sustenance.

As soon as the water truck parked in front of a tent, I'd jump out of the car and head in. These inhabitants of the interior, so lovable and so easy to startle, would always disperse quickly in fright when I, a total stranger, approached. Bashir would shout whenever he saw people inevitably fleeing at the sight of me. He'd round them up like sheep and make them stand before me. The men might come over, but the women and children were more difficult to coax. I never let Bashir force them to come closer. I probably couldn't have borne it if he had done that.

'Don't be afraid. I won't hurt you. Come here, don't be afraid of me.' I knew these people probably didn't understand Spanish at all, but I also figured my tone would comfort them. Even if they didn't understand, they might not panic any more so long as I spoke calmly.

'Here, I have beads for you!' I put a pretty beaded necklace around the neck of a little girl, pulling her over to pat her head.

After I'd given away most of my things, I started playing doctor.

I treated diseases of the skin with anti-inflammatory cream, headaches with aspirin. For eye infections, eyedrops. If someone was too skinny, they got extra-strength vitamins. More importantly, I gave them large quantities of vitamin C.

Whenever I got to a new place, I would never just take out my camera and start photographing like crazy without getting to know the people a bit. I believe that is a highly disrespectful act.

Once I gave two aspirin to an old lady who complained of a headache, along with a key to hang beneath her headscarf as jewellery. Less than five seconds after swallowing the medicine

I'd given her, she nodded to indicate that her head no longer hurt. Then she grabbed my hand and pulled me into her tent.

As an expression of gratitude, she called out hoarsely and invited in a few girls who had their faces entirely veiled. I figured they were her daughters and daughters-in-law. These women had intense body odour and were all wrapped in the same black cloth. I gestured at them to remove their veils. Two of them shyly did so, revealing their light brown skin.

These two beautiful faces had large eyes, blank expressions and full, sensual lips. I was wholly bewitched. I couldn't help but lift my camera. I assumed these women had never seen a camera before, let alone a Chinese person. Maybe these two strange things also bewitched them. They stared at me, unmoving, allowing me to take their photo.

Just then the man of the family came home and saw what I was doing. He gave a sudden shout and rushed over. He flailed and yelled, almost kicking over the old woman. Then he proceeded to curse at the girls, who were all huddled together now. Hearing his angry words, these young women were near tears, frightened into a small bundle.

'You,' he said in broken Spanish. 'You have taken their souls. They will be dead soon.'

'I *what*?' Hearing this was a major shock for me. Talk about an unjust accusation.

'You, you woman, know how to cure sickness and steal souls,' he boomed. 'You catch them all in here.' He pointed at my camera and looked like he was about to strike me.

Seeing that the situation was not in my favour, I slipped out with my camera and ran to the car, calling out for Bashir, my protector.

Bashir was in the middle of delivering water. When he saw what was happening, he immediately blocked the man who was chasing me. Regardless, a crowd began to form excitedly around us.

I knew that under these circumstances, we could threaten to not deliver water or use the desert corps or other deeper superstitions to deter them and secure the safe passage of my camera and me. But on the other hand, since they believed these women had already lost their souls, couldn't this crowd do anything to help recover them from me somehow?

If I'd sneaked a few photos and driven off at that point, the psychological damage I could have inflicted on those women would have been immense. Now they were moaning as though they were close to death.

'Bashir, let's not argue any more. Please tell them that their souls really are in this box. Now I'm going to take them out and return their souls to them. Tell them not to be afraid.'

'Señorita, they're stirring up trouble! They are too ignorant. Don't bother.' Bashir's attitude was very condescending. I felt disgusted. 'Go on!' He waved his sleeve in the air. 'Get out of here!' The people reluctantly began to disperse.

Seeing that we'd started up the car and were about to leave, the women whose souls I'd taken immediately knelt down, their faces pale as death. I patted Bashir on the shoulder and asked him to hold on. 'I will release your souls now,' I said to the women. 'Don't you worry.'

I opened my camera in front of the group and pulled out the film from inside as though doing a magic trick. Then I jumped out of the car, holding the film to the light so they could see that the negatives were white on top. No human figures. They breathed a sigh of relief, seeing this. Everyone was smiling contentedly by the time we took off.

On the road, I put in another roll of film, chuckling with Bashir. I sighed and looked back at the two old Sahrawi people riding with us. 'Long ago, there was a thing,' one of them said. 'And when you put it next to someone, it would completely absorb their soul. It was even more powerful than your box!'

'Bashir, what are they talking about?' I asked, leaning over Bashir's shoulder, my head bobbling in the open air.

Once Bashir had explained it, I retrieved a hand mirror from my bag without a word and gently raised it in front of the old people. They took one look at the mirror and almost tumbled out of the car in fright. They pounded on Bashir's back, telling him to stop the car. They scrambled out in haste as soon as he pulled over. I was dumbfounded by their actions. Then, looking around Bashir's water truck, I realised there wasn't a rear-view mirror or anything like that.

Material civilisation isn't really necessary for humankind. But I was truly shocked and amazed that there were people who lived in the same world as me and had never even seen a mirror before. Then I couldn't help but feel a twinge of pity for them. Was this kind of ignorance due to geographical limitations or human factors? I couldn't figure out the answer for a long, long time.

The next time I went into the desert, I took a medium-sized mirror. I took this shiny object with me out of the car and propped it up with a pile of rocks. Everyone was so scared to look into it they stopped caring about my camera altogether. The mirror became the truly powerful soul-stealing device.

Fooling people for the sake of taking photos didn't seem like noble behaviour, so I often squatted before the mirror to brush my hair, wipe my face and check myself out, before getting up to leave like nothing was wrong. I showed that

I wasn't at all afraid of the mirror. Over time, even groups of children were willing to come over. They walked very quickly past the mirror and, discovering that nothing had happened, walked past again and again. Soon the mirror was completely surrounded by shrieking Sahrawi people. This was how the matter of stealing souls disappeared.

After getting married, it wasn't just me that became José's property. My camera, of course, also fell into his hands.

When we cut straight across the desert on our honeymoon, my master didn't let me lay a hand on my precious even once. He became the soul-stealer of the desert. The souls he stole often turned out to be those of our beautiful female neighbours.

One day we took our rented Jeep over to the desert on the Atlantic coast. This was already over a thousand kilometres away from the town where we lived. The desert was black in some parts, white in some parts or yellow-brown and red in other parts. I preferred the black sand because it looked majestic. José liked the white sand. He said it looked like a fine snowscape beneath the hot sun.

At noon, we drove slowly past a swathe of sand that was almost pure white. On the other side of the desert was the deep blue ocean. Out of nowhere a pink cloud appeared overhead, slowly descending towards the sea. Soon the rays of a setting sun were spreading across the sky.

I thought it incredibly strange, gazing closely at this odd phenomenon in the firmament. How could there be a dusk scene appearing all of a sudden at noon? I looked closer. My God! Goodness! It was a large flock of flamingos, crowded together in enormous numbers, all of them lowering their heads to eat who knows what from the beach.

I gently placed a hand on the camera. 'Give it to me!' I said to him quietly. 'Let me take a photo. Don't make a noise. Don't move.'

José was faster than me and had the camera up to his eye in no time.

'Hurry and take the photo!'

'I can't get it right. It's too far. I'm getting out.'

'Don't get out,' I hissed at José. 'Be still!'

Before I could say anything else, José took off his shoes and scurried towards the bay. He looked like he was going to sneak up on a group of heavenly guests. Before he could get close, that pink cloud rose into the air and flew off without a trace.

It was too bad that we didn't get a shot of the flamingos. But the beauty of that moment remains in my heart, something I will never in my life forget.

One time we paid a visit to someone's tent, along with a Sahrawi friend. That day the host had slaughtered a goat with great ceremony and invited us to eat. This manner of eating goat is very simple. You cut up the goat into a few dozen pieces and throw it, dripping blood and all, to roast on a fire. Once it's half-cooked, you put it in a clay basin the size of a bathtub and sprinkle on some salt. Everyone gathers around to eat together.

All of us picked up big pieces of meat to gnaw on. After gnawing for a bit, we set it down, going out to drink tea and play board games with small stones. About an hour later, we were all called together again. We convened by the already gnawed-on meat, picking up pieces at random, regardless of who had had it before. We redoubled our efforts at eating. Only after many rounds of gnawing and tossing and gnawing and tossing did this one goat get eaten to the bone.

I asked José to take a picture of me gnawing on the bones. But photos are just a still frame. I didn't know how to photograph this phrase: 'The piece of meat I'm gnawing on already has saliva from three or four people or more.'

Another time, José and I went to see a camel give birth because we heard that baby camels just tumble down from their upright mother when they're born. It promised to be extraordinary. So, of course, we took a camera.

Who knew that the baby camel would take forever, refusing to come into this world? I got bored waiting so I went to walk around in the sand. That was when I saw the old Sahrawi man who managed the camel fall to his knees, then rise to stand again.

His movements made me suddenly think of something rather amusing. There's no toilet paper out in the desert, so what do people do after they defecate? Even though this wasn't a very constructive question, I pondered it for some time.

I ran over to José and whispered, 'José, how do they do it?'

'You see him kneeling and rising because he's peeing, not pooping.'

'What? Who on earth kneels to pee?'

'There are two ways of doing it, kneeling and squatting. Don't tell me you didn't already know that?'

'Go take a photograph for me!' I insisted that there should be a record of this grand discovery.

'He's covered by a robe when he kneels. It'll just be a picture of a person kneeling. Totally boring!'

'I think it's interesting. What other people also pee in such a strange way?' I really thought this was a fascinating matter.

'Is there artistic value in this? Sanmao?'

I didn't know what to say.

The number one most amusing episode with my photography also happened out in the desert.

We were camping in a place not far from El Aaiún. Someone saw that we'd set up our tent and came over to chat. It was a young Sahrawi man, who was also very friendly. He knew how to speak Spanish and told us he used to help out with a mobile clinic run by nuns. He repeatedly informed us that he was a 'civilised' person.

This guy really liked having his soul stolen by us. He politely asked if José could lend his clothes to him for the photos and was very careful when slipping on José's watch. He tousled his hair again and again, then posed in a way that was completely not his style. He looked like a boorish imitation of a European.

'May I ask if your camera is colour?' he asked politely.

'What?' I was taken aback.

'May I ask if this is a colour camera?' he repeated.

'You mean the negatives? There's no such thing as a colour camera.'

'Yes, there is. The nun I used to work with only had a black and white one. I prefer colour cameras.'

'You mean the film? Or the actual machine?' I started having doubts myself, talking to him.

'The machine. You don't understand. Ask your husband. I see that the camera he has can shoot in colour.' He looked disdainfully at me, a woman asking too many questions.

'It can! Don't move. I have the world's best natural colour camera in my hands.' José solemnly raised his hands and took a photo of this graceful young man who considered himself a civilised person.

I watched from the sidelines as José deceived him without correcting his mistake. I was laughing so hard I had to bury my head in the sand like an ostrich.

Lifting my head up, I realised José had his camera pointed at me now. I covered my face and yelled, 'The colour camera is going to take my clean white soul! Please have mercy on me!'

Sergeant Salva

One summer evening, José and I decided to go for a stroll in the cool outdoors. It had been an unbearably hot day. The desert, at this hour, was pleasantly refreshing. Our Sahrawi neighbours were all eating dinner outside with their children. The night had already grown quite dark.

As we neared the cemetery on the outskirts of town, we saw there was a group of young Sahrawi not too far away, clamouring around something in the moonlight. It wasn't until we made our way through the crowd that we discovered it was a Spanish soldier who lay completely still on the ground. He would have looked dead, were it not for the rosiness of his face. With his big beard, riding boots and military uniform, it was clear he was part of the desert corps. There was no insignia by which to identify him.

He had been sprawled there for quite some time, it seemed. The crowd that surrounded him was speaking loudly in Arabic. They snuck up on him and spat mischievously, tugging at his boots, stepping on his hands. One of the Sahrawi even put on his military cap and clowned around, pretending to be drunk. Facing a soldier who was in no position to resist, the Sahrawi were bold and impudent indeed.

'José, go back and get the car, quick,' I said under my breath, looking around nervously. How I wished there were another soldier or a Spaniard nearby. However, no such person was around. While José ran back to get the car, I kept staring at the gun slung around the officer's waist. I decided I would start screaming if anyone tried to take it. I didn't know what I would do after that.

Around this time, the youth of the Spanish Sahara had organised themselves into the Polisario People's Liberation Front. Their headquarters was in Algeria, but pretty much every young person in town was on their side. Relations between the Spanish and the Sahrawi were dangerously tense. The desert corps and the locals hated each other even more.

José drove over in a hurry not long after. We parted the crowd in order to drag this drunkard into the car. This guy was big and beefy. It was no mean feat to carry his weight. We were soaked in sweat by the time we managed to get him situated in the backseat. Closing the door, we muttered apologies and drove slowly away from the crowd. A few people still banged on the roof of the car as we left.

José sped along towards the main gate of the desert corps. The army camp was deathly quiet. 'Flash your lights, José, and honk the horn. We don't know the password. They'll get the wrong idea. Let's park a bit farther away.'

José parked quite a distance from the guards. We opened the doors and got out of the car in a hurry. 'We're bringing home a drunk person,' we called out. 'Come over and take a look!'

Two guards rushed over. They loaded their guns with a clatter and pointed them at us. We pointed into the car and didn't budge. Looking inside, the two guards immediately recognised the fellow. They went in and began to take the soldier out. 'Him again!' they said.

Just then, a spotlight from above swept over and shone down on us. I was incredibly frightened by this and scrambled into the car. As José was about to drive off, the two guards saluted us and said, 'Thank you, *compadre*!'

Fear still lingered in my heart on the way home. It was the first time in my life that someone had pointed a gun at me up close. Even though these were our own troops, it still made me very nervous. For many days after, I kept thinking about the heavily guarded camp area by night and that stupidly drunk officer.

A few days later, two of José's co-workers came over to hang out at our home. I poured a big jug of cold milk for them as an expression of our sincere hospitality. These guys chugged it down like oxen drinking water. I went to open two more cartons right away.

'Sanmao, if we drink it all, then what will you do?' They stared sadly at the milk but continued to drink, looking embarrassed.

'Relax and drink up! This stuff is hard to come by for you guys.'

Food was a topic that concerned everyone in the desert. It wasn't enough to be on the receiving end of hospitality. People would always ask where the good stuff came from. That afternoon, José's co-workers drank all the cartons of fresh milk I had. Seeing that my expression hadn't changed, sure enough, they asked where I'd bought it.

'Heh! I've got a place.' I kept them in the dark, feeling very pleased with myself.

'Please tell us where?'

'Ah, you can't buy it there yourselves. Just come over when you want milk!'

'We want lots of it. Sanmao, please tell us where!'

'I bought it at the canteen of the desert corps.'

'The barracks?!' they shouted, gaping like yokels. 'A woman, all by yourself, buying groceries at the barracks?'

'Don't the army wives shop there? Of course I go there, too.'

'But it's against the rules. You're just a commoner!'

'Commoners in the desert are different from commoners in the city,' I chuckled. 'The soldiers don't draw distinctions between us.'

'Are the soldiers polite to you?'

'Very polite. Much better than most people in town.'

'Would it be a problem to ask you to buy milk on our behalf?'

'No problem at all, just give me a list tomorrow for how many cartons you need.'

When José got home from work the next day, he gave me a list of requests for milk. On it were the names of eight single men, each of them hoping I could provide ten cartons of milk to them per week, a total of eighty cartons. I bit my lip, looking over the list. I'd already talked it up so much, but I couldn't imagine asking for eighty cartons of milk at the barracks. Under such circumstances, I would rather lose face and buy the shameful eighty cartons all at once, then never come again. It would be better than buying ten cartons a day.

The following day, I went to the canteen and bought a big case of ten cartons of milk. I asked someone to help me set it aside in a corner, then turned and went straight back in to buy another case. I put this case in the corner again. After a while, I went in yet again. I did this four times in total. The young soldier at the till looked befuddled.

'Sanmao, how many more times do you need to come and go?'

'Four more times. Please bear with me.'

'Why don't you buy it all at once? Is it all milk?'

'It's against the rules to buy it all at once,' I replied, rather embarrassed. 'It's too much.'

'Don't worry. Let me get it for you. May I ask what you need this much milk for?'

'I was sent by others to buy milk. It's not all for me.'

Once there were eight big cases of milk piled in the corner, I got ready to call a taxi. Suddenly a Jeep swooped past and parked. I looked up and had quite a fright when I saw the soldier sitting in the car. Wasn't it that drunkard we'd brought back to the camp area the other night?

This man was tall and robust. The uniform fitted him well. I couldn't tell how old he was beneath that big beard. There was a bit of an aggressive glint in his eye when he looked at me, an overly intense focus. The top two buttons of his shirt were left undone. He had a crew cut beneath a green boat-shaped military cap, which displayed his ranking – sergeant.

I hadn't seen him clearly that night, so I looked him over deliberately. Without waiting for me to speak, he jumped out of the car and started moving the small mountain of milk cases into the car, one by one. Seeing that the milk was already in the car, I stopped hesitating and got into the front seat.

'I live in the Cemetery District,' I said to him very politely.

'I know where you live.' With that curt reply, he started the engine.

We said nothing on the road. He drove very steadily, two hands gripping the steering wheel. As the car passed the cemetery, I turned my head to take in the landscape, worried he might remember and feel embarrassed about how we had picked him up in such a pitiful drunken stupor the other night.

He slowed the car to a stop as we came to my neighbourhood. Before he climbed down, I tumbled out and called loudly for my friend Salun, who ran the small grocery store nearby, since I couldn't very well trouble this sergeant to help move all that milk again.

Hearing my voice, Salun rushed out in his slippers, a shy smile on his face. When he got to the Jeep and discovered there was a soldier standing next to me, he paused ever so briefly. Then he lowered his head and hurriedly began moving the cases for me, looking as though he'd seen a ghost.

At this point, the sergeant who'd brought me home saw that Salun was helping me and glanced over to Salun's little shop. His eyes shifted to me with a gaze full of contempt. I was keenly aware that he must have misunderstood. My face turning red, I clumsily spoke up in my defence. 'This milk isn't for resale, really! Please believe me, I'm just...'

He climbed into the car and set his hands on the steering wheel with a pat. He looked like he might say something, but he just started the engine instead. Only then did it occur to me to run over and thank him. 'Thank you, Sergeant! May I ask your name?'

He stared at me as though he'd already exhausted all of his patience. 'To friends of the Sahrawi, I have no name,' he said quietly. Then he stepped on the gas. The car sped off into the distance.

I gaped at the dust, feeling wronged deep down but unable to articulate why. It had been unfair of him to not give me a chance to explain. And then he'd rudely refused after I asked his name.

'Salun, do you know this person?' I turned and asked.

'Yes,' he said softly.

'Why are you so afraid of the desert corps? It's not like you're a member of the guerrilla troops.'

'It is not that. This sergeant hates all of us Sahrawi.'

'How do you know he hates you?'

'Everybody knows. Only you do not know.'

I looked closer at the earnest Salun, who never cast judgement on anyone. He must have had a reason for saying something like that.

After the misunderstanding with the milk, I was too embarrassed to buy groceries at the barracks for a long time. Much later, I ran into a young soldier from the canteen on the street one day. He told me that his whole troop thought I was gone for good and asked why I hadn't been buying groceries recently. Seeing that they hadn't misunderstood my intentions, I happily started going back there again.

As luck would have it, the first day I went back to the barracks for groceries, the sergeant strode in with his big boots. I bit my lip and looked at him nervously. 'Good day!' he said, nodding to me before going to the till.

I had decided that this man was a racist for harbouring such hatred of the Sahrawi. I didn't have the energy to bother with him. Standing aside, I focused on telling the soldier what groceries I needed and paid no more attention to the sergeant. Later, as I was about to pay, I noticed the sergeant had a large tattoo on his forearm under his rolled-up sleeve. It was a pretty tacky drawing of a string of dark blue hearts above a row of medium-sized words: *Don Juan de Austria*.

I found it very weird. I thought for sure there would be a woman's name beneath the tattooed hearts. I didn't expect it would be a man's name.

'Hey! Who's Don Juan de Austria?' I asked the soldier behind the counter after the sergeant left. 'What does it mean?'

'Ah! That used to be the name of a battalion in the desert corps.'

'It's not a person's name?'

'It was the name of someone during the time of Carlos I, back when Austria and Spain were one kingdom. The legion used his name for one of the battalions. But that was a long time ago.'

'But the sergeant that was just here had the name tattooed on his forearm!'

I shook my head, took my change and went out the front door of the canteen. Who knew I'd run into the sergeant there at the doorstep. He was waiting for me. He lowered his head when he saw me, following me for a few strides before speaking. 'Thank you, and your husband, for the other night.'

'For what?' I asked, confused.

'You brought me home when I... I drank too much.'

'Ah, that was so long ago!'

This man was so strange, suddenly thanking me for something I'd already forgotten about. How come he hadn't thanked me last time, when he drove me home?

'May I ask why there's a rumour among the Sahrawi that you hate them?' I asked boldly.

'I do hate them.' He looked me in the eye. The directness of his answer caused me quite a fright.

'There are both good and bad people in this world,' I said, naively spouting a cliché. 'There's no such thing as a people who are especially bad.'

The sergeant's gaze swept past a large group of Sahrawi squatting on the sand. His face showed a frighteningly intense focus again, as if a terrible, uncontrollable hatred were burning inside him. I stopped with my platitudes, staring at him. A few seconds later, he snapped out of it, gave me a deep nod and then strode away.

This tattooed sergeant still had not told me his name. He had the name of an entire battalion on his arm, but why a battalion from a long time ago?

One day, our Sahrawi friend Ali invited us to a place outside of town, where his father lived in a large tent. Ali was a taxi driver in town and only had time to visit his parents at the weekend. The place where Ali's parents lived was called Lemseyed. Perhaps it had been a wide river tens of millions of years ago, but now it had dried up into a canyon with cliffs on both sides. There were a few coconut trees in the riverbed and spring water flowed continuously. It was a tiny oasis in the desert. Such a vast land with quality fresh water, and yet only a handful of people resided there. I couldn't understand it at all.

In a cool twilight breeze, we sat with Ali's father outside his tent. He leisurely puffed on a long pipe. The red cliffs looked especially majestic in the sunset. A lonely star rose in the sky above.

Ali's father served us a big plate of couscous and thick sweet tea. I grabbed some couscous, pressed it into a greyish ball and stuck it in my mouth. With this kind of view, it seemed only fitting to sit on the ground and eat the food of the desert people.

'What a great place, and with spring water, too. How come there's practically nobody living here?' I asked the old man, curious.

'It was once lively here. That is how this place came to be called Lemseyed. But then it was struck by tragedy. The people who lived here left and outsiders refused to come. Only a few families like ours insist on staying here.'

'What tragedy? How come I don't know about this?' I pressed. 'Did the camels die of a plague?'

The old man glanced at me and continued to smoke his pipe. He looked into the distance, his mind seemingly far away now. 'Murder! People were murdered! There was so much blood that no one dared drink from the spring for a time.'

'Who murdered whom? What incident was this?' I couldn't help but lean closer to José. The old man's voice had become full of mystery and terror. Night had fallen.

'The Sahrawi murdered soldiers from the desert corps,' the old man said quietly, looking at José and me. 'Sixteen years ago, Lemseyed was a beautiful oasis. Even wheat could grow here. The ground was full of dates. There was plenty of drinking water. Almost all Sahrawi took their camels and goats to pasture here. The tents numbered in the thousands...'

As the old man described the bygone days, I looked out at the few remaining coconut trees and could barely believe that this desiccated land had once flourished. 'Then the Spanish desert corps also came,' the old man continued. 'They set up camp here and did not leave...'

'But the Sahara Desert didn't belong to anyone back then,' I interrupted. 'It wasn't against the law for anyone to come.'

'Yes, yes. Please hear what I have to say.' The old man made a gesture with his hands. 'The desert corps came. The Sahrawi did not allow them to access the water. The two sides often had disputes over this. Then...'

Seeing that he'd stopped speaking, I urged him on. 'Then what happened?'

'Then, a big group of Sahrawi people raided their camp. In one night, they slaughtered the entire unit in their sleep with knives.'

My eyes widened. I looked at the old man over the flickering fire. 'You mean they were all killed?' I asked quietly. 'The entire unit, murdered by Sahrawi?'

'Only one sergeant survived. He had got drunk that night and fell asleep outside the camp. When he woke up, his companions were all dead, nobody left.'

'Did you live here at the time?' I almost asked, *Did you participate in the killing at the time?*

'The desert corps are so vigilant,' José said. 'How can this be true?'

'It was unexpected. They had worked too hard during the day. There were not many guards, either. They did not expect the Sahrawi would come with their knives to kill.'

'Where was the military camp set up at the time?' I asked.

'Just over there!' He pointed at an area above the spring. There was only sand, not a trace of any former habitation. 'From then on, nobody has wanted to live here. Of course, the murderers escaped. A fine oasis has been wasted into what you see now.'

The old man lowered his head to smoke. A piercing wind rose, filled with whining cries, setting the coconut trees a-tremble. The tent's support beam began to squeak.

I raised my head and looked out into the darkness at the place where the desert corps had set up camp sixteen years ago. I could picture the crowd of Spanish soldiers in military uniform fighting the headscarved Sahrawi with their knives raised. One by one, they each fell to the ground in slow motion as though in a film scene, piles of bleeding bodies crawling along the sand, hundreds of helpless hands reaching for the sky, bloodstained faces screaming silent cries. In the black wind of night, there was only the hollow laughter of death reverberating across the vast and lonely land...

Startled, I made a great effort to blink. The vision disappeared. Everything around me was as serene as ever. We sat in front of the fire, no one speaking.

I suddenly felt freezing cold. My heart was unhappy. This wasn't some ghost story that the old man had told us; it was a vicious massacre from recent history.

'The sergeant who survived – he's the one with a tattoo on his arm, who always stares like a wolf at the Sahrawi?' I asked softly.

'They were a battalion of great unity and fraternity. I still remember how the sergeant shook as he threw himself onto the bodies of his slain brothers, after awakening from his drunken state.'

'Do you know what his name is?' I asked.

'After this incident, he was sent to the camp in town. Ever since he has refused to speak his name. He says all his brothers in the battalion are dead. How could he deserve a name? Everyone just calls him "Sergeant".'

Even though this had happened many years in the past, thinking about it still disturbed me greatly. In the distance, the sandy ground seemed to writhe.

'Let's go to sleep!' José said loudly. 'It's late.' He turned and went into the tent without another word.

This event had already become a tragedy of the past. I almost never heard anyone in town talk about it. Every time I saw the sergeant, my heart would skip a beat. How long would it take for such a bitter memory to dissipate in his heart?

About a year ago, things became even more complicated in this desert that the world had all but forgotten. Morocco to the north and Mauritania to the south wanted to partition the Spanish Sahara. Meanwhile, the native tribes of the desert had organised into guerrilla troops and gone into exile in Algeria. They wanted independence. The Spanish government was unsure of its next move and behaved ambivalently. There had already been so much bloodshed to maintain this territory, but they didn't know if they wanted to hold on to it or let it go.

During this time, Spanish soldiers were getting murdered when they travelled alone. Wells were poisoned. Timed explosives were discovered on an elementary school bus. The conveyor belt at the phosphate mining company was set on fire. Nightwatchmen were hanged on electric wires. A landmine on the highway outside of town exploded and destroyed a passing car...

This kind of unceasing turmoil made the whole town jittery. The government shut down schools and evacuated children back to Spain. Martial law was enacted by night. Tanks rolled in one after another. Multiple layers of barbed wire fences went up around military institutions. Particularly terrifying was that we were surrounded by hostile forces on three sides. When incidents flared up in town, it wasn't clear which party could have been responsible.

Given this situation, many women and children returned to Spain almost immediately. José and I didn't have any dependents, so we bided our time. He went to work as usual while I stayed home. Besides mailing letters and buying groceries, I didn't spend much time in public places for fear of explosions.

People began selling their furniture cheaply in our once peaceful town. There were long lines at the airline office every day, everyone vying for tickets. The cinema and stores were always closed. Handguns were distributed to all the Spanish civil servants who remained. There was endless anxiety in the air, stirring up great unrest even though there hadn't been any direct military confrontations in town.

One afternoon, I went into town to buy the Spanish daily. I wanted to know exactly what the government had in mind for this land. The newspaper didn't say much; every day it was the same thing over and over. I walked home slowly and glumly. When I saw military trucks bearing many coffins heading towards the cemetery, I was deeply shocked and assumed that conflict had already erupted at the Moroccan border.

I had to pass by several cemeteries on my way home. The Sahrawi had two graveyards of their own. The cemetery for the desert corps was enclosed by a snow-white wall and had an ornate black metal gate. Rows and rows of crosses stood within these walls, stone slabs below them marking the graves. The metal gate to the cemetery was open as I walked past. The first row of graves had already been dug up. Many soldiers from the desert corps wanted to take out their fallen brothers and put them into new coffins.

Seeing this, I understood instantly. The Spanish government had long refused to make an announcement about their decision. The soldiers here lived in the desert, died in the desert, were buried in the desert. Now they were digging up the deceased in order to take them away. Spain was going to let go of this land, after all!

Some of them had been dead for many years, but because the desert is so dry, they weren't just a pile of white bones. Horribly enough, they had become shrivelled corpses that looked like mummies. The soldiers carefully lifted them out beneath the glaring sun. They gently placed them into new coffins, nailed them shut, pasted some paper on top and then moved them into the truck.

The crowd of onlookers made a little path to allow the coffins to pass through, squeezing me into the cemetery. At that moment I realised the nameless sergeant was sitting in the shade of the wall. I wasn't uneasy at all about seeing dead people, but the noise of the coffins being nailed together was ear-piercing. Seeing the sergeant there, I remembered that he was also near the cemetery the night we found him drunk on the ground. The tragedy had happened so long ago. Could it be that his pain hadn't diminished at all over the years?

When the third row of graves was being unearthed, the sergeant stood as though he'd been waiting for this moment for a long time. He strode over, jumped into a hole and pulled out a corpse that had not yet rotted into an embrace like a lover. He gently held the body in his arms and gazed calmly into the dried face. There was no hatred or anger in his expression. What I saw was only a sorrow that verged on tenderness.

Everyone waited for the sergeant to put the corpse into the coffin. Beneath the scorching sun, he seemed to forget about the world around him. 'It's his younger brother,' a soldier said quietly to someone else holding a pickaxe. 'He was killed with all the rest.'

It felt like a century passed before the sergeant started to move towards the coffin. As if handling an infant, he gently laid the body of his beloved family member, dead for sixteen years, into his resting place for eternity. When the sergeant was passing through the gate, I looked away, not wanting him to think of me as a nosy and unfeeling spectator. He abruptly stopped in the midst of the crowd of onlooking Sahrawi people. The Sahrawi scattered with their children in tow.

Row after row of coffins were sent on to the airport. Now that the brothers in the ground had been transported away, only the neat crosses remained, shining white under the sun.

One morning, José worked an early shift and had to leave home by five. The situation had worsened to such an extent that I needed the car that day to pack up some things and ship them out of the desert. We had agreed that José would take the shuttle bus to work so I could have the car. But I still woke up at the crack of dawn to drive José to the bus stop.

On the return trip, I didn't dare take shortcuts for fear of landmines and drove on the tarmac the whole way. As I neared the slope that led into town, I saw that the petrol tank was nearly empty, so I thought I might as well pull into the petrol station. Looking at my watch, I saw that it was ten minutes before six. It wouldn't be open. I turned around and decided to head home. Just then, not far from me on the street, there was an incredibly low boom, the sound of an explosion. A pillar of black smoke rose into the sky afterwards. I was very close to it. Even though I had been in my car, my heart was beating like crazy from the fright. I drove quickly home, hearing the sound of ambulances in town rushing to the rescue.

'Did you hear the explosion?' José asked when he came home in the afternoon.

I nodded. 'Was anyone hurt?'

'That sergeant died,' José said abruptly.

'The guy from the desert corps?' I knew it couldn't have been anyone else, of course. 'How did he die?'

'He was driving past the place where the explosion happened this morning. A group of Sahrawi kids were playing with a box. There was a small guerrilla flag stuck in the box. I guess the sergeant thought there was something fishy about it. He got out of the car and ran over to the kids to chase them away. And then one of the kids ripped the flag out and the box exploded...'

'How many of the Sahrawi kids died?'

'The sergeant threw himself over the box. He was blown to bits. Only two of the kids were hurt.'

In a daze, I began making dinner for José. I couldn't stop thinking about the events of the morning. At a critical moment, this man, who had had a hatred gnawing away at him for sixteen years, gave up his own life to protect a few children of those whom he regarded as enemies. Why? I hadn't ever thought that he would die in this way.

The next day, the sergeant's corpse was put in a coffin and quietly laid into a grave that had already been dug. His brothers had left long ago and now rested in another land, while he hadn't managed to catch up with them. He was now buried silently in the Sahara. This place he both loved and hated would be his home for eternity.

His gravestone was very simple. A long time later, I went to take a look. On it was inscribed:

SALVA SANCHEZ TORRES, 1932–1975

While walking home, I passed Sahrawi children banging on rubbish bins in the public square, singing a rhythmic tune. You couldn't tell from this scene, so peaceful in the waning daylight, that war was on its way.

Hitchhikers

I often hear this song – the title I don't know, the tune I can't quite hum – but the first two lines go something like: 'When I think of the desert, I think of water / When I think of love, I think of you.' It's left quite an impression on me, that's for sure.

It's normal to have this kind of mental association. Water and love are both supremely important for living in the desert. I just don't know what the rest of this song is about. When my friend Mai Ling wrote to me, she said she often fantasised about me with a colourful Arabian rug over my shoulders and bells on my feet, walking with a huge jug on my head to draw water from a well – and what a beautiful image it was.

Mai Ling is so sweet. She even drew me a picture called 'Slave Girl Drawing Water from the Well', full of charm and romance. In reality, walking to fetch water is a thoroughly miserable affair. There's nothing comfortable about it, nor would I prop up a tank of water on top of my head.

My father and mother write to me every week, also exhorting me:

Even though water and Coca-Cola are the same price, and you must have resigned yourself to drinking Coke every day instead of water, water is necessary for the human body. If you drink only Coke, over the years you'll find it becomes nowhere near as refreshing anymore. Make sure you remember to drink water, no matter how expensive it is…

Everyone who doesn't live in the desert always brings up the matter of water. But very few people ask me what it's like to live in this vast and boundless sea of sand with no access to transport, or how one manages to set sail on the wind and waves to the world outside of town.

Being shut away for a long time in this tiny town with just one street, you feel the same kind of loneliness as a person with a broken leg living in an alley with no exit. In such a humdrum existence, there's no such thing as excessive joy, yet nor is there much sorrow. This unchanging life is like the warp and weft of a loom, days and years being woven out line by line in an ever-monotonous pattern.

The day José pulled up in our car that had been shipped over by sea, I dashed out in a frenzy to meet him. Even though it wasn't anything like the highly practical but expensive Land Rover, nor remotely suitable for travelling through the desert, it was, for us, the perfect car. I caressed this treasure inside and out, overwhelmed with joy. In my mind there suddenly appeared the image of a desert landscape at sunset, with the catchy theme song from *Born Free* playing in the background. Oddly enough there seemed to be gusts of wind blowing on the car just then and tossing my hair about.

I loved our newly arrived Boat of the Desert with all my heart. Every day after José came home from work, I would carefully polish the car with a clean piece of cloth, not letting a single speck of dirt or grime remain. I would even take tweezers to extract the little rocks that got embedded in the tyres. I just worried I wasn't fully dedicated to servicing this companion, who was bringing us so much joy and happiness.

'José, how was she running when you went to work?' I asked, mopping the car's big eyes.

'Better than fine. She rides like the wind. She's also pretty polite when you give her some grub. Only needs a little.'

'Now we have a car, but do you remember how we used to hitchhike?' I asked José. 'Anxiously waiting in the wind and rain, hoping someone would stop and take pity on us.'

'That was Europe,' José chuckled. 'You didn't have the guts to do it in America.'

'Public safety is different in America. Plus, you weren't with me back then.' I wiped the tender right eye of the new car as we bantered idly. 'José, when will you let me drive?' I asked, full of hope.

'Didn't you try it out once?' he retorted.

'That doesn't count. You sat next to me and made me drive badly. You got me all nervous. The more you scold me, the worse I drive. You don't understand psychology.' I was about to get worked up talking about this again.

'I'll drive for another week. From then on, I'll take the shuttle bus to work and you can come and pick me up in the afternoon. How about it?'

'Amazing!' I jumped for joy, feeling an urge to give the car a great big hug.

A round trip to José's workplace took almost two hours, but the desolate road was straight as an arrow. You could drive as fast as you wanted to. There was also no traffic to speak of. The first time I went to pick up José, I was late by almost forty minutes. He was pretty annoyed from the wait.

'Sorry I'm late.' Dripping with sweat, I jumped out of the car and used a sleeve to wipe my face.

'I told you not to be nervous. It's such a straight road, you could put the pedal to the metal and still not hit anyone.'

'So many parts of the road were buried in sand. I got out of the car and dug two ditches so I wouldn't get stuck. Of course that took up time, and then that person had to live so far away…' I moved to the passenger side to let José drive home.

'Who's "that" person?' He tilted his head and looked at me askance.

'A Sahrawi man who was walking.' I threw my hands up.

'Sanmao, in the last letter my father wrote to me, he said you can't even trust a Sahrawi who's been dead and buried for forty years. And yet when you're trekking through the desert, all by yourself…' José's undiplomatic tone really made me unhappy.

'He was really old!' I snapped back at him. 'What's wrong with you?'

'Old or not, it's still not OK!'

'You'd better not fault me for this. How many cars stopped to pick up the two of us back in the day, even though we looked like young bandits? If those strangers weren't holding on to the tiniest bit of faith in humanity, then they must have been blind or plain crazy.'

'That was Europe. We're in Africa now. The Sahara Desert. Let's be clear about that.'

'Oh, I'm clear, alright. That's why I picked that person up.'

It was different here. Back in civilisation, life was too complicated. I wouldn't have thought other people or things had anything to do with me. But in this barren land, fierce winds howling the year round, my spirit was moved by the mere sight of a blade of grass or a drop of morning dew, let alone a human being. How could I turn a blind eye to an old man tottering on his own beneath such a lonely sky?

José understood this, of course. He just refused to think too much about it.

Now that we had a car, we could go out into the wilderness on the weekends and drive all over the place. We were much happier, naturally. It really changed our whole world. But on most days José went to work. He didn't keep his promise and seized the car for days at a time. I still had to walk the long way into town, braving the intensity of the sun. The two of us often fought over the car. Sometimes I'd hear him sneak out and drive away in the early morning. By the time I ran out in my sleeping gown to chase after him, it was already too late.

The neighbouring children used to be my friends, but once they saw José acting cocky in the car – coming and going, reversing, spinning in circles, like a circus clown doing tricks for the audience – the whole nest of them went to worship this amazing person. I always hated the sight of clowns because they make me uncomfortable. This was no exception.

One day at dusk, I heard the sound of José parking outside after getting home from work and assumed he would be coming in. Who knew that a few moments later, he'd drive off again. He didn't get in until after ten, looking a dreary mess.

'Where were you? Food's cold.' I glared at him unhappily.

'Out for a stroll!' he answered with a chuckle. 'I went for a walk.' With that he went to take a shower, whistling as if nothing happened.

I ran out to look at the car. It was still in one piece, inside and out. Opening the car door, a very particular smell wafted out immediately. The cushion in the front seat was conspicuously covered in snot. There was a pee stain on the backseat. Little handprints were all over the windows. The inside of the car was littered with biscuit crumbs. It was a total catastrophe.

'José, are you running a children's amusement park?' I shouted from outside the bathroom.

'Ah! Sherlock Holmes.' The sound of water drifted out merrily.

'Sherlock who?' I yelled. 'Go look in the car.'

José turned up the water a bit, pretending he couldn't hear me.

'So you took a few dirty kids out for a spin, huh? Speak!'

'Eleven of them!' he giggled. 'Even squeezed in little Khalifa with the rest.'

'I'm going to wash the car now. You eat dinner. From now on, we each get the car for a week. You have to be fair.' While I had him cornered like this, I seized the opportunity to bring up the matter of sharing the car again.

'Fine, then! You win!'

'This is for good. A done deal, then!' I didn't trust him and wanted to confirm again.

He stuck out his sopping wet head and made an ugly face at me.

Even though I had insisted on getting the car, I actually just ended up driving in circles around the post office in the morning. Afterwards, when I got home, I'd wash and iron clothes, tidy up and do all the usual household chores. Around three in the afternoon, I'd change into my going-out clothes, wrap a wet rag around the boiling hot steering wheel and put two thick books on the seat. Only then could I start doing what I'd waited to do all day, under a sun so hot it made you dizzy.

'This sort of entertainment might be totally meaningless for someone who lives in the city. Faced with a long afternoon of idleness in the dead solitude of our little home, however, I'd rather sit in the car and drive through the wilderness and back. There practically wasn't even any choice in it.

Tents were scattered here and there along nearly a hundred kilometres of this narrow tarmac road. When the people who lived out here needed to go into town for errands, there were no other options besides trudging along for an entire day. Around these parts, the endless undulating sand was the true master of the land. Humans who survived here were mere pebbles mixed up in the sand.

Driving through this great wasteland, so peaceful in the afternoon it was almost frightening, it was hard not to feel some measure of loneliness. But, by the same token, to know that I was wholly alone in this unimaginably vast land was totally liberating.

Occasionally, I'd see a little black dot moving slowly at the edge of the horizon. Without fail, I'd unconsciously slow down my speeding car each time. The figure seemed so small and frail underneath the great dome of sky. My heart could never bear it. I'd raise my head high and drive, kicking up clouds of dust, whipping past the person who was walking along with such difficulty. In order to not frighten the person, I'd always drive past first, then stop, roll down the window and wave to them.

'Come on in! I'll give you a lift.'

More often than not, they'd look at me with shy hesitation. It was usually a really old Sahrawi carrying a sack of flour or grain on their shoulder.

'Don't be afraid. It's too hot. Get in.'

The people I picked up always thanked me with utmost respect when I dropped them off. Even after driving far in the distance, I still saw these humble people waving at me beneath the expanse of sky. I was often touched by the look on their face as I drove away. What honest and innocent people they were!

One time, I had driven more than thirty kilometres out of town when I saw an old person in front of me dragging a big goat tied with a piece of cloth. He was struggling along on the side of the road, his long gown filled with wind like a blown-up sail, getting in the way of all movement.

I stopped the car. '*Sahābi*,' I called, using the Arabic word for friend. 'Get in!'

'My goat?' He seemed quite embarrassed as he said this, grabbing a tight hold of his goat.

'You can bring the goat, too!'

We stuffed the goat into the backseat. The old gentleman sat next to me. Meanwhile, the goat's head just happened to rest against my neck. Throughout the journey, the goat's strained breathing kept tickling my neck like crazy. I stepped on it so I could get these two to their scrappy roadside tent as soon as possible. When they were getting out, the old man grabbed my hands tightly, his toothless mouth babbling expressions of gratitude to me. He didn't let go for a long time.

I started laughing. 'No need to thank me,' I said to him. 'Just get your goat out! He's been chewing on my hair like it's straw.'

'Now you've got goat shit in the car. You yelled at me last time for running a children's amusement park. You clean it. I'm not touching this.' José ran inside as soon as we got home. I suppressed a smile and followed him in, grabbing a broom. I collected the goat shit and dumped it in our flower pots as fertiliser. Who said there was nothing to be gained from picking up hitchhikers?

Sometimes José's work schedule would change and he'd go in at two in the afternoon, coming back at ten at night. Under those circumstances, if I still wanted to drive the hundred kilometres there and back, I'd have to leave with him around half past noon. Once we reached the office, he'd get out of the car and I'd come back alone.

During sandstorm season, noon was scorching hot and the air was full of yellow dust. I would choke horribly, my lungs pained as though they were filled with sand. Visibility would be down to zero. The car would thrash like it was on stormy seas. Sand and rocks would rain down on all sides, furiously pounding the car, a deafening sound.

It was on one of these days after I'd taken José to work that I saw a figure riding a bike through the hazy yellow sand. Shocked, I stepped on the brakes. The person on the bike immediately jumped off and ran towards me.

'What is it?' I opened the window and shielded my eyes.

'Señora, may I ask if you have water?'

I peeled away the fingers that were covering my eyes and, to my surprise, saw a young boy of ten or so. His desperate eyes stared at me with great need.

'Water? I don't have any.'

When I said this, the boy was so full of despair that he looked as though he might cry. He wrenched his head away.

'Get in, quickly!' I rolled up the window in a haste.

'My bicycle...' He was unwilling to leave his bike behind.

'You'll never make it into town in this kind of weather.' I slipped on anti-wind goggles, opened the door and ran to get his bike. It was an old-style bicycle, impossible to get into my little car, no matter what I tried.

'It's impossible,' I yelled to him over the wind. 'How come you didn't bring any water? How long have you been riding?' Grains of sand immediately flew into my mouth and nose.

'Since this morning,' the kid said in practically a whimper.

'Get in the car. Let's leave your bike here for now. Once you get home, you can find another car in town to come back and get your bike. How does that sound?'

'I can't. The sand will cover it soon and I won't be able to find it. I can't leave my bike.' He was stubborn and protective of his beloved old bicycle.

'Fine! I'm going then. Take these.' I took off the anti-wind goggles, handed them over and helplessly climbed into the car.

I tried to do some chores when I got home, but the figure of the little boy, like an apparition, had mesmerised me. Hearing the mournful wind outside the window, I sat for a few minutes and realised I didn't have the heart to do anything. I angrily opened the refrigerator and took out a bottle of water and a sandwich. Then I got one of José's duckbill caps, went out and jumped in the car. I retraced my steps to go looking for the little lad whom I couldn't forget.

The guard at the checkpoint ran over when he saw me. He leaned in to talk. 'Sanmao, are you going to take a walk in this kind of weather?'

'It's not me who's taking a walk, it's that odd little rascal who's asking for trouble.' I stepped on the gas. My car flew into the haze of the sandstorm like a bullet.

'José, you can drive the car! I don't need to any more.' It was the third time in one day I'd driven along this road, now frigid at night.

'You can't handle the heat!' he laughed, pleased with himself.

'I can't handle the people on the road. So annoying, so many problems.'

'What people?' José asked with bemusement.

'I run into them every few days, don't you know?'

'Why don't you just ignore them?'

'If I ignore them, then what? Should I have just stood by and watched that little rascal die of thirst?'

'So you're done with it?'

'Ah, forget it!' I slouched in the car seat and looked out of the window.

I'm a woman of my word. For quite a few weeks, I stayed in the peace of my home mending clothes. After I finished sewing almost a hundred pieces of printed fabric into a colourful patchwork quilt, I started feeling impulsive again out of nowhere.

'José, the weather's so nice today, no sandstorms or anything. I'll drive you to work!' Standing outside in my nightgown, I looked out at the car in the morning.

'It's a public holiday today,' José said. 'You should go into town and have fun.'

'Ah! Really? Then why are you going to work?'

'The mining doesn't stop. Of course I have to go.'

'A holiday probably means there'll be hundreds of people crowded in town. Can't stand it. I won't go.'

'Get in the car then!'

'Let me change.' I flew into the house, put on a blouse and jeans and grabbed a plastic bag on my way out.

'What's the bag for?'

'The weather's so nice. While you're at work, I'm going to collect bullet casings and goat bones and come back a bit later.'

'What's the point in collecting those things?' José started the car.

'If you freeze the bullet casings on the roof overnight and bring them back down the next morning while it's still dark out, you can stick them on your eyes to treat styes. Didn't I treat yours last time?'

'That was a coincidence. Some bogus method you invented yourself.'

I shrugged and withheld comment. Actually, picking things up was just a ruse. The real pleasure was wandering in the fresh air of the open land. Too bad the days of nice weather were so few.

I watched José get out of the car and walk on to the floating platform. Then I sighed and drove away from his work site.

The desert in the morning looked like it had been washed clean, the sky a crystal blue without a thread of cloud. Soft dunes spread out as far as the eye could see. During moments like these, the sand always made me think of the body of a gigantic sleeping woman, almost seeming to rise and fall as if it were breathing lightly. Such quiet serenity and profound beauty inspired an emotion close to pain.

I drove the car off the road, following in the tracks of others who'd gone to the shooting range before. After picking up some bullet casings, I lay down for a while and looked up at the semicircular dome of sky that enclosed us like a bowl. Then I walked along the sand for a long time looking for dried bones. I didn't get any complete skeletons, but I did unexpectedly find a huge fossilised shell that looked like a pretty folding fan spread out.

I spat on it, wiping it clean on my trousers before getting in the car and going home. Somehow the sun had already climbed high in the sky above.

Windows down, warm wind blowing, it was so lovely out that I didn't even want to listen to the news on the radio, as it would intrude upon the peace and calm of this day and this land. The road stretched out like a shimmering river, flowing in a straight line beneath the firmament.

On the horizon, there was a small black dot, clear and unmoving against the sky. As I whooshed past this person, he suddenly raised his hand to get a ride.

'Good morning!' I slowed the car to a stop.

It was a young Spanish soldier, impeccably dressed as though he were about to attend a flag ceremony, standing on the side of the road all by his lonesome.

'Good morning to you, señora!' He stood ramrod straight, obviously a bit surprised to see me in the car. His grass-green soldier's uniform, wide leather belt, riding boots and boat-shaped cap would make any old bumpkin look heroic. The funny thing was that he still couldn't hide the innocence on his face no matter how he dressed.

'Where are you heading?' I asked, raising my head up high.

'Umm! To town.'

'Come on in!' This was my first time giving a ride to a young person, but I had no qualms about it after looking at him for just a moment.

He got in the car and self-consciously took a seat next to me, two hands resting neatly on his knees. To my great surprise I saw that he was wearing the snow-white gloves exclusively used for grand ceremonies.

'Going into town so early?' I asked casually.

'Yes, I wanted to see a movie,' he answered earnestly.

'The cinema doesn't open until five, though!' I tried my hardest to speak normally, but secretly I thought this kid was probably up to no good.

'That's why I left early in the morning.' He fidgeted shyly.

'You were planning to walk for a whole day just to catch a movie?' This was truly unbelievable.

'We're on holiday today.'

'Military transport wouldn't take you?'

'I didn't sign up in time. There wasn't space on the bus.'

'So you're walking?' I looked at the endless road, a strange feeling passing through my heart out of nowhere.

We both grew quiet for a long while, not knowing what to say.

'You're serving in the army?'

'Yes!'

'Still feel good?'

'Great. I'm a ranger who lives in the tents, always switching campsites. It's just that there isn't enough water.'

I peered once more at the uniform that he kept so pristine. It must have been an important occasion to him, as he probably wouldn't have worn these clothes otherwise. Once we got into town, the joy on his face spilled forth, unable to be contained. He was a young kid, after all. After he got out, he gave me a solemn military salute that nonetheless had a childish quality to it. I nodded and sped off.

I can never forget that pair of white gloves. This big child lived in a scarcely populated and depressing wasteland all year long. Yet to him, at that moment, there was no more magnificent an occasion than watching a movie in this dilapidated nowhere town.

On the way back, a helpless ache came over me. This person had touched a part of my heart that wasn't often touched. He must have been the same age as my younger brother who lived so far away, my brother who was also serving in the military. I practically got sucked up into a vacuum of time, stupefied for a moment. Then I shook my head and stepped on the gas, speeding towards home.

Even though José often said I was meddling in too many things, he was really just giving me a hard time. Whenever he drove himself to and from work, he would also pick up passers-by on the road. If you ask me, when you're driving in a remote place and see someone on the side of the road making a difficult journey like a snail beneath the hot sun, you simply can't disregard them.

'Today was such a headache,' José moaned as he walked into the house. 'These old men are really fearsome. I picked up three old Sahrawi men and had to deal with their body odour the whole way. I almost fainted. Once we got to their destination, they said something in Arabic. I didn't even know they were talking to me, so I kept driving. You want to know what they did to me? The guy sitting behind me got so worked up, he took off his stiff shoe and started whacking me furiously on the head. He almost killed me.'

'Ha! You gave them a lift and still got beaten up!' I was beside myself with laughter.

'Feel for yourself,' José said, gnashing his teeth and rubbing his head. 'There's a big bump.'

The happiest times were when we ran into foreigners in the desert. Even though the land we lived in was vast and open, our spirits were isolated and enclosed. When we came across people from out of town who spoke about the fast-paced world that was so distant from us, I always felt excited and inspired.

'I gave a lift to a foreigner on the way to work today.'

'Where was he from?' My curiosity was piqued.

'America.'

'What did he have to say?'

'He didn't say much of anything.'

'You didn't speak at all during that long ride?'

'Firstly, we couldn't really communicate. Also, when this lunatic got in the car, he kept banging rhythmically on the dashboard with a stick in his hand. I got annoyed and wanted to drive as fast as I could so he'd get out. Didn't think he'd come with me to work.'

'Where did you pick him up?'

'He had a big backpack with the American flag sewn on it. I picked him up just where the freeway starts at the edge of town.'

'Your ferocious security guard let him enter the work site? Even without a permit?'

'They wouldn't let him in at first, but he said he had to go and see the mine.'

'You can't just go in and look around as you please,' I asserted.

'They blocked him for a while. Eventually this guy raised his backpack and said, "I'm an American…"'

'And he just got in?' I opened my eyes wide at José.

'He just got in.'

'Hmph!' I looked at José with great surprise.

Afterwards, José went to take a shower. Out of nowhere, beneath the sound of running water, he started singing in a strange voice in English. 'I wannaaa beeee an A–me–ri–can, I wannaaa beeee an American…'

I ran in, pushed aside the curtain, and started hitting him with a spatula. He sang with even greater vigour, changing the lyrics. 'I wannaaa marryyyy an A–me–ri–can, oh, I wanna marryyyy…'

From then on, whenever I drove past the checkpoint at his work site and saw that security guard, I would put my hand over the permit on my windscreen, stick my head out and, affecting a weird accent, shout to him in English, 'I'm an American!' Then I'd step on the gas and drive in. I didn't blame this guy for being annoyed with me. I deserved it.

At the beginning of the month, there would always be a long queue for the cashier window at the phosphate company. After every person's turn, they'd squeeze their way out of the crowd with a wad of cash in hand and a smile on their face like strawberry ice-cream melting in the sun. We used to get cash out too, because the pleasure of touching real paper money was decidedly different from a bank statement. But then we became tired of queuing, so we had the company deposit the salary directly into the bank.

However, all the labourers wanted cash. They refused to deal with the bank.

Towards the beginning of the month, there were always gorgeously dressed women flying in from the nearby Canary Islands. With great fanfare, they would get down to business. During these times, you could hear the sound of coins jingling all over town like that song from the movie *Hotel*: 'Money, money, money, money...' How nice it all sounded!

One evening I went to pick up José after a night shift. When I arrived, I saw him coming out of the company cafeteria.

'Sanmao, I have to do a shift at the last minute. I won't finish until tomorrow morning. You should go home.'

'How come you didn't say anything earlier? I already drove all this way.' Hugging myself through a thick sweater, I handed over the coat I had brought for José.

'There's a boat that got stuck. We have to work through the night to get it free. Tomorrow there are three ships coming in to load ore.'

'Alright, then, I'll be off!' I reversed the car, turned my headlights onto full beam and started on the way home. The desert was so big, driving a hundred kilometres a day felt as simple as taking a short walk.

It was a clear evening. The moon shone down on sand dunes that looked like the sea. It always made me think of those dreamlike and mysterious paintings by the Surrealists. Such scenes truly exist in the desert at night!

My car headlights illuminated the empty road ahead. Occasionally another car would appear driving towards me. Some cars also overtook me. I stepped on the accelerator and opened the windows, hurtling into the nocturne.

Once I was nearing twenty kilometres from town, I suddenly saw someone waving in my car headlights. Instinctively I stepped on the brakes and pulled over, shining my lights on this person. Out of the blue, in such an unexpected place, I saw that it was a beautiful and well-dressed woman with red hair standing on the side of the road. It was even more startling than seeing a ghost. I sat there in silence, afraid to move, examining her cautiously.

This woman used a hand to shield her face from the bright headlights. She clopped over to the car in her high heels. When she came near and saw me, she hesitated. It looked like she wouldn't be getting in.

'What's going on?' I asked, tilting my head.

'Umm… nothing! You can go on!'

'Didn't you wave because you needed a ride?' I ventured.

'No, no, I got it wrong. Thank you! Please go on! Thanks!'

I immediately drove off in a fright. This female demon was choosing a human to possess. I had better run for it before she had any regrets! As I fled down this road, I started noticing that there were similar women with curly hair, green eyes and red lips standing in the sand at regular intervals, looking to hitchhike. I didn't dare pull over and drove faster into the night.

After speeding along for some time, I saw another woman in a purple dress and yellow shoes, smiling sweetly and standing in the middle of the narrow road. Even if she wasn't human, there was no way I could run her over. I had to slow down and stop very far away, shining my headlights on her. I honked the horn and asked her to get out of the way. What a bunch of mysterious women!

All smiles, she ran to the car in her loud heels. 'Ah!' She made a noise when she saw me.

'I'm not who you want. I'm a woman.' I smiled, looking at her powdery face that was already middle-aged. It dawned on me then what was happening on this road by night. It was the beginning of the month!

'Ah, sorry!' A polite smile broke out on her face.

I gestured at her to please move aside and slowly started up the engine. She looked around for a moment, then ran back and slapped a hand on my car. I stuck my head out.

'Alright, I'm pretty much done. Let's call it a day! Can you take me into town?'

'Hop in!' I said helplessly.

'Actually, I recognise you,' she said brightly. 'You were mailing a letter at the post office the other day, wearing a Sahrawi man's white gown.'

'Yep, that was me.'

'Did you know we fly in here every month?'

'Yes, but I didn't know you did business outside of town.'

'We have no choice – nobody in town wants to rent rooms to us, and there isn't enough space at the Didi Hotel.'

'Business is booming?' I shook my head and laughed.

'Well, only at the beginning of the month. After the tenth, there's no more money, so we head back!' Her voice was honest and clear, without a trace of sadness.

'How much do you charge per person?'

'Four thousand. If we're staying overnight at the Didi, eight thousand.'

Eight thousand pesetas is probably around US$120. It was difficult to imagine how those labourers could bear to part with the money they'd toiled so hard for. I hadn't expected that the women would be so expensive.

'Men are stupid!' She leaned against the car seat and laughed loudly, self-satisfied as though she were a successful businesswoman.

I didn't respond and drove faster towards town, the lights already visible in the distance.

'My lover also works for the phosphate company!'

'Oh!' I made a perfunctory noise.

'You must know him. He works the night shift in the electrical department.'

'I don't know him.'

'He was the one who told me to come. He said business would be good around here. I used to work just in the Canary Islands. I made much less money back then.'

'Your lover told you to come here because business is good?' I didn't believe my ears and had to repeat the sentence.

'I've already made enough for three houses!' She raised her hands with great pleasure, examining her fluorescent purple nail polish.

I felt like roaring with laughter at this person's mindless chatter. She said men were stupid and she'd earned three houses' worth of money. But she still stood pitifully in the sand looking for clients, thinking herself to be very clever.

For the woman sitting beside me, prostitution wasn't about making a living or a question of morality. She'd simply become numb to it all.

'Actually, female housekeepers around here can make around twenty thousand a month,' I said disapprovingly.

'Twenty thousand? Sweeping, making beds, doing laundry. You'd work yourself half to death for only twenty thousand. Who wants to do that?' Her voice was contemptuous.

'I feel like you're the one who's working hard,' I said slowly.

She started guffawing with glee.

Meeting this type of precious character was better than seeing a prostitute in tears, I suppose.

When we reached town, she thanked me sincerely and wriggled out of the car. She had only taken a few steps before a labourer gave her a strong slap on the bottom, hooting and hollering. She laughed and yelled some nonsense, chasing after him to hit him back. The quiet nightscape quickly became lively and thick with gaudy colour.

The whole way home and even while reading later, I kept on thinking about that cheerful prostitute.

Day after day, I drive along the one tarmac road in this wilderness as usual. At first glance, it looks totally deserted, devoid of life, without joy or sorrow. In reality, it's just like any other street or tiny alley or mountain stream in this world, carrying the stories of its passers-by who come and go, crossing the slow river of time.

The people and moments I encounter on this road are normal as anything that anyone walking on the street might see. There's really no greater meaning to it, nor is it worth recording. But Buddha says: 'It takes a hundred years of self-cultivation to be in the same boat, and a thousand years if you want to share the same pillow.' All those hands that I've shaken, all those brilliant smiles exchanged, all those boring conversations, how could I just let a wind blow through my skirt and scatter these people into nothingness and indifference?

Every little stone in the sand, I still know how to cherish. Every sunrise and sunset, I'm reluctant to forget. Not to mention these real, living faces, how could I just erase them from my memory?

Actually, even trying to explain it is too much.

The Mute Slave

The first time I was invited to dine at the house of this affluent Sahrawi man in town, I didn't actually know the host. According to Ali, whose elder sister was married to the guy's cousin, this rich man didn't invite just anyone to his home. It was because we, along with three other Spanish couples, were friends with Ali that we got to feast on kebabs of camel hump and liver.

After we arrived at the wealthy man's large and labyrinthine white estate, I didn't just sit still on the beautiful Arabian rug like the other guests, waiting to eat delicacies that might make some want to throw up. The rich guy came out to exchange a few pleasantries, then retreated into his own room. He was an older Sahrawi who looked very shrewd, smoking his hookah, speaking French and Spanish elegantly and fluently. He had an air of great ease and no small amount of arrogance. As for entertaining our group of dinner guests, he left this task to Ali.

Once I'd examined the handsome books on display, I politely asked Ali if I could meet the rich guy's wives. 'Of course. Please come. They also want to meet you, they're just shy.'

I wandered around the back rooms by myself and saw one opulent bedroom after another, full-length mirrors, beautiful women, Simmons beds, as well as countless fabrics of gold and silver that one rarely comes across in the desert. I really wished José could have met the rich man's four gorgeous young wives. Too bad they were shy and didn't want to come out to greet the guests.

I covered my face with a scarlet veil and leisurely made my way back into the living room. The men sitting in there jumped up in surprise, thinking I had become the fifth wife. I thought my appearance perfectly matched the ambience of this home, so I decided not to take off the veil. I just lowered it from my face in anticipation of the grand desert feast.

In a short while, a little child who wasn't even as high as the chairs brought over a red-hot charcoal stove. He had a deferential smile on his face and couldn't have been more than eight or nine years old. He carefully set the stove in the corner by the wall, then went out again. A few moments later he returned, walking unsteadily with a gigantic silver tray. He set this down before us on the big red carpet that was woven with all sorts of colourful patterns. On the tray there was a silver pot of tea, a silver box of sugar, bright green fresh mint leaves, perfumed water and another miniature stove that warmed the tea. I was full of praise, totally mesmerised by this pristine and ornate tea set.

The child gently knelt before us, then stood up again with the silver-white bottle of perfumed water in order to sprinkle some on each person's head. This was one of the desert's grand rituals. I lowered my head to let the child pour water on me. He didn't stop until my hair was completely soaked. For a moment, the fragrance filled this Arabic palace, the atmosphere stirring and solemn. The strong body odour of the Sahrawi vanished, thanks to this.

After a few more moments, the child calmly brought in a big plate of raw camel meat and set a metal grill on the charcoal stove. Our group had been talking loudly. Two of the other Spanish wives were chatting about the circumstances under which they had given birth. Only I was quietly observing the boy's each and every movement.

He did things in a neat and orderly fashion, first skewering the meat, then putting it over the fire to roast. At the same time he kept an eye on the tea brewing over the other stove. When the water began to boil, he added mint leaves and a few hard cubes of sugar. Then he lifted the teapot higher than his own head and poured, perfectly angling the tea into little cups. His posture was extremely graceful. Once the tea had been poured, he knelt before us again and offered us each a cup with both hands. The tea was aromatic and full of flavour.

After the kebabs were cooked, the boy removed the first batch of meat onto a big dish and served it to us. Camel hump turned out to be a fatty meat. We managed to force down the liver and the other meat, as well. The male guests and I each took a skewer to eat. The child watched us all. I smiled and winked at him to let him know it was tasty.

While I was eating the second skewer, those two uncultured Spanish wives started grumbling with absolutely no sense of propriety. '*Dios mío!* I can't eat this! I'm going to throw up! Somebody fetch some soda water, quick!' I felt very embarrassed on their behalf, witnessing their lack of manners.

This lavish meal had been prepared for us and I was the only woman who was eating. What a shame, I thought, that this child was serving us while we sat like useless rubbish. I decided I might as well move closer and sit next to the boy. I could help him put meat on the kebabs and grill it for myself. I figured if you put a little more salt on it, the camel taste wouldn't be so noticeable.

The boy kept his head lowered, working silently. The hint of a smile remained at the edges of his lips. There was a look of great cleverness about him. 'You put together one piece of meat, a slice of hump, then liver and add salt, right?' I asked him.

'*Haqq!*' he answered quietly. (Meaning yes, correct and so on.)

I showed him great respect, checking with him before fanning the flame or flipping the meat since he really was a capable child. His face became flushed from happiness, I noticed. I imagined it was probably rare that someone made him feel so important. The people around the fire, on the other hand, seemed utterly uninterested. Ali had invited us to eat some authentic desert cuisine, and here were these two irritating female guests with a steady stream of complaints. They didn't want tea, they wanted soda water; they wanted to sit in chairs, not on the ground.

For each of these things, Ali sharply rebuked the child and made him remedy the situation. He had to manage the stove, then rush out to buy soda water. After buying soda water, he had to bring over chairs. After bringing the chairs, he had to hurry back to grilling meat. His face was full of bewilderment from being so busy.

'Ali, you're not doing anything and neither are those women,' I declared. 'It's unfair to make the littlest one work so hard!'

Ali swallowed a piece of meat and pointed the meat fork at the kid. 'He has more responsibilities than these,' he said. 'He got lucky today.'

'Who is he? Why does he have to do so many things?'

José immediately changed the topic of conversation. After José was done talking, I continued to ask questions over the flame. 'Who is he? Ali, tell me!'

'He's not a member of this family,' Ali said awkwardly.

'If he's not a member of this family, then why is he here? Is he a neighbour's kid?'

'No.'

The room fell quiet. No one made a sound. At the time, because I hadn't been in the desert for long, I naturally didn't understand why everyone seemed so uncomfortable. Even José wasn't speaking. 'Well, who is he then?' I grew impatient with this hemming and hawing.

'Sanmao, come here.' José waved his hand at me. I set down the kebab and went over to him. 'He's a slave,' José said softly, so that the child would not overhear. I put a hand over my mouth. I stared at Ali, then surreptitiously at the child with his lowered head and didn't say anything more.

'Where did the slave come from?' I asked Ali, my face cold.

'They are born into it and passed on from generation to generation.'

'Are you telling me the first black person who was born had "I am a slave" written on his face?' I looked at Ali's light brown complexion, refusing to give up on this enquiry.

'Of course not. They were captured. When they saw black people living in the desert, they went out to capture them. They knocked them out and tied them up with ropes for a month so they did not escape. With the whole family captured, there is even less of a chance. Like this, they become property passed on from one generation to the next. Now you can also buy or sell them.' Seeing the look of unbearable injustice on my face, Ali quickly added, 'We do not mistreat slaves. Like him, this kid, he goes back to his parents' tent at night. He lives outside of town. He is very happy to go home every day.'

'How many slaves does the master of this home have?'

'Over two hundred, all sent out to build roads for the Spanish government. At the beginning of the month, the master goes to collect wages. That is how he got so wealthy.'

'What do the slaves eat?'

'The Spanish agency for contracted projects gives food to them.'

'So you make money from the slaves, but you don't provide for them.' I gave Ali the side-eye.

'Hey, let's get a few for ourselves!' one of the female guests whispered to her husband.

'Shut your damn mouth!' I heard her husband scold her angrily.

As we were saying goodbye to this wealthy household, I took off the veil and returned it to one of the beautiful wives. The rich guy walked us out. I thanked him but had no desire to shake his hand. I didn't want to see this kind of person ever again.

The group of us walked about a block or so before I noticed the little black slave had come out after us and was watching me from a corner by the wall. His large clever eyes were tender as those of a deer. I left behind the group and jogged towards him, taking out two hundred pesetas from my purse. Pulling over his hand, I put the money in his palm. 'Thank you!' I said to him before turning and walking off.

I felt really ashamed of myself. What good was money? Was money the only means I had to express something to the child? I couldn't think of anything else, but it truly was a low-level form of goodwill.

The next day I was collecting mail at the post office when I remembered the matter of slaves. I decided to go upstairs to the courthouse and pay a visit to the old secretary.

'Ah, Sanmao, you haven't come in a while, but I see you still remember me.'

'Señor Secretary, that you openly allow slavery in a Spanish colony is truly admirable.'

The secretary let out a long sigh, hearing this. 'Don't say another word,' he said. 'Every time a Sahrawi and a Spaniard get in a fight, we always lock up the Spaniard. We can barely keep up with appeasing these violent peoples. Who wants to meddle in their affairs? We're scared to death of them already.'

'You are all accomplices. More than just not meddling, you're using slaves to build roads and you give their owners the money. What a joke!'

'Hey, what's it got to do with you? Those slave owners are all heads of their tribes. The most powerful Sahrawi serve as representatives in the congress in Madrid. What can we say about it?'

'A dignified Catholic country where divorce is illegal, but still you can own slaves. How absolutely bizarre. *Felicidades.* Hmph! My second motherland, my God…'

'Sanmao, stop stirring up trouble! It's so hot…'

'Fine! I'm going! Goodbye!' I strode quickly out of the courthouse.

That same evening, there was a knocking on my door: a courteous series of three gentle raps, then nothing. I was truly puzzled. How could there be someone so civilised coming to see me?

Opening the door, I saw a middle-aged black man whom I didn't recognise standing before me. His clothes were ragged and dirty, practically scraps of cloth hanging on his body. He didn't wear a turban, his long grey hair fluttering in the wind. When he saw me, he immediately bowed with great humbleness, hands folded at the chest as if in worship. His manners were in stark contrast to the rudeness of the Sahrawi.

'You are?' I waited for him to speak.

He couldn't speak. Hoarse sounds came from within his mouth. He pantomimed something at the height of a child, then pointed at himself. I couldn't grasp his meaning.

'What?' I asked gently. 'I don't understand. What is it?'

Seeing that I didn't understand, he quickly took out two hundred pesetas and pointed in the direction of the rich guy's home. Then he pantomimed again. Ah! I understood. He was the father of that child. He insisted on giving me back the money, but I absolutely refused. I also gesticulated that I wanted to give it to the kid because he had grilled meat for all of us. He was very smart. He understood right away. This slave obviously hadn't been born mute because he could make some sounds with his mouth. It was just that he was deaf, so he had never learned to speak.

He looked at the money as though it were an extremely large amount, thought it over, then tried returning it to me once more. We pushed it back and forth for quite some time. Finally he bowed to me again, pressed his hands together and smiled at me. He thanked me over and over before leaving. That was the first time I met the mute slave.

Less than a week later, I got up bright and early one day to see José off to work beneath the starry heavens. As usual, it was around quarter past five. When we opened the front door, we unexpectedly discovered a head of lush green lettuce sitting there, still dripping with water. I carefully picked up the lettuce, waiting until José was in the distance before closing the door. I found a wide-mouthed bottle and stuck the lettuce upright inside like a flower. Then I put it in the living room, reluctant to eat it.

I knew exactly who this present was from.

Around here we were lending out or giving away innumerable things to the Sahrawi neighbours every day. But the person who'd repaid me happened to be a slave, so poor that not even his body belonged to him. This touched my heart even more than the lesson of the widow's mite in the Bible. I really wanted to find out more about the mute slave, but he didn't reappear for a long time.

About two months passed. The neighbour behind us was about to build a room on their roof. All their cement blocks were shipped and piled on our doorstep, then hoisted up.

The scene in front of my house was a complete mess. Our powder-white walls had also been scraped into oblivion. I was afraid to bring it up when José came home. I wanted to avoid incurring his wrath and hurting our neighbour's feelings. I could only hope that they'd begin construction quickly so we could have peaceful days once more.

Sometime later, there was no sign that the project was starting. Whenever I went to hang clothes up on the roof, I would go over to the neighbour's square hole and peer down, asking them why they hadn't started.

'Almost there. We are renting a slave. In a few days he will come, once we agree on a price. His master's asking price is very expensive. He is the best bricklayer in all the desert.'

This first-class bricklayer arrived a few days later. I went up to the roof to take a look and found the mute slave up there, squatting and mixing cement. Pleasantly surprised, I walked towards him. He saw my shadow and looked up. Seeing it was me, a sincere smile emerged on his face like a blooming flower. This time I extended my hand as soon as he bowed. I shook his hand, then gesticulated my thanks to him for the lettuce. His face reddened when he saw that I knew he'd sent it. He pantomimed to ask if it tasted good.

I nodded vigorously and said José and I had eaten it. He smiled happily again and gestured that our kind of people must eat lettuce or else our gums would bleed. I was stunned. How could a slave in the desert have this sort of common knowledge? The mute slave used simple and straightforward hand gestures, the language of a thousand countries. Most convenient indeed. His face was also very expressive. One glance at him and his meaning was clear.

After the mute slave had been working for a few days, a wall about half a person's height had been built. It was a scorching hot August at the time. At noon, the poisonously hot sun poured down like lava from a volcano. I was inside with the windows and doors shut tight, pasting strips of paper into the window joints so waves of heat wouldn't burst indoors. I wiped down mats with water, wrapped ice cubes in a towel and put it on top of my head. But still, that temperature, close to fifty-five degrees, could make a person go insane.

Whenever this wild heat was tormenting me, I would lie on the straw mat, counting down the minutes and seconds until sunset. Only when the cool winds blew at dusk could I manage to sit outside for a moment. This was the greatest pleasure to which I could look forward.

Many days passed before I thought about the mute slave working on the roof. Somehow I'd forgotten him. What was he doing when it was scorching hot? I steeled myself and immediately ran up. When I opened the door to the roof, a wave of heat surged at me and I felt severe pain in my head right away. I rushed forth to find the mute slave. There was not a sliver of shade to hide in on this open rooftop.

The mute slave leaned against the side of the wall, a torn straw mat from the goat pen covering his body. He looked like an old dog that couldn't put up a struggle, fallen to his knees. I walked over quickly, calling him, pushing him. The sun scorched my skin like molten iron. It had only been a few seconds, but my head was whirling, unable to bear it any longer.

I pulled the straw mat from the mute slave and pushed him again. Slowly he raised his pitiful face, which looked like he had been crying, and gazed at me. I pointed to my home. 'Let's go down,' I said to him. 'Quickly. Let's go.'

He stood up weakly. His pallid face seemed uncertain, unsure of what to do.

I couldn't take the heat and gave him a forceful shove. Finally he bowed with great embarrassment, passed under the canopy that José had built and slowly made his way down the stone steps. I closed the door to the roof and descended quickly after.

The mute slave stood under the makeshift ceiling cover by our kitchen, holding a piece of bread that was hard as a stone in his hand. I recognised it as old bread that the Sahrawi get from the military camp. Usually they shredded it and gave it to the goats to eat. Now the neighbour who'd rented the mute slave for labour was giving it to him to sustain his life. He seemed enormously nervous standing there, afraid to move. It was still unbearably hot under the ceiling cover. I told him to come into the living room, but he wouldn't budge at all, pointing at himself and his skin colour. There was no way he would enter.

I gesticulated to him again. 'You, me, we're the same. Please go in.' No one had ever regarded him as human before. No wonder he was scared out of his wits.

Eventually I saw how upset this poor man had become and decided not to force him. I let him stay in a cool spot of the hall and set out a straw mat for him. I brought out an ice-cold bottle of orangeade from the refrigerator, a soft and fresh piece of bread, a piece of cheese and a hard-boiled egg that José hadn't had time to eat that morning. I put them all next to him and gestured that he should eat. Then I walked away into the living room, closing the door so that he could eat undisturbed.

At half past three, lava was still pouring down from the heavens. It was boiling hot indoors; hard to imagine what it was like outside. Worried that the mute slave's owner might scold him, I went over and told him to continue working. He sat in the hallway, still as a statue. He had drunk a little of the orangeade and eaten his own dry bread. The other things were untouched. Seeing that he hadn't eaten, I crossed my arms and looked at him calmly. He got the picture, immediately standing up and gesturing to me not to get angry. He hadn't eaten because he wanted to take it home to his wife and children. He had three kids, two boys and a girl.

Then I understood. I found a bag, put the things in it and sliced a large chunk of cheese and half a watermelon. I also put two bottles of Coke in there. I didn't have much stored myself, or else I would have given him more. When he saw that I was putting things in the bag, he hung his head low, a complicated mix of shame and happiness on his face. I really couldn't take it.

I shoved the whole bag into the half-empty fridge and pointed out the sun to him. 'Take it when the sun goes down,'

I said. 'For now let's store it here.' He nodded eagerly, then bowed to me again, nearly crying tears of joy. He quickly made his way up to continue working. He must really love his kids, I thought. He must have a happy family, or else he wouldn't have been so pleased about this little bit of food. I hesitated for a second, then opened a box of José's favourite toffees, grabbed a large handful and put them in the bag. We didn't have much food ourselves, in reality. What I was able to give him was really too little.

On Sunday, the mute slave was still working. José went up to the roof to see him. This was the first time he had met my husband. He threw down his tools and stepped nimbly over the bricks, calling out hoarsely. A few steps away, he extended his arm to shake José's hand. I felt very happy seeing that he first offered his hand to José, instead of bowing. Around us his sense of inferiority was naturally diminishing, while conversely human compassion rose, bit by bit, in his heart. Smiling, I went down from the roof. The shadow of José speaking to him in sign language fell at an angle onto the ceiling.

José came down at noon, the mute slave happily trailing behind. José had dust all over his face. I figured he must have been helping him with the work. 'Sanmao, I invited the dummy to eat with us.'

'José, don't call him that!'

'He can't hear.'

'He can hear with his eyes.'

I picked up the spatula and spoke to the mute slave in Hassaniya Arabic, making big, slow movements with my mouth: '*Sa–hā–bi.*' (Friend.) I pointed to José and said once more, '*Sa–hā–bi.*' Next I pointed at myself. '*Sa–hā–bu–ti.*' (Female friend.) Then I sat the three of us in a circle.

He understood everything. I was touched once again by his unguarded smile. He seemed excited and a little nervous. José gave him a push and he stepped into the living room. He pointed at his dirty bare feet. Waving my hands at him, I said it didn't matter. I paid no further notice to him, letting the two men speak amongst themselves.

A while later, José came into the kitchen. 'He knows the constellations.'

'How do you know?'

'He drew them. He saw the stars on one of our books and drew a picture with almost everything in the right place.'

I went to set out cutlery in the living room later and saw José and the mute slave sprawled out on a world map. Without even having to search, the mute slave pointed out the Sahara. I was stunned. Next he found Spain and pointed to José. 'What about me?' I asked him. He looked at me. I jokingly pointed to Spain, as well. He pantomimed a roar of laughter and waved his hands, moving to search the part of the map that showed Asia. After a while, he couldn't find it and gave up.

I pointed to his temple and made a face. *Stupid!*

He almost laughed himself to the ground.

The mute slave was clearly most intelligent.

Rice with stir-fried beef and green peppers, I thought, would be hard for him to digest. In his whole life, he'd probably only eaten camel or goat a few times at most. He probably couldn't bear the taste of beef. I invited him to eat white rice with some salt, but he refused. The look of nervousness was back. I told him to eat with his hands. He finally lowered his head and ate it all. I decided next time I wouldn't ask him to eat with us, so that he wouldn't have to suffer like this.

Word got out very quickly. The neighbouring kids saw the mute slave eating in our home and immediately told the adults, who spread the news to other adults. In an instant, everyone around us knew and, we soon found out, felt hostility towards both the mute slave and us.

The little girl I detested the most among our neighbours was the first to warn me, her voice full of hatred and scorn. 'Sanmao, you shouldn't talk to him. He is *haloof!* A dirty person!' (*Haloof* means pig.)

'Mind your own business. If you call him *haloof* one more time, José will catch you and hang you upside down on the roof.'

'He is a pig. His wife is crazy. He is a pig that works for us!' Upon saying that, she ran over and spat on the mute slave, then looked at me with a challenge in her eyes.

José rushed over to grab this little monster. Shrieking, she fled from the roof and went to hide in her own home. I was very upset. The mute slave, without speaking, gathered his tools. Raising my head, I realised that my neighbours were staring darkly at José and me. We didn't say anything and went down from the roof.

One day around sunset, I went up to gather up the clothes I'd hung to dry. I waved at the mute slave, who was already completing the roof of the room. He waved back at me. Just then José returned from work. He came in through the front door and up to the roof, too.

The mute slave put down his tools and walked over. There were no sandstorms that day. A flock of little birds sat on our electric wires. I pointed to a bird and told the mute slave to look. I mimicked their flying, then pointed at him and gesticulated. 'You are not free, working yourself half to death while earning no money.'

'Sanmao, that's enough!' José scolded. 'What's the point in riling him up?'

'That's exactly what I want to do. He has skills. If he were free, he could provide for a family, no question.'

In a daze, the mute slave looked at the sky for a while. He examined the colour of his skin, then sighed. A few moments later, he was smiling again. He pointed at his heart, then at the little birds and made a flying motion. I knew what he wanted to say was this: *Though my body is shackled, my heart is free.*

That he could communicate such wisdom gave me quite a shock.

As dusk approached, he firmly insisted on inviting us to his home. I hurriedly went down to find some things to eat. I put together a bottle of milk powder and white sugar and followed him home.

His home was on the edge of a sandy valley outside town. It was a tattered tent, looking even more lonesome and sad in the light of the setting sun. Just as we were approaching, two naked children burst out of the tent, yelling and laughing, and rushed to the side of the mute slave. Immediately full of smiles, he picked them up in his arms. A woman also came out from the tent. She was so wretched that she didn't even have fabric to wrap around her body; she wore just a ragged skirt from which her feet poked out.

The mute slave repeatedly invited us to go inside and sit. We stooped and went in, finding that the tent only had a few hemp bags spread on the ground. The bags didn't provide enough cover, so half of the floor was sand. Outside the tent was an oil drum, which was only partially full.

The wife was so shy that she stood with her back against the canvas of the tent, afraid to even look at us. The mute slave went over to fetch water and start a fire. He used an ancient kettle to boil water, but there weren't any cups for us to drink from. Extremely embarrassed, he got so worked up that his face soon became sweaty. José laughed and told him not to worry. Once the water cooled down a bit, we could just drink it directly from the kettle and pass it around. Then he seemed to relax, smiling. This was already the greatest hospitality he could provide for us. We were incredibly touched.

It was clear their older son was still working at the rich man's house and hadn't come home yet. The two little ones snuggled close to their father, sucking their fingers and looking at us. I quickly took out what I'd brought and gave them each something. The mute slave also passed the bread to his wife, who sat behind him. After sitting for a while, it was time to leave. Holding one of his kids, the mute slave stood outside the tent and waved goodbye to us. José clasped my hand tightly. Then he turned to look at that poor family who barely had a speck of land to call their own. For some reason we felt even closer than before. 'At least he has a happy family,' I said to José. 'He's not that poor a person, after all!'

Family is the wellspring of joy for all people, providing warmth in the face of bitterness. Even for a slave, I wouldn't think he was too pitiable so long as he had a family. Eventually we bought some cheap fabric for his wife and kids. When the mute slave finished working, we slipped it into his hands and told him to go quickly before his master scolded him.

At the next Muslim holiday, we gave him a hemp bag full of charcoal and a few kilos of meat. I always felt embarrassed giving him these handouts. I went during the day when he wasn't home and put them outside his tent before running off. His wife was kind but not very bright. She was always smiling at me, wrapped in the blue fabric that I'd bought for her.

The mute slave wasn't like those mannerless Sahrawi people. He didn't have anything to repay us with, but he surreptitiously repaired the ceiling that the goats had stomped into disrepair. At night, he'd steal water and wash our car. When the wind became intense, he'd quickly gather my laundry, put it in a newly washed bag, lift the ceiling board and throw it down into our home.

José and I kept hoping we could help the mute slave obtain his freedom, but to no avail. Everyone said that this was impossible. If we did manage to free him, we didn't know how we could bear the responsibility. And what would happen to him if we left someday? Actually, we hadn't really considered that the mute slave's fate could be even more tragic than his current condition. For this reason we didn't actively try to free him.

One day a great storm swept through the desert, raindrops pelting our ceiling. I awoke and gave José a shove to rouse him. 'Listen! It's raining. It's coming down really hard.' I was scared to death.

José jumped up, opened the door and ran out into the storm. The neighbours were all awake. Everyone had come out to look at the rain. 'Holy water!' they cried. 'Holy water!'

I felt ice cold, frightened by this anomaly in the desert. Having not seen rain in so long, I shrank nervously into the doorframe, afraid to go outside. Everyone had brought out barrels to catch the rain. They said it was divine water and drinking it could cure illness. Heavy rain fell relentlessly. The desert became a sludge and our home was totally destroyed by all the leaks. A downpour in the desert was that bad.

The deluge lasted for one whole day and night. Even Spanish newspapers carried stories about the great storm in the desert.

The mute slave's project was also completed the week after the rain.

I was reading around sunset that day. José had to work an extra shift and wouldn't be back until early the next morning. Suddenly I heard unusually noisy children outside the door, along with the sound of adults speaking. My neighbour Gueiga knocked urgently at the door. When I opened it, she told me excitedly, 'Come and see, quick. The dummy was sold off. He is about to leave.'

I heard a pounding in my ears and grabbed Gueiga. 'Why was he sold?' I asked. 'Why was he sold so suddenly? Where is he going?'

'After it rained, a lot of grass grew in Mauritania,' Gueiga said. 'The dummy knows how to herd sheep and deliver baby camels. Someone came to buy him and take him there.'

'Where is he now?'

'In front of the house of the people who have the construction project. His owner is also here, counting money inside.'

I ran out in great haste, my face transformed by anger and worry. I ran all the way to my neighbour's doorstep, where I saw a Jeep parked nearby. The mute slave sat next to the driver's seat. Rushing over to the side of the Jeep, I saw that he was gazing numbly ahead like a person made of clay. His face had no expression on it. I looked at his hands and saw that they'd been tied with ropes. His ankles were also tied loosely in hemp rope.

I put a hand over my mouth, looking at him. He didn't look at me. Glancing in all directions, I saw there were only kids gathered around. I barged into the neighbour's home and found the respected rich guy leisurely drinking tea with a group of well-dressed people. I knew this business transaction was over. There was no hope of rescuing him any more.

Running outside again, I saw that the mute slave's lips were trembling. His eyes were completely dry. I ran back home, grabbed the only cash I had and looked around. I saw the colourful desert blanket spread on my bed and, without thinking, pulled it down. With the blanket in my arms, I hurried back to the Jeep where the mute slave sat.

'*Sahābi*, I'm giving you some money and this blanket,' I cried, piling these things into his lap.

He only noticed me then, along with the blanket. Suddenly he clutched at the blanket, making a crying noise. He jumped out of the Jeep, holding this beautiful blanket, and ran desperately in the direction of his home. Because the rope around his feet hung loose, he could run in small steps. I saw him running towards home at unbelievable speed.

The children saw that he was running. 'Escape!' they cried immediately. 'He's escaping!'

The adults rushed out from inside. A young person swiftly grabbed a big wooden board and ran after him in pursuit.

'Don't hurt him! Don't hurt him!' I almost fainted in panic. I ran yelling after them. Everybody was chasing the mute slave. I ran for my life, forgetting that I had a car parked at my doorstep.

As we drew near the mute slave's tent, everyone saw him open up that riotously colourful blanket into the wind in the distance. Stumbling, he spread it over his wife and children. The ropes around his arms had broken. He cried out garbled noises while firmly wrapping the blanket around his wife and kids. Grabbing his simple wife by the hand, he made her touch the blanket to feel how nice and soft it was. He put the money I'd given him in her hand. Against the wind, I could hear only the sound of his voice and the red blanket flapping.

A few young people went over to capture him. The Jeep had also been driven there. He got in the car blankly and pressed his hand against the window. There was an expression of both joy and sorrow on his face. His white hair whipped in the wind. A distant look was in his eyes, which were still completely dry with no trace of tears. Only his mouth was still trembling beyond his control.

The crowd stepped aside as the Jeep began to go. The silhouette of the mute slave gradually disappeared into the sunset. His family members didn't cry or scream. They held each other in a tight embrace, shrinking into the big red blanket like three stones formed in a sandstorm. Rivers of tears flowed down my face. I slowly walked home, closed the door and got into bed. Before I knew it, the roosters were already crowing.

Crying Camels

How many times in one day I'd woken from deep, dull slumber, I'd lost count. Opening my eyes, I saw a room already swathed in darkness. There were no voices coming from the street, nor cars passing by. All I heard was the clock on the table, its ticking clear and indifferent just like every other time I woke up.

I was really awake, then. Everything that happened yesterday wasn't just a bad dream in the end. Each time I regained consciousness, my memory forced me to bear witness to a torrent of confused images. I had to relive, over and over again, the tragic event that had made me go mad.

I shut my eyes. The faces of Bassiri, Afeluat and Shahida drifted before me in waves, the hint of a smile rippling across each of them. I jumped up, turned on the light and looked at myself in the mirror. In the span of one day, my tongue and lips had become dry, my eyes swollen, my face haggard.

I opened the wood-framed windows that faced the street. The desert outside looked like a landscape of snow and ice, cold and lonely and devoid of life. This unexpectedly bleak view came as a shock. I stared dumbly at this vast and merciless world, forgetting where I was.

Yes, they were still dead, truly dead. Whether in a few short days or over the long span of a life, everything disappears in due time: tears, laughter, love, hate, the ups and downs of dreams and reality. On the sand, pure white like snow, there was no trace of the dead. Not even the nocturnal wind could carry aloft their sighs.

Turning back around to face the deathly emptiness of the room, I could almost make out Bassiri sitting cross-legged in the dim light. He slowly peeled away layer after layer of black fabric covering his head as I looked on in bewilderment, not knowing what to do. A hint of a suggestive smile flashed over his face, tanned to a dark brown that underlined the cold stars of his eyes.

I blinked. Suddenly there was Shahida sitting in profile beneath the bookshelf. Her long eyelashes were like a patch of cloud projected onto her thin and elegant visage. I stared at her. Still she took no notice, indifferent as though she were no longer part of this world.

I was completely oblivious to the car parking outside and the person rapping on my door until a voice startled me to my feet. 'Sanmao!' someone called gently.

'I'm here,' I said to the person outside, grabbing on to the lattice window.

'Sanmao, there are no more plane tickets, but I'll still take you to the airport tomorrow morning.' It was the general director of José's company who spoke quietly to me through the window. 'I've arranged for two standby tickets. Maybe you can squeeze in. Just be prepared. José already knows. He says to lock the door when you leave. Who is the second ticket for?'

'There's only me. No need for the other ticket. Thank you!'

'What? I had to beg and plead for these, and now you don't need it?'

'The other person is dead,' I said flatly. 'They're not leaving.'

The general director froze and gave me a look. Then he glanced nervously at his surroundings. 'I heard there have been incidents with the locals. Do you want to come into town and stay at my house for a night? There are no Spaniards here. It's not safe.'

I became silent for a moment, then shook my head. 'I have to take care of some things. There won't be any trouble. Thank you!'

He stood there for a while, then flicked away the cigarette butt in his hand. 'Well, shut your windows and doors tight,' he said, nodding to me. 'Tomorrow morning at nine, I'll come and get you to go to the airport.'

I closed the window and locked the dual hinges. The sound of the Jeep slowly faded into the distance and finally disappeared altogether. Heavy silence made the tiny room feel completely empty, not at all like the ambience of times past.

It felt like only yesterday that I used to stand here in just my long nightgown, a crowd of Sahrawi girls giggling and talking to me through the window. 'Sanmao, open the door! We have waited all day. Why are you still sleeping?'

'No class today. You're on a break.' I stretched and took a few deep breaths, my gaze leisurely falling on the bright and clean sand dunes in the distance.

'No class again,' the girls clamoured unhappily.

'Those explosions nearly made me and José fall out of bed at three in the morning. We ran out to see what happened, but there was nothing. We couldn't sleep until daybreak because of this. So, heh, no class. No more fussing.'

'Let us come in, even if there is no class! Just for fun.' The girls banged on the door again. I had to open it.

'You sleep like dead people. That loud and you still didn't hear anything?' I asked them, smiling and sipping my tea.

'Of course we did, there were three explosions,' they piped up eagerly. 'One in front of the military camp, another at the elementary school of the mining company, one more in front of Ajyeiba's father's store—'

'News sure gets around fast. You guys don't ever leave this street and still manage to hear about everything.'

'It is the guerrillas. They are getting more and more fierce.'

The girls spoke completely without fear as though it were a great show, twittering and pantomiming and bubbling over with life. The room became filled with the sound of chatter and laughter.

'Actually, the Spanish government has made reassurances on national self-determination. So what are they causing this ruckus for?' I sighed, picked up a brush and started brushing my hair.

'Let me braid your hair.' A girl squatting behind me smeared saliva on her hand, then started putting my hair in thick braids with great care.

'This is all because of Shahida,' the girl behind me said loudly. 'This is what happens when men and women love whoever and however they want. Ajyeiba's store got blown up in the end.' When she said 'love' the whole lot of them started shoving and teasing.

'Shahida who works in the hospital?' I asked.

'Who else? Shameless woman. Ajyeiba loves her, she doesn't love him. She still talked to him, so Ajyeiba pursued her. Then she had a change of heart and got close to Afeluat. Ajyeiba got together a group of people to teach her a lesson, but she told Afeluat. They had a fight several days ago. Then, last night, there was a bomb thrown at Ajyeiba's father's store.'

'That's bull. Afeluat isn't that kind of person.' I disliked this group of girls the most. At every turn, they used their imaginations to judge matters that were completely beyond their comprehension.

'Ay! Afeluat isn't, Shahida is! That whore knows the guerrillas…'

I grabbed my braid of hair back. 'The word "whore" is only for cruel, dishonest women,' I said sternly. 'Shahida is one of the best midwives among you Sahrawi girls. How can you call her a whore? This word is truly terrible. Never call her that again.'

'She talks to every man,' said Fatima, Gueiga's younger sister. An ignorant and slovenly mess, she sat in front of me biting her blackened nails, her hair hardened with red mud.

'What's wrong with talking to men?' I growled. 'I talk to men every day. Am I also a whore?' How I wished I could knock open their silly little closed minds.

'Not only this,' spoke up a rather shy girl. 'Shahida, she… she…' She grew red in the face and couldn't continue.

'She sleeps with different men,' Fatima said deliberately, rolling her eyes. She barked a cold laugh.

'"She sleeps with different men". You've seen it with your own eyes?' I sighed, not knowing whether to laugh at or be angry at this group of girls.

'Hmph! Of course she does! Everyone talks about it. In town, nobody wants to be friends with her, except men. The men won't marry her, though, they just want to play with her…'

'That's enough! No more talk. You're too young to be a bunch of gossipy housewives.' I turned around to go and pour my tea out in the kitchen, irritation unexpectedly rising in my heart. First thing in the morning and they had to talk about these silly things.

The girls sat in a shapeless mass on the ground, some sooty and barelegged, others with terrible body odour or wild hair. All of their mouths were busy chattering. I didn't understand Hassaniya, but I often heard Shahida's name jump out from their sentences. They all bore expressions of resentment and disdain. It was really horrible to witness, this unspeakable jealousy and hatred.

I leaned against the door, looking out at them. I saw a flicker of Shahida, pale and elegant, beautiful as a flower in spring, pass before my eyes. This lovable girl from the desert had been brought up with such refinement, but her own community treated her contemptuously. It was truly difficult to understand.

In this town, we had many Sahrawi friends: the stamp-seller at the post office, the security guard at the courthouse, the company driver, the store assistant, the beggar pretending to be blind, the donkey wrangler who delivered water, the powerful tribal chief, the penniless slave, male and female neighbours young and old, policemen, thieves; people from all walks of life were our *sahābi*.

Afeluat was our beloved friend, a young policeman. He had received a high school education, then ended his studies after becoming a police officer. He had a childlike face and a mouth full of white teeth. People were drawn to his kind and sunny disposition, not to mention his sincerity.

In town, bombs were going off frequently these days, while business bustled on as usual. Everyone was talking about the political situation, consciously or not. But nobody was seriously bothered by these crises. Everyone took it lightly as though these troubles were far away.

One day, I was walking back from buying vegetables when Afeluat drove past me in the police car. I waved at him. He swooped out of the car.

'Afeluat, how come you haven't visited us in so long?' I asked him. He laughed but didn't say anything, walking by my side. 'José is working the early shift this week. He's home after three in the afternoon. Come over for a chat.'

'Alright, I'll definitely come by soon.' Still smiling, he helped load my basket of vegetables into a taxi I hailed, then walked off.

A few days later, Afeluat indeed paid us a visit at night. As luck would have it, a bunch of José's co-workers were over. He glanced in from the window. 'Ah, you have guests!' he said quickly. 'I'll come another time!'

I ran out to greet him and insisted that he come in. 'We're grilling beef kebabs. Come and eat with us. These are all old friends. Don't worry about it.'

Afeluat smiled and pointed behind him. Only then did I see a girl dressed in a light-blue desert robe slowly descending from his car. Her face was covered, but a pair of eyes like autumn water shone at me warmly.

'Shahida?' I asked him with a chuckle.

'How did you know?' He looked at me with surprise. Rather than reply, I walked quickly over to welcome this rare guest whom I couldn't have been more pleased to see. If it had been anybody but Shahida, I wouldn't have dragged her in there since the room was all men. But Shahida was an open-minded girl. After a moment of hesitation, she crossed the threshold.

José's co-workers had never seen a Sahrawi girl up close before. They all stood up politely. 'Please sit, don't go to any trouble.' Shahida nodded with perfect poise. I pulled her down to sit on the mat, then spun around to pour soda water for her and Afeluat. When I looked at her again, the headscarf had already come off quite naturally.

In the light, Shahida's features gave off an inexplicably intense appeal. Her cheeks were close to ivory, offsetting the deep black wells of her eyes. Beneath her straight nose were her clear lips, slim lines that had the flawless elegance of a statue. She unconsciously shifted her gaze around the room. The serenity of her small smile was like a freshly risen moon in the sky, enveloping the room in its brilliance. Everyone slipped into a stupor. Even I, in that sliver of a moment, was frozen in place by her radiance.

Compared with her bright and beautiful appearance in the hospital, Shahida dressed in local garb exuded a different kind of charm altogether. She transported us into an ancient reverie just by sitting there without speaking.

Everyone strained to start talking again. We all felt a bit distracted because Shahida was in the room. Afeluat sat for a while, then bade farewell with Shahida at his side. Long after she'd left, the room was still swathed in silence. This must be how it feels to witness an eternal beauty!

'So beautiful,' I sighed with emotion. 'Such a beautiful woman really exists in the world. It's not a fairy tale.'

'She's Afeluat's girlfriend?' someone asked quietly.

'I don't know.' I shook my head.

'Where is she from?'

'I heard she's an orphan. Her parents are both dead. She learned midwifery from the nuns at the hospital.'

'She's got a keen eye if she picked Afeluat. What an upstanding guy.'

'Afeluat isn't a good match for her.' I shook my head. 'He's lacking something. I can't quite put my finger on it, but it's not there.'

'Sanmao, are you judging a book by its cover?' José said.

'I'm not talking about outward appearance. Just a feeling that she won't end up with him.'

'But Afeluat is still high society. His father owns thousands of goats and camels in the south—'

'Although I don't know Shahida very well, I know she doesn't care much for wealth. I guess nobody in this desert is good enough for her!'

'Didn't Ajyeiba also want her?' José spoke up again. 'He even got in a fight with Afeluat over her a while ago!'

'That merchant's son does nothing all day,' I said scornfully. 'He lords it over everyone in town just because of his father. How can you mention such a terrible person in the same breath as Shahida?'

That first night when Shahida came to my home, a mere glimpse of her shook everyone to the core. We were reluctant to change the subject. Even I was wholly intoxicated by this stunning girl.

Gueiga was upset with me the following day. 'How could you let that whore into your house? If you continue like this, the neighbours will shun you,' she warned. I laughed and shrugged it off. She went on: 'We were all watching when she got out of the car with that man. She even smiled and waved at my mother. My mother pulled us all inside and shut the door. Afeluat went red in the face.'

'You're all too much,' I said. I was startled by this. I had no idea that this had happened yesterday as they were entering my home.

'I hear she is Catholic, not Muslim. This type of person will go to hell after they die.'

I stared silently at Gueiga, not knowing how best to enlighten her. I walked out with her. Hamdi was just getting home from work. The Spanish military uniform emphasised his silver hair and brown face. He looked really rather dignified.

'Sanmao, I am not scolding you. My daughters are at your home every day, so I hope you will teach them to be good. Now you and your husband have befriended some of the more dubious Sahrawi in town. How can I comfortably let my daughters remain your friends?' This heavy language came to me like a slap. I grew purple in the face, unable to speak.

'Hamdi, you must be a bit more open from having been with the Spanish government for over twenty years. Times are changing…'

'Times change, but Sahrawi traditions do not. Your people are your people, our people are our people.'

'Shahida is not a bad woman, Hamdi. You're middle-aged, you must see things more clearly than others…' I was so angry I couldn't find the words and stopped speaking altogether.

'Is there anything more shameful than someone who betrays the religion of their people? Ay…' Hamdi stomped his foot, then walked towards his home with Gueiga in tow, her head lowered.

'Fool!' I cursed, walking into my own home and slamming the door shut.

'It's going to take a lot more patience and time to civilise these people,' I couldn't help but say to José at dinner.

'The guerrillas say in their broadcasts all the time that they'll liberate slaves and educate girls. But the townspeople only hear the bit about independence. They ignore the rest.'

'Where are the guerrillas broadcasting? How come we haven't heard it?'

'It's in Hassaniya. Every night there's a broadcast from near Algeria. All the locals here are listening.'

'José, how long do you think this situation will last?' I asked pensively.

'I don't know. The Spanish governor has agreed to their national self-determination.'

'But what happens if the Moroccans don't agree?' I tilted my head, playing with my chopsticks.

'Ay! Eat your food!'

'I don't want to leave,' I sighed, persisting on this topic.

José gave me a look but didn't say anything else.

Summer in the Sahara meant endless dust filling the sky. It felt like the same day on repeat. Time became sticky in this torrid heat that made you wish for death. These slow, helpless days rendered a person lazy and tired, unable to keep interested in anything amid that sludge, mind blank and body simmering in sweat. Most of the Spanish people around here had already gone, escaping the heat for their hometowns. All that remained was a bleak and deserted ghost town.

There was news about the Sahara in the papers every day. In town there were intermittent explosions where no one got hurt. On the Moroccan side, King Hassan's clamouring grew louder by the day. The future of the Spanish Sahara was uncertain. Meanwhile, the people who actually lived here seemed unconcerned, as though borders meant nothing to them.

Sand was still sand, sky was still sky. Tornadoes were still tornadoes. In this prehistoric piece of land isolated at the edge of the world, the United Nations, the international court at The Hague and self-determination were unfamiliar terms, wispy and unreal as a thread of blue smoke.

We lived on as usual with a wait-and-see attitude. We refused to believe that other people's rumours might one day have any special connection with our fates and our future.

In the scorching heat of the afternoon, whenever the car was available, I would always gather a bunch of snacks and drive to the hospital to hang out with Shahida. The two of us would hide out in the cool and dark basement, breathing in the smell of disinfectant. We sat cross-legged while mending clothes, eating and talking about any number of things, all sorts of nonsense, completely unrestrained as though we were sisters. Shahida often spoke to me about her childhood, the good old days living in a tent. Her stories would quietly come to a halt at the death of her parents. Everything after that seemed to be a blank. She never talked about it, nor did I ask.

'Shahida, if the Spaniards withdraw, what will you do?' I asked one day out of the blue.

'What kind of withdrawal? To give us independence or to let Morocco partition us?'

'Both are possible,' I said with uncertainty, shrugging my shoulders.

'If it's independence, I will stay. Partition, then no.'

'I thought your heart belonged to Spain,' I said slowly.

'This is my land, the place where my parents are buried.' Shahida's eyes clouded over with untold secrets and hidden pain. She sat there, dazed and silent, seeming to have forgotten to speak. 'What about you, Sanmao?' she asked after a long pause.

'I don't want to go. I like it here.'

'What attracts you to this place?' she asked me sceptically.

'What attracts me to this place? The wide openness of the earth and sky, the hot sun, the windstorms. There's joy in such a lonely life, there's sorrow. I even love and hate these ignorant people. It's so confusing! I can't quite make sense of it myself.'

'If this land were yours, what would you do?'

'Probably the same as you, learn some medical care. Actually – what difference does it make whether it's mine or not?' I sighed.

'You haven't thought about independence?' Shahida asked softly.

'Sooner or later, colonialism will be a thing of the past. The real question is how long it'll take to set things up once you're independent. I'm not optimistic at all.'

'One day it will happen.'

'Shahida, you can only say these things to me. Whatever you do, please don't go mouthing off to anyone else.'

'Don't worry,' she laughed. 'The nuns also know.' She brightened, smiling at me, completely carefree for a moment.

'Do you know they're arresting guerrillas in town?' I asked her anxiously.

She nodded pensively, standing up to brush off her clothes. The rims of her eyes were moist all of a sudden.

One afternoon, José came home and started talking as he entered the door. 'Sanmao, have you seen it?'

'Seen what?' I asked dully, wiping a trickle of sweat from my neck. 'I haven't gone out today.'

'Get in the car and I'll show you.' José dragged me out gravely and we took off straight away. He kept silent as he drove by the outskirts of town. A torrent of messages in blood red overflowed on every wall we could see, like water from a burst dam.

'What's this?' I was completely dumbstruck.

'Look closer.'

Get out of our land, Spanish dogs! Long live the Sahara, long live the guerrillas, long live Bassiri! No Morocco, no Spain, long live national self-determination! Spanish robbers! Robbers! Murderers! We love Bassiri! Spain, get out!

Line after line flowing like blood on the white walls rushed out at us, gloomy indictments that brought forth cold and sticky sweat beneath the hot sun. The surge of panic I felt was like someone in deep slumber being awoken by a bayonet.

'The guerrillas are back?' I asked José quietly.

'They don't need to come back. All the Sahrawi who live here are on their side.'

'Are these slogans all over town, too?'

'They even appeared on all the walls at the barracks. It happened in the span of just one evening. Who knows what happened to the guards.'

Fear grabbed hold of us. As we drove through town, every single Sahrawi on the street made me feel jumpy and paranoid. We didn't go back home. José took us to the cafe at his company.

The employees were all gathered in a dense mass in one room, smiling stiffly at each other in greeting. The sleepy summer seemed to have totally vanished. Besides panic and tension, everyone's face bore varying degrees of shame and embarrassment from having been insulted.

'The United Nations mission is coming. Of course they want to cause a ruckus. They want to express their views on the Sahara at any cost.'

'I heard Bassiri was educated in Spain all the way through law school. After so many years, how could he come back and oppose us as a guerrilla?'

'What's going to happen to the company? Do we hold on or should we split?'

'I'm sending my wife away tomorrow. I'm not going to wait until things get bad.'

'It's not just their own guerrillas, I heard. A whole bunch of them came over from Morocco long ago.' Confused chatter rose and fell around the room, everyone groping in the dark about a hotchpotch of matters.

Suddenly, a rough-looking Spaniard I didn't recognise pounded on the table and stood up. Face red, he spoke with great agitation, gesticulating wildly, spittle flying everywhere. 'Fuck, these bastards don't know how to eat or take a shit, but they dream of independence. We Spanish are being too lenient. If you ask me, we should be able to kill them if they dare to insult us. Bah! Only seventy thousand people. It wouldn't be too hard to sweep them with a machine gun. What did Hitler do to the Jews...?'

He was so angry his eyes looked like they might burst out of their sockets. His rage went far beyond mere hatred. 'Slaughtering a Sahrawi is no different than killing a dog. Dogs are better than them. At least they know to wag their tails for the people that feed them...'

'Uh... uh...' I listened to him say these inhumane things. Originally I'd been siding with the Spaniards, but his extreme comments pushed me far in the opposite direction. José was frozen in place, staring at this guy.

Unbelievably the majority of people in the room started clapping and shouting their support for this man's mad rhetoric. He swallowed spit, picked up a glass and took a big gulp of booze. Then he saw me. 'We Spaniards are not the only colonialists,' he added. 'Those Chinese in Hong Kong are anxious to please England. After this many years, the Chinese are at their beck and call. The Sahrawi aren't able to see this example, but we are…'

Before I could even jump up, José banged loudly on the table and stood to drag the guy out for a fight. Everyone stared at us. I desperately pulled José towards the door. 'He's just a redneck, he has no sense. Why bother going to the trouble?'

'This lunatic is talking trash, and you want me to leave?' José started shouting. 'According to him, people who aren't subjugated by foreign powers should just die off in waves like flies. Does he know how you Chinese resisted Japan back in the day?' I kicked him out the door.

'José, I also disapprove of colonialism, but what can we say about Spain in this regard? If you clash with your own people, you'll end up with a reputation for being unpatriotic. And where's the good in that?'

'These kinds of bad apples… Ay, no wonder the Sahrawi don't like us.' José seemed surprisingly sad. 'We're not doing well with either side. The guerrillas call us dogs on one hand, but then hearing my own people speak drives me nuts. Ay! *Dios!*'

'This could have been resolved peacefully if Morocco hadn't wanted to partition them. Then they wouldn't have become as agitated as they are for independence.'

'The observer mission will be here soon, Sanmao. Do you want to leave for a while and come back once the upheaval is over?'

'Me?' I laughed coldly. 'I'm not going. As long as this place is under Spanish occupation, I'll be here. Even when Spain leaves, I'll probably stay.'

That night, all of town was under martial law. The atmosphere of disturbance submerged every street corner and alleyway. During the day, Spanish police pointed their guns at Sahrawi pedestrians on the streets. One by one, they were pushed up against the walls and ordered to take off their loose-fitting robes. The youth had long ago disappeared. The only ones left were pitiful old people who stared blankly with arms raised as they were being frisked. There was nothing to be gained from this except a feeling of disgust. Would the guerrillas really be so stupid as to carry handguns that could easily be found?

I went to the hospital to find Shahida. The concierge told me she was on the second floor assisting in a birth. After I got up there, I hadn't taken more than a few steps when Shahida walked out, all flustered. We nearly collided full on.

'What is it?'

'Nothing, let's go!' She dragged me down the stairs.

'Don't you have a baby to deliver?'

'The woman's family members don't want me,' she said, her lower lip trembling. 'It's a difficult birth. She was near death when she got here. As soon as I walked in, they started cursing me. I…'

'What do they have against you?'

'I don't know. I…'

'Shahida, why don't you just get married? Coming and going with Afeluat doesn't sit well with the community.'

'It's not Luat,' she clarified quickly, lifting her head.

'Eh?' I was puzzled.

'It's because Ajyeiba and his gang of thugs kept wanting to get me. I had no other option... Who could I tell my pain to...' Tears rushing from her eyes, she shot off quick as an arrow.

I slowly walked down the hallway and through the compound where the nuns lived. A group of children were obediently drinking milk. Among them was a little Sahrawi boy with milk bubbles all over his upper lip like a funny white moustache. I picked him up and walked into the sunlight to play with him.

'Hey, where are you carrying him off to?' A young nun rushed after us anxiously.

'It's me!' I laughed and gave her a wave.

'Ah! You gave me quite a scare.'

'This little guy is really handsome. So strong.' I looked deeply into the kid's large black eyes and tousled his curly hair.

'Alright, hand him over!' The nun reached out and took him in his arms.

'How old is he?'

'Four,' the nun said, giving him a kiss.

'Shahida was already grown up by the time she got here, right?'

'She arrived when she was older, sixteen or seventeen.'

I smiled and bade the nun farewell, giving the little guy another kiss. He shyly bowed his head as low as he could. The expression sparked a flicker of a memory in my mind. Who was it that this kid reminded me of?

On the road we saw loads of military convoys driving into town. The government buildings were tightly enclosed by barbed wire. A huge crowd was queuing patiently at the tiny airline office. Suddenly a group of journalists I didn't recognise caused a commotion by rushing forward like a bunch of hooligans. The anxious racket cast an ominous cloud over this once peaceful town. A storm was brewing.

I quickly walked home and found Gueiga waiting for me on the stone steps. 'Sanmao, Tebrak wants to know if you're giving Khalifa a bath today?' Khalifa was Gueiga's youngest brother, who had dermatitis. Every few days they brought him over and asked me to bathe him with medicated soap.

'Yep!' I replied, absentmindedly opening the door. 'I'll give him a wash. Bring him over!'

In the bathtub, large-eyed Khalifa wriggled about disobediently. 'Time to stand up!' I was sprawled on the ground washing his feet.

He picked up a wet brush and banged it against my lowered head. 'First kill José, then kill you,' he sang like a nursery rhyme while knocking my head. 'First kill José, kill José...' The words were unmistakable. As soon as I realised what he was singing, I heard a loud pounding in my ears. I made a great effort to calm myself.

After I finished bathing Khalifa, I wrapped him up in a big towel and carried him to the bedroom. I felt a sense of unreality during these few short steps, like I was walking on cotton, my footing unsteady. How I got into the bedroom, I have no idea. I gently wiped down Khalifa, my body in shock.

'Khalifa, what did you say? Good boy, say it again.'

Khalifa reached out a hand to grab the book by my pillow. Looking at me, he grinned and said, 'The guerrillas will come, mm, mm, to kill José and kill Sanmao. Heehee!' Then he went to grab the alarm clock at the bedside, completely unaware of what he was saying.

Dazed, I wrapped Khalifa in one of José's old shirts and slowly walked over to Hamdi's house where the door was open. I handed the child over to his mother, Tebrak.

She lovingly took him in her arms right away. 'Ah! Thank you! Khalifa, say, *Gracias!*' she said to her child, all smiles.

'The guerrillas kill José, kill Sanmao.' The little kid pointed at me and started singing again, bobbling excitedly in his mother's lap.

When she heard this, Tebrak flipped her child over and made to strike him. 'I'll kill you!' Her earnest face grew red an instant.

'What's the use in hitting him?' I sighed helplessly. 'The child doesn't understand what he's saying.'

'Sorry! Sorry!' Tebrak was practically in tears. She looked at me, then immediately lowered her head.

'Don't look upon us differently! We are all children of *Maulana*!' (*Maulana* is the name of God in Hassaniya Arabic.)

'We do not do that. Gueiga and my children are all friendly with you. We are not those kind of people. Please forgive us. Sorry, sorry.' As she went on and on, tears of shame rolled down Tebrak's face. She kept on wiping her eyes with her shirt sleeve.

'Tebrak, what nonsense you are talking. Don't be absurd.'

Gueiga's older brother Bashir entered, chiding his mother. He laughed coldly and looked at me askance. Flinging aside the curtain, he walked out.

'Tebrak, don't feel bad. Young people have their own ideas. You don't need to say sorry.' I patted her and stood, feeling wronged but unsure of what to do, just like when I was bullied as a kid. I floated out in a trance.

At home, I sat listlessly, my mind a total blank. I didn't even notice when José came in with Afeluat. 'Sanmao, I need a favour from you. Please drive me out of town on Sunday.'

'What?' I was still drifting in another world and hadn't heard him clearly.

'Help me leave town to go home,' Luat said, straight to the point.

'I can't. The guerrillas are out there.'

'I guarantee your safety. Please, I beg of you!'

'Don't you have your own car?' That day I'd somehow lost not only my spirit, but also my manners. I was not remotely in the mood to talk to anyone.

'Sanmao, I am a Sahrawi,' Afeluat said, looking at me patiently. 'They are not giving car passes to local people now. Usually you are the most level-headed person. What's the matter today? It seems you are angry.'

'Aren't you a police officer? Yet you're still asking me.'

'I am a police officer, but I am also a Sahrawi.' He smiled bitterly.

'If you want to leave town, don't get us involved. No matter what, they'll murder us and feed our hearts to the dogs.' I don't know where my temper came from. I couldn't keep myself from yelling. Upon saying this, tears burst forth from my eyes. Might as well just cave in and sit bawling on the ground.

José had been changing his clothes. When he heard me cry out, he rushed over to my side. He and Afeluat looked at each other speechlessly.

'What's wrong with her?' José said, brow furrowed.

'I don't know,' Afeluat said, puzzled. 'I was just speaking normally and she got like this.'

'Fine. I've gone crazy. It's none of your business.' I snatched a tissue to wipe my face and nose. Then I took a deep breath and sat on the sofa, staring into space. Thinking back to how well Afeluat's parents and siblings had treated me in the past,

I began to regret my rash behaviour. I couldn't help but start talking again. 'And why do you have to leave town right at this moment? It's a mess out there.'

'The entire family is getting together one more time on Sunday. It's going to get worse soon. We won't be able to go into the desert very often.'

'Are the camels still there?' José asked.

'We sold them all. My older brothers needed money, so they sold everything. They just have a few goats with them.'

'Why do they need so much money that they're selling off family property?' I felt much better after crying for a spell and had calmed down a bit.

'Luat, we'll drive you out of town on Sunday,' José said, cool and collected. 'You guarantee that we get home by night. Don't disappoint your friends.'

'I won't,' Luat said with sincere gratitude, patting José's shoulder. 'It really is a family gathering, trust me.' It was settled then.

'Luat, how will you guarantee our safety since you're not a member of the guerrillas?' I asked pensively.

'Sanmao, we are true friends. Please believe that I am asking you only because I have no other choice. If I didn't have a handle on things, I wouldn't dare put you to the trouble. We all have parents who worry after us.'

Hearing the sincerity of his words, I decided not to press the issue further.

At the checkpoint, they took identification cards from all three of us, two in blue from José and me and a yellow one from Afeluat. 'Pick these up when you get back to town tonight. Watch out for Bassiri on the road.' The guard waved and let us go. His last words got my heart pounding like crazy.

'Drive quickly! It'll take us more than three hours round trip. Let's go and come back soon.'

I sat in the backseat, while José and Luat sat up front. For ease of travel, we were wearing desert garb. 'How come you wanted to go home all of a sudden?' I asked, feeling apprehensive again.

'Sanmao, don't be nervous,' Afeluat laughed. 'You've been saying the same thing over and over for the past few days.' He had become much livelier since we left town.

'How come Shahida isn't coming along?'

'She's at work.'

'You might as well say you're afraid for her safety.'

'Guys, stop talking. Luat, you navigate so I can drive faster.'

A vast grey sky surrounded us on all sides. Through the thick layers of clouds, the newly risen sun could only give off a dim light in pale orange. A substantial chill lingered in the desert in the morning. A few lone birds cawed and circled above our car, deepening the sense of desolation.

'I'm going to sleep a bit. Got up too early.' I curled up in the backseat and closed my eyes, feeling like a piece of lead was weighing on my heart and keeping me from being at ease. It was better not to look out at the desert for now. If I looked, I'd be afraid of seeing something I didn't want to see on the horizon.

After dozing off for what seemed like just a short while, I felt the jostling of the car slow and then stop. I felt hot and flung the blanket from my body. Suddenly the back door of the car opened. I cried out in surprise.

'Who is it?!'

'My little brother, Sanmao. He came to get us from afar.'

I sat up groggily, rubbing my eyes. Before me was a fresh and innocent young face, smiling at me in greeting.

'It's really Muhammad? Ah…' I smiled and reached out a hand. 'Are we almost there?' I sat up and opened the window.

'It's just up ahead.'

'You moved again. You didn't live here last year.'

'We sold all the camels. Wherever we live it's pretty much the same.'

In the distance, I saw the large brown tent of Afeluat's family. Finally I let go of the suspense I'd felt during this whole trip. Luat's beautiful mother came out with his two sisters. Beneath the open sky, the three dots of their figures flew towards us.

'*Salaam alaikum!*' his little sister called as she threw herself onto her brother. She immediately hugged me after, two hands encircling my neck. Her face was beautiful and innocent, her long gown spotless. Her teeth were clean and white, her braids thick and shiny. An earthy freshness emanated from her entire body.

With small steps, I hurried over to Luat's mother's side. She was just detaching herself from her son's embrace. '*Salaam alaikum!* Yasmin!'

Wrapped in a deep blue fabric, hair in a low bun, she slowly opened up her arms and greeted me with warm affection. Her eyes were filled with sincere feeling. The greyness of the morning had disappeared; the sky behind her was now awash in bright blue.

'Little sisters, get the fabric from the car,' I called out to the girls, shooing a flock of goats out of my way. 'I also brought some multi-coloured glass beads for you.'

'This is for Luat's father.' José brought out two large jars of powdered tobacco.

'There's also a small box of biscuits. Go and get it. They're made from cocoa powder.'

Everything felt peaceful and orderly, like I was going home or visiting relatives, the same atmosphere as on every previous visit to Afeluat's home. Not a thing had changed. I moved past a crowd of people and ran towards the tent.

'I'm here, Chieftain!' I stepped in. Afeluat's father had a full head of white hair. He raised his arm without standing. '*Salaam alaikum!*' I dropped to my knees and crawled over. Raising my right hand from afar, I gently touched the top of his head. This old man was the only person to whom I offered the most respectful greetings.

José entered. He also walked close to the old man and knelt down, touching his head briefly before sitting cross-legged below him. '*Combien de temps est-ce que vous restez cette fois-ci?*' the old man asked in French.

'*La situación no es buena,*' José answered in Spanish. '*Volveremos por la noche.*'

'You will soon leave the Sahara?' the old man asked with a sigh.

'We have no choice at this time,' José said. 'We have to go.'

'Ah, war! No longer the peaceful days of the past.'

The old man fumbled around in his pocket for a while, then took out a pair of heavy silver anklets and gestured at me. I crawled over to sit by his side. '*Porte-les, je les laisse à toi.*' I didn't understand French, but I understood the glint in his eye. I accepted with both hands. Slipping off my sandals, I put on the anklets and stood up, walking awkwardly for a few steps.

'*Zwayna! Zwayna!*' the old man said in Hassaniya. 'Beautiful!'

I understood. '*Haqq!*' (Yes!) I answered gently, unable to hold back from admiring my exquisitely adorned ankles.

'Each of the daughters has a set,' Afeluat said amiably. 'My little sisters are still too young, so we give this to you.'

'May I step out?' I asked Afeluat's father. He nodded. I ran out to show Yasmin my feet. The two sisters were in the middle of catching a goat to slaughter. Blue smoke curled upward from the dry brambles that were already burning. Yasmin stood with me, looking out at the open wilderness. In the past, they had lived farther south with many neighbours all around. Now they had relocated to an even more desolate place for some reason.

'The Sahara is so beautiful,' Yasmin said, sweeping both hands into the sky in a casually elegant gesture. She was praising her land as always, just like when I had come to stay with them before. Through the magic of her raised hands, the world around us became full of poetic sighs, threading into the whole of my heart.

There is no other place in the world like the Sahara. This land demonstrates its majesty and tenderness only to those who love it. And that love is quietly reciprocated in the eternity of its land and sky, a serene promise and assurance, a wish for your future generations to be born in its embrace.

'Time to slaughter the goat. I'll go and get Luat.' I ran back to the tent.

Luat came out. I lay quietly on the ground, lightly breathing in the usual faint scent of tobacco from the carpet. The people in this family didn't have any of those body odours that I found repellent. They were quite unlike the others.

After a long while, Luat tapped me. 'It's been slaughtered. We can go out to look.' When it came to killing livestock, I could never force myself to watch the actual slaughter.

'These two goats are huge! Can we eat this much?' I asked Yasmin, squatting by her side.

'It is not enough! The brothers will come home soon. Take a portion back with you when you leave here. I still have to make a pot of couscous so we can really enjoy a good meal.'

'I've never met Luat's older brothers, not once,' I said.

'They have all been gone for many years now and rarely come home. You both have been here three or four times, but they have come only once. Ah…'

'Times like these, and they still haven't come.'

'They're here!' Yasmin said softly, kneeling back down to continue to work.

'Where?' I asked, finding it strange. 'I don't see anyone!'

'Listen, will you?'

'Listen to them talking in the tent right now?'

'No good!' Yasmin laughed. 'You have no ears.'

After a while, I finally noticed there was a cloud of yellow dust rising like smoke in the distance, dissipating into the sky. I couldn't tell who or what was coming towards us. Were they walking or running? Riding on camels or in cars?

Yasmin stood slowly. The image that gradually appeared on sand turned out to be row after row of yellow-brown Jeeps driving straight towards us with a show of great might. The cars drew closer and closer. Just as they got near enough for me to almost catch sight of the people inside, they slowly dispersed and encircled the tent from afar. One by one, they drove off until they couldn't be seen clearly any more.

'Yasmin, are you sure those are your family members?' I felt there was something sinister in the air from the imposing manner of this scene. I unconsciously grabbed on to the corner of Yasmin's robe.

Now there was only one Jeep, inside which sat a group of people with their faces hidden, driving calmly straight at us.

A shiver went through me. I was unable to lift my feet; it was as though they were nailed in place. I could feel the people inside the car staring at me like vultures from beneath their headscarves. The younger sisters and brother immediately ran towards the Jeep. 'Older Brother! Older Brother!' they exclaimed jubilantly, seemingly close to tears. When they pounced on the group of people who had just got out of the Jeep, they did actually start to cry.

Yasmin opened up her arms, burbling the names of her sons. I noticed then that her slim and beautiful face had become drenched in tears. One after the other, the five sons quietly and lovingly embraced their petite mother. Everyone grew still and silent for a long spell.

Afeluat had come out a while ago. He calmly moved to hug his brothers. It was quiet all around us. I stayed in place, unmoving as though somebody had stuck pins in me. One brother after another prostrated himself and then entered the tent, kneeling to gently touch the top of their elderly father's head. Reunited after a long separation, the old man also had tears all over his cheeks, losing himself in joy and sentimentality.

At last they approached José gravely and shook his hand. Then they turned to me and shook my hand. 'Sanmao!' they called in greeting.

'These are my older brothers,' Luat said happily. With their headscarves off, they all looked very similar to Luat, extremely handsome and tall, their teeth straight and white.

Soon they wanted to shed their gowns, and they looked at Luat inquisitively. I saw Luat's gentle nod and immediately it all became clear. After they carefully took off their outerwear, five brown guerrilla uniforms seared my eyes like fire.

José and I didn't even have time to look at each other; both of us turned to stone. I felt as though I'd been cheated. All the blood in my body rushed to my face. José didn't make a move, silent as a wall. His face was expressionless.

'José, please do not misunderstand,' Luat explained with urgency, face reddening. 'Today is purely a family reunion. There is no other meaning to it. Please, I beg you for forgiveness and understanding.'

'They are all *waladi*,' said Yasmin. 'Please don't think otherwise, José. They are my *waladi*.' In situations like these, only a woman would know how to open up the impasse like flowing water. (*Waladi* means boy.)

I rose and followed Yasmin out to slice up the goat meat. Thinking it over, I still felt angry and decided to run back to the entrance of the tent to have a few words. 'Luat, you made fools out of us. How could you be so reckless with such matters?'

'Actually, Luat did not need to trick you, even if it was hard for him to leave town,' said one of his brothers. 'The truth is that we brothers wanted to meet you two. Luat has often spoken of you. It is rare for us to have a reunion, and it just so happened that we asked him to invite you. Please do not misunderstand. Let us make friends for once beneath this tent!' He shook José's hand again after this sincere explanation. José finally seemed relieved.

'*Ne parlez pas de la politique!*' the old man suddenly thundered.

'Today we drink tea, eat meat and spend time in each other's company, enjoying a day of familial love and affection,' continued Luat's brother. 'Tomorrow we will go our separate ways!' He stood up and strode out of the tent to receive the pot of tea that his little sister was carrying.

Almost everyone spent the entire afternoon doing house-hold chores. We gathered a small mountain of dry kindling and herded the flock of goats into its pen. Since most of the family was a bit older, José and a few of the brothers pitched a tent for the younger siblings to sleep in. They put a hose in the water bucket, set up a wall of rocks in upwind areas, elevated the stove, made cushions out of sheepskin. The father even cheerfully asked his oldest son to give him a haircut.

Luat's second eldest brother was busying himself with household chores like the rest of us, but his pace, demeanour, bearing and open manner were striking, almost regal. He was polite and mild in speech and extremely attentive. His worn and ragged uniform couldn't conceal the radiance that emanated from him. His gaze was sharp and focused, so much so that it was almost hard to look him directly in the eye. His mature face was handsome and refined in a way that I'd never seen among the Sahrawi.

'I'm guessing you're going into town to stir up some trouble,' José said to Luat's brothers against the wind as he gathered a bundle of wood.

'Yes, we will go back the day the observer mission comes. We place great hope in the United Nations and want to demonstrate to them the decision that the Sahrawi people have made about this land.'

'Make sure you don't get arrested,' I cut in.

'The locals will aid us. We are hard to catch. As long as we don't have bad luck, it probably will not happen.'

'You're such idealists, full of romantic notions about establishing your own country,' I called out, sitting on the ground with a little goat in my lap. 'And what if you really become independent? Dealing with the huge and ignorant mobs in town, you'll really be at a loss then!'

'The first step is to develop resources and educate people.'

'Who's going to do the developing? Even if all seventy thousand people go and block off the borders, they still wouldn't be able to cover all of it. You'd just become a protectorate of Algeria. Things would only get worse from there.'

'Sanmao, you're too pessimistic.'

'You're too romantic. It's one thing to fight as a guerrilla. It's another to establish a country.'

'It does not matter if we succeed or fail, so long as we've made every effort,' they answered me calmly.

Once the day's housework had ended, Yasmin called everyone over to drink tea in the new tent. The floor was already covered in carpets.

'Luat, the sun is setting,' José said quietly, gazing at the sky. A reluctant expression swept over his exhausted face. 'Let's go! We have to get home before night falls.' I immediately stood. Seeing that we had to leave, Yasmin paused mid-motion, still holding the teapot, then hurriedly wrapped up a lamb shank for us.

'You cannot stay a bit longer?' she implored softly.

'Yasmin, we'll see you next time,' I said.

'There won't be a next time,' she said gently. 'This I know. This is the last time. José and you will leave the Sahara for good.'

'If you manage to gain independence, we will come back.'

'We will not become independent,' the old man said ruefully under his breath, shaking his head of white hair. 'The Moroccans will be here soon. My children are dreaming, just dreaming…'

'Let's go, the sun is setting so fast!' I urged them to get on the road. The old man slowly walked us out, one hand draped on José, the other on Afeluat.

I took the lamb shank and put it in the car, then turned to hug Yasmin and the sisters silently. Lifting my head, I gazed intently at Afeluat's older brothers, countless unspoken words passing between us in one helpless glance. In the end, we were people from two different worlds.

I was just about to get in the car when Luat's second eldest brother came near me. He shook my hand very seriously. 'Sanmao,' he said softly. 'Thank you for taking care of Shahida.'

'Shahida?' I was completely taken by surprise. How did he know Shahida?

'She is my wife. I entrust her to you once more.' Suddenly his eyes were filled with tenderness and deep sentimentality. We looked at each other, sharing a secret. He smiled sadly in the twilight. Dumbfounded, I stayed rooted in place. Then he turned around and strode off. The first brisk wind of dusk sent a shiver through me.

'Luat, so Shahida is actually your second eldest brother's wife?' On the car ride home, it was like I'd woken up from a dream. Secretly nodding to myself, my heart sighing – yes, only this kind of man was worthy of Shahida. There really was a Sahrawi man in this world who was worthy of her.

'She is Bassiri's only wife,' he nodded sadly. 'Ah, seven years!' He must have been secretly in love with Shahida himself!

'Bassiri?' José stepped on the brake.

'Bassiri!' I yelled. 'Your second eldest brother is Bassiri?' All the blood in my body was whooshing and whirling about. The elusive, cunning and mighty leader of the guerrillas these past years, the spirit of the Sahrawi people, happened to be none other than the man who had just shaken hands with me and called out Shahida's name.

We sank into a deep shock, so much so that we couldn't find the words to speak any more.

'Your parents seem to not know about Shahida.'

'They cannot know. Shahida is a Catholic. If my father knew, he would condemn Bassiri to death. Also, Bassiri is afraid that the Moroccans will kidnap Shahida and hold her for ransom. So he does not speak of her to others.'

'The guerrillas are surrounded by enemies. They have to fight Morocco, fend off Spain and also watch out for Mauritania to the south. Such an exhausting life, and it might be futile in the end!' José had pretty much made his thoughts known about the guerrillas' dreams.

I stared blankly out at the desert flying behind us. Hearing José talk like that, I was struck by a phrase from *Dream of the Red Chamber*:

The disillusioned to their convents fly,
The still deluded miserably die.
Like birds who, having fed, to the woods repair,
They leave the landscape desolate and bare.[1]

My heart grew sombre. I don't know why, but suddenly I felt that Bassiri would die soon. In my lifetime, this kind of intuition had often surfaced and I'd never been wrong. For a moment I froze and stared out of the window, thinking about this unlucky omen and not knowing what to do.

'Sanmao, what's wrong?' José woke me from my reverie.

'I want to lie down. This day has been too much.' I covered myself with the blanket and buried myself in it, feeling depressed and unable to relax.

The day the United Nations observer mission flew to the Sahara, the Spanish governor reiterated his guarantee that the Sahrawi people could freely express their positions so long as they maintained order. Spain would not make things difficult for them. The Sahrawi people's self-determination, already in discussion for over two years, was reaffirmed.

'I hope they're not lying. If I were the government, I wouldn't be so generous.' I started feeling worried again.

'Colonialism is in decline. It's not that Spain is being generous. Spain is also in decline.' José always seemed glum lately.

The small UN team intervening in the Spanish Sahara was composed of three people from different countries: Iran, Côte d'Ivoire and Cuba. Early in the morning, the road into town from the airport was lined with a dense crowd of Sahrawi people. Facing off with the Spanish policemen who stood guard, they didn't make any trouble and waited patiently for the motorcade.

When the governor and the delegation were about to enter town in their convertible, an order sounded and all the Sahrawi began to shout thunderously. 'National self-determination, national self-determination! Please, please, national self-determination, national self-determination...'

Guerrilla flags of all sizes, sewn together from thousands of rags, rose up as if by a fierce wind. Men and women, young and old, were dancing wildly and screaming and crying their hopes. It was like the sky was falling and the earth had opened up. As the car drove slowly past, the Sahara was roaring its final struggle...

'Idiotic nonsense!' A pained sigh came over me as I stood on the roof of my friend's house in town. Would they give up their lives for such a hopeless matter, like moths to a flame? Would they never understand what was happening?

The Spanish government's understanding of the lie of the land was leaps and bounds ahead of the Sahrawi's. They let them grab at the UN to their hearts' content, neither blocking nor opposing them. Spain would eventually withdraw, after all. Who would be the next to come? It wouldn't be Bassiri. Never would he be the leader of this small, weak nation of 70,000 people.

The UN observer mission left the Spanish Sahara very quickly and flew to Morocco. The Sahrawi and Spaniards in town shared a strangely intimate coexistence, perhaps even more peaceable than previously. In face of the clamour from Morocco, Spain adhered to the promise it had made to the Sahara. National self-determination would soon be realised, it seemed. Both sides, under the menace of Morocco's intense drums of war, began to collaborate again in a spirit of fraternity.

'What matters is Morocco, not Spain.' Shahida was sinking deeper into gloom with every passing day. She was not a naive person. She saw things more clearly than anyone else.

On the other hand, most Sahrawi were blindly optimistic. 'Morocco? If the UN says the Spanish Sahara should allow us national self-determination, then Morocco shouldn't be afraid of it. Who do they think they are? If it gets down to it, Spain will go to court with them in The Hague!'

On 17 October, the question of the Spanish Sahara, after being dragged out for who knows how long, finally came to a conclusion at The Hague's international tribunal after the ruckus and a lengthy waiting period.

'Ah! We have won! We have won! Peace is here! Hope is here!' When the Sahrawi in town heard the broadcast, they grabbed everything they could bang or drum on and started jumping and hooting like they'd gone crazy. Spaniards and Sahrawi, regardless of whether they knew each other or not, hugged each other and laughed and caroused loudly. The streets were full of people in mad celebrations.

'Did you hear that? Let's just stay here if Spain manages to resolve things with them peacefully.' José, full of smiles, gave me a hug. My heart remained anxious. I don't know why, but I had the feeling that disaster was on the doorstep.

'It won't be that easy. It's not little kids playing house.' I still wasn't buying it.

That evening, the announcer on the Sahara radio station reported with great bitterness: 'King Hassan of Morocco is recruiting a volunteer army. Starting tomorrow, they will advance towards the Spanish Sahara.'

José slammed the table and leapt to his feet.

'Time to fight!' he boomed. I buried my face in my knees.

The frightening thing was that Hassan, that devil, was aiming to recruit 300,000; by the second day, 2 million people had already signed up. The evening news on Spanish television even began broadcasting footage of the march from Morocco. 'We'll take El Aaiún on 23 October!' They were out in force like wasps leaving their nest. Encouraged by Hassan, men and women of all ages made moves, full of song and dance, gradually pressing towards the border with terrible force. One step at a time, they steadily advanced on the fearful minds of those of us watching television here.

'Dance, dance, dance yourselves to death, you bastards!' I cursed hatefully at the men and women on television who were dancing and clapping.

'Time to fight!' All the heroic youths in the desert corps had lost their minds, it seemed, driving off towards the border. The border was only forty kilometres away from El Aaiún.

By 19 October, the Moroccan forces were increasing unabated in number.

By 20 October, the arrow on the newspaper map was drawing closer.

By 21 October, the Spanish government was using megaphones on every street and alleyway to call for an emergency evacuation of all Spanish women and children. The collective spirit collapsed like river water bursting forth from a dam.

'Get out of here! Sanmao, quick, we don't have much time.' Our friends in town got rid of all their home furnishings and rushed over to say goodbye to me before fleeing to the airport.

'Sanmao, get out, go quickly.' Everyone I ran into urged me like this. They banged on my door before jumping into their cars and heading away.

The Spanish policemen vanished from the streets. Apart from the crowds huddled outside the airline office, the town emptied out.

During this critical juncture, José was working day and night at the mining company's floating embankment, withdrawing arms and troops. He didn't have time to come home to check up on me. On 22 October, a Moroccan flag suddenly rose on Hamdi's roof deck. After that, Moroccan flags began appearing around town in droves. 'Hamdi, you're really jumping the gun here.' I was disheartened to the point of tears when I saw him.

'I have a wife and children. What do you want me to do? You want me to die?' Hamdi scuffed his feet around, head lowered, and moved quickly on.

I was startled when I saw Gueiga, whose eyes were swollen like walnuts from crying. 'Gueiga, you—'

'My husband Abeidy is gone. He's joined the guerrillas.'

'A man of character is truly hard to come by.' One may as well go into exile instead of dragging out an ignoble existence.

'Shut the door tight. Make sure you know who's there before opening it. The Moroccans won't be here tomorrow. They're still too far away! I bugged Jaime about your plane ticket again. He won't forget about you. I'll come home whenever I have a moment. In case things get bad, head to the airport with the little suitcase. I'll think of a way to find you. Be brave.' José's eyes were bloodshot. I nodded. He left again, travelling more than a hundred kilometres to help withdraw troops. All of the mining company had been mobilised to coordinate with the troops, putting the most precious of goods into shipping cargo as fast as they could. Not a single worker left his post or complained. All the Spanish civilian vessels from the Canary Islands had sailed here and were waiting on standby at the coast.

That very night, I was home alone when somebody knocked softly on the door.

'Who is it?' I asked loudly, immediately turning out the lights.

'Shahida. Quick, open the door!'

I rushed over to open the door. Shahida darted inside, followed by a man with his head covered. I shut the door and locked it securely.

Once she'd entered, Shahida hugged herself, trembling with immense fear. She stared at me and exhaled a big breath. The stranger who sat on the mat slowly removed his headscarf and nodded at me with a smile – Bassiri!

'You two are looking for trouble. Hamdi is with the Moroccans now.' I jumped up and turned off the light, pushing them towards the bedroom where there were no windows. 'The rooftop is public and there's a hole in the ceiling. They can see you.' I firmly shut the bedroom door before going to turn on the lamp.

'Give me something to eat!' Bassiri sighed heavily. Shahida made to go into the kitchen.

'I'll go,' I said quietly, stopping her. 'You stay in here.'

Bassiri was famished, but he only had a few bites before he couldn't eat any more. He heaved another sigh. His face was so emaciated he barely looked human.

'Why are you back here? Now, of all times?'

'To see her!' Bassiri looked at Shahida and sighed deeply once more. 'The day I found out about the march, I started making my way from Algeria, travelling day and night to get here in time. I've been walking for so long...'

'By yourself?'

He nodded.

'What about the other guerrillas?'

'They scrambled over the border to block the Moroccans.'

'How many in total?'

'Just over two thousand.'

'How many of your people are in town?'

'I'm afraid there might not be a single one who hasn't fled in fright by now. Ay, the human heart!' Bassiri sat upright. 'I must go before curfew.'

'What about Luat?'

'I'm leaving to meet him.'

'Where?'

'At a friend's house.'

'Are you sure? Is this friend trustworthy?'

Bassiri nodded.

I thought for a while, then reached my hand out to open a drawer and grab a set of keys. 'Bassiri, these are for an empty apartment that a friend passed on to me. It's next to the hotel. The roof is a semicircle, painted bright yellow. You can't miss it. If you end up without a place to stay, go and hide out there. It's a Spaniard's home. No one will suspect a thing.'

'I cannot put you to the trouble. I will not go.' He refused to take the keys.

Shahida pleaded bitterly with him. 'Take the keys so you have one more place to go, no matter what. Now there are all sorts of spies for Morocco in town. Listen to Sanmao. She has the right idea.'

'I have places to go. Sanmao, Shahida has a bit of money and can work as a nurse. You take her, our child will go with the nuns. Split up into two groups and you won't attract attention. The Moroccans know that I have a wife in town.'

I froze and looked at Shahida. 'Your child?'

'I'll explain later.' Shahida was trembling so hard she couldn't speak, tugging at Bassiri as he made to leave. Bassiri cupped Shahida's face, calmly studying it for a few seconds. Then he sighed heavily and ran his hands tenderly through her hair before turning abruptly and striding out.

Shahida lay with me in silence. After a sleepless night, day broke and she insisted on going to work. 'My child is leaving for Spain today with the nuns. I want to see him.'

'I'll come and find you this afternoon. As soon as I hear about plane tickets, we'll go.' She nodded dispiritedly and slowly walked out. 'Wait a minute. I'll drive you.' I'd somehow forgotten about my own car.

I spent the day in a daze. Around five o'clock in the afternoon, I was about to drive to the hospital when I realised I was almost out of gas. I had no choice but to go to the gas station. After going a whole night without sleep, I felt dizzy and heard a ringing in my ears. I couldn't stop sweating. I was weakened as though I were about to collapse from illness. My mind thickly clouded, I pressed on until I suddenly found myself driving head-on into the barricades outside of town.

I urgently slammed on the brakes, breaking out in a cold sweat from the fright.

'Why is this side blocked?' I asked a Spanish soldier standing guard.

'There's been an incident. They're burying people.'

'What does burying people have to do with traffic control?' I asked, dead weary.

'The dead ones include Bassiri, the leader of those guerrillas!'

'You— You're lying!' I yelled.

'It's true. Why would I lie to you?'

'You're wrong,' I cried out again. 'Absolutely wrong.'

'How could I be wrong? Headquarters verified his corpse. His little brother also confirmed it before he was taken into custody. Who knows if he'll get out?'

'How could this be true? How could it?' I was almost begging this young soldier to disavow the reality of what he had just said.

'His own people started some trouble and he got killed. Ay, he was badly mutilated. His face was a bloody mess.'

I started trembling, wanting to reverse but unable to shift into gear. My body shook relentlessly. 'I don't feel well,' I said to the soldier. 'Help me reverse the car.' I got out limply.

He gave me a strange look but obliged nonetheless. 'Drive carefully! Get home quick!'

I was still trembling all the way to the hospital. After shuffling out of the car, I ran into the old porter and could barely formulate words. 'Where is Shahida?'

'She's gone!' He regarded me calmly.

'To where? Is she looking for me?' I asked haltingly.

'I don't know.'

'And the nuns?'

'They left this morning and took a few children with them.'

'Is Shahida in the dormitory?'

'No, I'm telling you she's not there. At three this afternoon, she left looking very pale and without speaking to anyone.'

'What about Afeluat?'

'How would I know?' the porter replied impatiently.

I left, feeling helpless. I drove in circles around town until I came upon another gas station and, in a trance, decided to get gas again.

'Señora, you should get out of here! The Moroccans will be here any day now.'

Ignoring the guy at the gas station, I drove on and asked endless questions near the police unit.

'Have you seen Afeluat? May I ask if you've seen Luat?'

Everyone shook their heads sombrely.

'The Sahrawi police officers split days ago.'

I drove over to the public square where the Sahrawi liked to congregate. An old man sat inside a half-open store. I used to buy local products from him all the time.

'May I ask if you've seen Shahida? Have you seen Afeluat?'

Afraid of getting involved, the old man gently nudged me towards the door. He seemed like he wanted to say something and sighed.

'Please tell me—'

'Leave quickly! It is not your business.'

'I'll leave as soon as you tell me, I promise,' I begged him.

He glanced at his surroundings for a moment before speaking. 'Tonight, they will put Shahida on trial.'

'Why? Why?' Once more I was frightened beyond belief, not knowing what to do.

'She sold out Bassiri. She told the Moroccans that he returned. They took care of him in an alley.'

'Impossible. Who is detaining her? Let me talk to them. Shahida stayed at my house last night. There's no way. Besides, besides, she's Bassiri's wife...'

The old man gently pushed me out of the shop. I got back in the car and sprawled on the steering wheel, exhausted, unable to move.

When I got back to my doorstep, Gueiga immediately ran over from a crowd of people who were talking. 'Let us go inside to talk.' She gave me a push.

'You want to tell me Bassiri is dead,' I said, collapsing on the ground.

'Not only that. They will kill Shahida tonight.'

'I know. Where?'

'The place where they slaughter camels,' Gueiga said, sounding scared.

'Who are these people?'

'Ajyciba and his gang.'

'They did it on purpose, blaming her,' I cried again. 'Shahida was at my house last night.'

Gueiga sat in silence, dumb fear on her face.

'Gueiga, give me a massage! My entire body is in pain.' I lay on the ground letting out long sighs. '*Dios! Dios!*' Gueiga bent down next to me and began massaging.

'They invited everyone to go and watch,' Gueiga said.

'What time tonight?'

'Half past eight. They told everyone to come. They said it is not for fun!'

'Ajyeiba is with the Moroccans! Isn't it obvious?'

'He is nothing,' Gueiga said. 'He is a hooligan!'

I shut my eyes, my head spinning like a carousel. Who could rescue Shahida? The nuns had all left, the Spanish troops wouldn't get involved, Luat was gone, I didn't have the power, José wouldn't be coming home. There was no one to even discuss the situation with. I was utterly alone.

'What time is it? Gueiga, pass me the clock.'

Gueiga handed it over and I saw that the time was already ten past seven. 'Where have the Moroccans reached today?' I asked. 'Is there any news?'

'I do not know. I heard the desert corps at the border already took away landmines to let them through. Some soldiers refused to leave, joined up with the guerrillas and went into the desert with them.'

'How do you know?'

'Hamdi said it.'

'Gueiga, think of a way to rescue Shahida.'

'I do not know.'

'I'm going tonight, are you? I'm going to testify that she stayed at our house last night—'

'Not good, not good, Sanmao,' Gueiga stopped me anxiously, almost in tears. 'Don't say it. If you do, it will be very bad, even for you.'

I closed my eyes, holding on despite my exhaustion, waiting for half past eight to arrive quickly. I would go and see Shahida no matter what. If it was going to be a joint trial, there should be some leeway for others to speak. The worst case would be a brutal lynching. Forget about a joint trial; it would just be an assertion of Shahida's guilt so they could condemn her to death and be done with it, this girl that Ajyeiba could never have. Only in troubled times could there be such injustice.

I heard the noise of a crowd outside after eight. Everyone was sullen, their faces without expression. Some walked, some drove, all heading towards the slaughterhouse next to the valley of sand far away from town.

I got in the car and drove slowly in the midst of the Sahrawi. At the end of the road, where there was only sand, I left the car behind and followed the crowd of people onwards.

The slaughterhouse was one place that I always avoided, a place where the wails of camels waiting to be slaughtered echoed on and on. The rotten meat and white bones of dead camels filled an entire shallow valley of sand. The wind was relentlessly fierce here. Even coming here during the day made a person feel ghastly and unhappy. Now it was nearing the tail end of dusk, the setting sun just a pale streak of light shining weakly on the horizon.

The slaughterhouse was made of cement, long and rectangular. In the dim light it looked like a large coffin that a giant hand had taken from the clouds and set gently in the sand. Its slanted shadow was almost too terrible to behold.

Many people were already gathered there for the show, not panicked at all, more like a flock of sheep crowded together and bumping into one another. So many people, and yet not a single sound.

Before it was even half past eight, a mid-size Jeep sped aggressively towards the crowd. Everyone hurriedly stepped back and made a path. High up in the front, next to the driver's seat, sat Shahida, so still and pale she looked already dead.

I pushed people aside, reaching out my hand, calling for Shahida, but I couldn't get near her. The crowds pushed me back and forth like a wave. So many people stepped on my feet, shoving me forward and backward, forward and backward.

Everything around me was a blur. I didn't see a single person I recognised. Jumping up to get a better look, I saw Ajyeiba pulling Shahida out of the car by her hair. There was a commotion in the crowd. Everyone struggled to get to the front.

Shahida shut her eyes and didn't make a move. I thought her heart must have already broken when she heard about Bassiri's death. Now she was just seeking death and soon she would have it. The nuns had safely taken their child away. There was probably very little left in the world with which she couldn't part.

What kind of joint trial was this? Where were the people who would speak? Who would bring up Bassiri? Who would uphold justice? Once Shahida was dragged out, a few people began tearing her bodice. Her naked breasts were soon pitifully exposed.

She raised her head, closed her eyes, gritted her teeth and stayed absolutely still. Then Ajyeiba started screaming in Hassaniya. Another roar went through the crowd. I couldn't understand. I grabbed a man next to me and desperately asked him what was happening. He shook his head, refusing to translate. I squeezed my way over to ask a girl. 'They will rape her first before killing her,' she said in a whisper. 'Ajyeiba asked who wants to rape her. She is Catholic. It is not a crime to do it.'

'Ah! *Cielos! Cielos!* Let me through. Let me pass. I need to get through.' I fought my way past the people in front of me. Those few steps felt like a century, like I would never be able to squeeze through.

I jumped up to look. Ajyeiba and seven or eight of his men were ripping apart her skirt. Shahida tried to run, but several of them caught her and pulled her back forcefully. Her skirt had fallen. She was almost completely naked, rolling around in the sand. A few men jumped on top of her and seized her arms and legs, pressing them down, spreading them apart.

Shahida's bloodcurdling screams and cries drifted outward, sounding like a wild animal. *Ah... no... no... ah... ah...*

I wanted to yell out, but I couldn't. I wanted to cry, but I choked. I wanted to watch, but couldn't bear it. I wanted to not watch, but my eyes were fixed firmly on Shahida, unable to move elsewhere. *Don't... ah... don't...* I heard my own voice rasping and wheezing... Right at this moment I felt someone behind me fly past like a leopard, rushing through the crowd, pulling people aside one by one. He entered the scene like a flash of lightning and pulled off the men who were holding Shahida down. He dragged Shahida by the hair and retreated towards the empty slaughterhouse and higher ground behind him. Luat. He carried a handgun and looked like he'd gone mad. Foaming at the mouth, he brandished the gun at the crowd that was about to rush up there. Those seven or eight thugs flashed knives. The crowd started screaming and fleeing the scene. I desperately tried to get closer, but I got pushed and staggered backwards. I opened my eyes wide, looking at Luat surrounded on all sides. He was pulling Shahida along the ground, his eyes wild and alert, a ferocious glint in them. He waved his gun at the people who were pressing closer. Just then a person who had got behind him jumped up and threw himself at him. He fired a shot. The others took advantage of the moment and attacked. 'Kill me, kill me, Luat... Kill me...' Shahida screamed and kept screaming. I was so frightened I choked and started sobbing. Upon hearing another series of gunshots, everyone was crying and pushing and fleeing. I fell to the ground, people trampling over me. A few moments later, everything around me was open and empty, serene. I turned over and sat up. I saw Ajyeiba's men hurriedly helping someone into the car. There were two corpses on the ground. Luat lay there dead, his eyes open. Shahida was sprawled on the ground. From Luat's position, it looked like he had been trying to crawl towards Shahida to cover her with his body.

I squatted in the sand at a distance, shivering and shaking uncontrollably. It was so dark, you could barely make them out any more. The wind had suddenly gone silent. Gradually, I saw less and less. I only heard the screaming and braying of the camels in the slaughterhouse grow louder and louder, higher and higher. The entire sky slowly filled with the immense echoes of the camels' cries, coming down on me like thunder.

Lonesome Land

There were eight of us in total, with two cars and three tents. The last glimmers of the setting sun had disappeared. It was no longer twilight, but there was still a faint pigeon-grey colour in the sky. A bone-chilling wind began to rise up from the mournful wasteland. Night was spreading very gradually, but already we could see next to nothing of the woods behind us.

No one had a chance to appreciate the blur of a desert dusk while pitching tents and setting out cookware. This time, we had already got off to a late start because of the woman and child who were tagging along. Manolín was meditating off to one side. He was a tall figure with a light brown beard down to his chest. He wore an old white shirt, as always, along with knee-length shorts and a little hat that looked like a kippah. His feet were bare. There was a fiery flicker in his eyes. He sat cross-legged, two hands rooted to the ground, his body partially suspended in the air like an ascetic from India. He spoke not a word.

Miguel wore a striped shirt and a clean pair of over-washed jeans. His thick eyebrows, large eyes and thin nose complemented a sensual mouth. Of average height, he had elegant hands that were currently fiddling with his very expensive camera. No matter how much you looked, you could never find any flaws with Miguel. He looked picture-perfect, like an advertisement in Kodak colour. But for some reason, he could never blend into his surroundings. He was what you would consider a good companion, sociable, happy, open. No quirks or idiosyncrasies. He talked a lot, said mostly pleasant things. You'd never get into an argument with him. But there was something missing.

Jerry was always shy. This strong and sturdy youth from the Canary Islands was the son of a fisherman. Like a piece of thick strawboard, he was simple in nature and stiff in his mannerisms. He had never spoken directly to me before. At work, he was known for being quiet and honest. Yet he was married to Tania, who was as jumpy as a deer in the headlights. She used to work at a hair salon. It was only after she married Jerry that she reluctantly relocated to the desert. She rarely spoke to other men. For the moment, the two of them were shut away in their new tent, the cooing sounds of their baby Isabel drifting out from time to time.

José wore grass-green shorts with a khaki shirt. He had on basketball sneakers and a woollen cap for the winter. Bent over gathering firewood, he was the spitting image of a wretched farmer from an old Russian novel, or at least a foreigner from Eastern Europe. His Spanish air had pretty much entirely gone. José was always the one who did the most work. He liked it that way.

Yadasi sat sombrely atop a large rock, smoking. His eyes were small and bright. In the twilight, his gaunt face gave off a golden metallic glow. His expression was always lazy and contemptuous. He didn't get along with the Europeans at work, and he was also impatient with his own people. But he was fiercely loyal to José. His long blue gown dragged down to the ground, billowing in the wind. Looking closely at him, you wouldn't think he was Sahrawi, but Tibetan, rather, a product of the Himalayan plateau, exuding an air of mystery.

I had worn my bathing suit when we took off at noon. Now I put on one of José's big coats, along with white wool socks that went up to my knees. I'd loosened my braids long ago. I was gently beating a bowful of eggs with one hand.

Tania wouldn't come out. She was afraid of absolutely everything in the desert, including Yadasi. The only reason she joined our troop this time was because her mother had returned to the Canary Islands, Jerry was coming with us and she would be scared to stay home alone. So she grudgingly came, looking pitiful with her three-month-old child in her arms. She and the desert weren't meant for each other.

Once José got the fire going, I set the bowl down and ran off towards the forest in the distance. 'Where are you going?' called Yadasi, who usually didn't say much.

'Picking— pine— branches—' I said without turning around.

'Don't go into the woods!' The wind carried the sound of his voice to me.

'Don't— worry—' I still managed to run all the way there in one breath.

Once I got into the woods, I whipped my head back around. Their figures were as tiny as chesspieces, scattered on the sandy ground. Just a moment ago, the wind rustling through the treetops sounded like it was right behind our tents. Strangely, though, it turned out to be quite a distance away.

The woods were thickly forested. In a moment, my eyes became used to the darkness and I saw a pile of wood. But it was ironwood, not pine, so I went farther in, burying myself deeper in the shadows. In the dim light, something totally unexpected caught my eye through the thicket.

There was a house of white stone with a semicircular roof and no windows or door. The stillness of its gloom was eerie and unsettling, almost like it was concealing the signs of some monstrous life. A wind rustled past, then quietly blew back in my direction. Shadows flickered all around, forces of *yin* pressing against me.

I gulped and started backing up, my eyes fixed on the little house. When I was almost out of the woods, I pulled down a tree branch and started hacking wildly at it. Once I had hacked halfway through, I snapped off the branch with great effort and then turned to see if the mysterious thing was still there. I had a sense of déjà vu. This scene looked familiar to me, as though I'd seen it in a dream. I stood there gaping for a while. I felt like I could hear someone sighing quietly in the woods. The hairs all over my body stood up. I grabbed the branch and fled from the woods. I sensed a coldness behind me still giving chase, step by step. After running a few dozen paces, I saw and heard José's campfire light up with a whoosh, as though competing with the sun that had just set.

'I told you not to pour in any gasoline, and you still did!' By the time I made my way over, all out of breath, the fire was already reaching high into the sky.

'We can add the pine branches later when the fire dwindles.'

'It's not pine, it's ironwood.' I was still winded.

'Just one branch?'

'It's creepy in there,' I cried. 'Go and see for yourself, if you dare.'

'Give me the axe. I'll go.' Manolín came out of his yoga pose and took the machete from me.

'Don't go!' Yadasi said lazily.

'There's an incredibly creepy house in there. Go and take a look.'

Manolín still went. A little while later, he came out with a big pile of tree branches. 'Hey, something's not quite right in there,' he said.

'There are enough brambles here,' José said casually. 'No need to go back.'

I looked up at Manolín. He was silently wiping sweat away despite the coldness of the early evening.

'Miguel, come and help me with these kebabs.' I squatted down and laid out the skewers, then looked back at Jerry's tent. They had already lit their gas lamp, but there was no sign of them.

Soon the food was prepared. Only then did I surreptitiously bring out the enamel bowl in which I had been beating eggs. I crept around, my body lowered, to the back of Jerry's tent. 'The djinni has come!' I cried all of a sudden, banging on the bowl with a fork.

'Sanmao, don't scare us!' yelled Tania from inside the tent.

'Time for dinner! Come out, come out!' I pulled aside the tent flap. Tania was squatting with a coat draped around her. Baby Isabel lay on the ground. Jerry was filling a milk bottle.

'I'm not going out!' Tania shook her head.

'It's too dark out to see any more. If you can't see, then there's nothing to be afraid of. Just pretend you're not in the desert. Come on!' She hesitated. 'Are you eating or not?' I cried. 'If you are, then you have to come out.'

Tania forced herself to look outside for a moment, her eyes wide.

'There's a fire,' Miguel called out. 'Don't be afraid.'

'Jerry...' Tania turned, calling her husband's name.

Jerry scooped up his child and gave her a hug. 'Don't be scared,' he said quietly. 'Let's go out there.'

Right after sitting down, Tania started crying out again. 'What are you roasting? It's so black. Camel meat…?!'

Everyone laughed at this. Only Yadasi looked a little annoyed. 'Beef, with some soy sauce. Don't worry. I'll let you try the first one.' He passed over a skewer, which Jerry took for his wife.

José got the fire going good and strong. We even had to spread out some redwood branches on the fire or risk burning our eyebrows. It was still and silent all around us, except for the sound of barbecue drippings splattering on the firewood. 'Eat at your leisure. There's quiche.' I started beating eggs again.

'Sanmao likes to make grand gestures like this,' José said. 'It's a feast every time we eat. I get stuffed to death.'

'I just don't want you guys to starve!' I turned to Tania. 'Do you eat onions?' She immediately shook her head. 'Alright, I'll make a salad with no onions, then another with all the onions.'

'If you really don't mind?' Miguel sighed, clicking his tongue.

'When the fire gets small later, I'll throw on a bunch of sweet potatoes.'

'Are none of you planning to sleep at all?' Tania asked.

'Whether you want to sleep or not, you're free to do what you want.' I smiled at her. 'You can sleep for a while and then get up, or just go on sleeping. Whatever makes you happy.' I handed her another kebab.

'We want to sleep,' Tania said apologetically. No one said anything. Let them do as they please. I was still cleaning up after our meal when Tania said good night and walked off, dragging Jerry after her.

When they were at the edge of the fire's light, an impulse came over me. 'Hey!' I called out to Tania. 'There are eyes staring out at you over there!' Hearing this, Tania let go of Jerry and Isabel and fell to the ground with a yelp.

'Sanmao…' Manolín harrumphed and gave me a dirty look.

'Sorry, sorry, I'm messing with you.' I fell over on my knees, unable to stop chuckling. I must have seemed crazy to get so wound up by all this.

The night grew colder, even as the fire continued to burn. José and I sat for a while, then went into our own little tent. We both slipped into our sleeping bags, turning our faces to each other to speak.

'What did you say this place was called?' I asked José.

'I didn't catch the name from Yadasi.'

'Are there really crystals here?'

'He told us that the one he gave us is from here. There should be some.' After a brief silence, José turned over.

'Going to sleep?'

'Yep!'

'Wake me up in the morning. Don't forget, 'kay?' I also turned, back to back with him, and closed my eyes.

After a long while, José fell silent. I figured he was asleep. Unzipping the flap of the tent, I saw there were still three people sitting around the fire. Miguel was speaking quietly to Yadasi about something or other.

I lay for a bit, listening to the doleful desert wind fly high like it had wings. The stakes of the tent had been blown loose and the canvas kept covering my face. Feeling suffocated, I thought I might as well get up. I put on long trousers and a thick coat and crawled over José. Dragging my sleeping bag, I quietly opened the tent and went out.

'Where are you going?' José whispered.

'Out,' I replied, also in a whisper.

'People are still up?'

'Three of them still haven't gone to sleep!'

'Sanmao...'

'Hmm?'

'Don't scare Tania.'

'Got it. Go to sleep.'

Holding my sleeping bag, I scurried over to the fire in my bare feet. I spread it out on the ground, then slipped in and lay down again. The three others were still talking in hushed tones.

There were no stars or moon in the sky. The night was frozen black. A wind blew freely, making rustling noises in the forest behind us.

'He must have been stoned,' Miguel said to Yadasi, continuing a conversation I hadn't overheard. 'You can't trust everything he says.'

'He didn't used to smoke,' Yadasi said. 'After he got into it, he was never clear-headed any more. You know how messy his stall is.'

I pulled down the sleeping bag that had been covering my face and looked at them from the corner of my eye. Yadasi's copper-coloured face was expressionless in the firelight.

'Are you talking about old man Hanna?' I asked quietly.

'You know him, too?' Miguel seemed very surprised.

'Why wouldn't I? I've gone to him for help on multiple occasions, but he always ignores me. He acts like he rules the roost, squatting on his counter in a daze. There are always coins scattered everywhere. I've even sold things on his behalf once or twice. He ignores his customers. He's always tripping.'

'Tripping?' Miguel asked.

'What Sanmao means is that he's always floating in his happy haze,' Manolín cut in.

I turned over in my sleeping bag and lay on my stomach. 'One time, I went over there to him and said, "Hanna, Hanna, draw us a map to the djinni,"' I said to them in a low voice. 'He wasn't muddled that day. As soon as I asked, he started crying—'

'Why did you have to go to Hanna?' Yadasi asked disapprovingly.

'Don't you know that he was the djinnis' gravekeeper when he was young?' I retorted, widening my eyes.

'The other clansmen also know the way,' Yadasi maintained.

'Nobody else would dare to take us,' I said, forcing my voice down. 'Will you take us then, Yadasi?'

He laughed ambiguously.

'Hey, do you guys really believe in djinn?' Miguel whispered to Yadasi.

'They exist to those who believe in them. For non-believers, there's no such thing.'

'And you?' I raised my head to ask.

'Me? Not really.'

'You either believe or you don't. Tell us the truth.'

There was that ambiguous laugh again. 'You know, I—'

'And yet you eat pork,' I jabbed.

'Well, there you go, then,' Yadasi laughed, putting his hands up.

'That time Hanna started crying...' Manolín brought us back to the story I hadn't finished telling.

'I just wanted him to show us the way. He was waving his hands like crazy and said, "Señora, that is a forbidden place, you cannot go." Two years ago he took a journalist there to take pictures. When he returned home, his old lady died out of the blue. It was the djinni's vengeance. His wife paid with her life because he wanted that bit of money… After he told me this, he started weeping uncontrollably, slapping his hands and feet. And I could tell he wasn't stoned that day…'

'I heard that when Hanna's wife was dead, her entire body was black,' Miguel said. 'Maggots came out of her nose straight away.'

'Add some firewood.' I tucked myself deeper into the sleeping bag and stopped speaking. The four of us faced each other in silence. Outside of the firelight, you couldn't tell the sky from the ground. The wind blew more urgently, a cold and ghostly wail.

After a long while, Yadasi spoke again. 'The earth really did crack open. It cracks every time.'

'You've seen it?'

Yadasi nodded sombrely, his gaze directed at somewhere outside the fire. 'Before, Hanna would walk for days at a time, then hurry back to report to the town. You'd always hear him shouting from afar, "It is cracked again! Cracked!" It was terrifying. Our clansmen would be scared out of their wits. In just a few days, there would be a death. Sometimes more than one.'

'Somebody always died, without fail?'

'Without fail. Nowadays there is no gravekeeper. It actually feels a lot better this way.'

'Does the ground still crack open?' Manolín asked.

'Of course. When somebody dies and gets carried away, there's always a big hole in the ground waiting.'

'A coincidence. The ground's probably too dry!' Even I didn't believe these words coming out of my mouth.

'The ground is made of cement and held together firmly. Without an earthquake, how could it crack open?'

'Ay, you just said you didn't really believe in it. How come you're insisting now?'

'I've seen it with my own eyes, many times,' Yadasi said slowly.

'*Dios mío!* Who did the djinni send to the grave?' I asked him.

'My wife. She's also buried there. Fourteen years old. She was pregnant when she died.' Yadasi sounded like he was talking about somebody else. Everyone was rooted in shock, staring at him without knowing what to say.

'What are you talking about?' José had crept over to us, accidentally knocking over a plank.

'Shh, we're talking about djinn!'

'Ah, those things. Miguel, hand me the teapot!' In the glow of firelight, there was silence once more.

'Yadasi,' I called out, lying in my sleeping bag.

'Hmm?'

'Why are they called djinn? Can you explain?'

'In the past, there were many djinn. They are ghosts that live in the desert. In the Hassaniya language, they are considered spirits. They live in the groves of desert oases. Then when there were fewer and fewer oases, the djinn moved to the south. They say one has been living here in the Spanish Sahara for the past few decades at the tomb of the Mahmoud clan. Everyone always cried out, "djinni, djinni", so now the ghost and the cemetery have the same name.'

'Isn't your surname also Mahmoud?' José asked.

'He just told us his wife is buried there, you didn't catch it,' I whispered to José, before turning back to Yadasi. 'Why did the Mahmoud clan choose that land?'

'It was by accident. They buried seven people at once. Then when they discovered a djinni lived there and made the ground split open to foretell deaths in the clan, no one dared to move again. They even offer sacrifices every year!'

'I've seen photos,' I said under my breath.

'Are there photos of the djinni?' Miguel asked in astonishment.

'Just the photos that the journalist took,' replied Yadasi. 'Not of a ghost or anything, but the graveyard. He didn't take any of the outside. There were lots of photos of the interior. It was small, with a concrete floor covered by a red and black striped coarse cloth. He didn't see anything special about it. There wasn't a crack in the ground either. There were names written all over the walls.'

'How come the graveyard was indoors?' José asked.

'Originally there was no building, just a circle of stones. But then the ground would always split open where people had been buried. When people went to look, they could never find the bones, so they just buried the next one wherever the earth was cracked. After almost a hundred years, they still hadn't filled this tiny piece of land. It's just a few times the size of Sanmao's sleeping bag, but somehow all deaths in the clan have been buried there, year after year.'

I felt pretty uncomfortable with Yadasi using my sleeping bag for scale. I didn't dare move, my back pressed to the ground.

'They didn't look hard enough!' Miguel said. 'I hear that most corpses in the desert never rot.'

'They still have to dig deep whenever someone is buried. There really was nothing underground.'

'Add some firewood, Manolín!' I called out.

'Then eventually you built a house and put down a concrete floor, thinking it wouldn't crack, right? Ha...' José started laughing out of the blue. The tea water splashed onto the fire with a sizzle, making us jump.

'You don't believe it?' Manolín asked in a low voice.

'Everyone dies. Whether the ground cracks open or not, they'll die. Besides, the Mahmoud clan is pretty big.'

'The djinni casts omens for only your clan,' Miguel said softly. 'The two cemeteries by Sanmao's house don't have one.'

'Hey, don't talk a bunch of crap,' I protested. 'Our place is the picture of serenity.'

'Shh, speak softly.' José swatted me and shoved the hand I'd stuck out back into the sleeping bag.

'The townspeople are quite odd. They won't hang out near your home.'

'People who aren't part of the Mahmoud clan won't get consigned to their deaths there. The djinni only recognises the Mahmouds because they're always the one offering sacrifices. No one else is allowed to be buried there!'

'One time, a father and two sons from another clan were travelling. During the journey, the father died of illness. The sons were close to where the djinni was. They carried their father and buried him with the Mahmouds. There was still no concrete at the time, so they just put stacks and stacks of large rocks on the grave. When the sons walked back to where they'd tied their camels, a new grave had appeared right there. There was no one anywhere around. The two sons could hardly believe it. They dug up the grave and were shocked to find their father inside, whom they had buried hundreds of metres away. They stumbled and tottered their way back to the djinni. The father's grave was empty. There was nothing at all in there—'

'Let me tell the rest,' Miguel cried. 'So this time they carried their father back to bury him in the original spot. After burying him, they returned and found another new grave in their path. When they opened it up, it was the father again. They—'

'How do you know?' I interrupted.

'I've heard this one before. It was an ancestor of Lwali, one of the drivers at the company. He used to talk about it all the time and wouldn't stop until everyone was upset.'

'Hey, how about roasting some sweet potatoes?' I asked, sticking out my head.

'Where are they?' José asked quietly.

'In the bucket, quite a few kilos. Stoke the fire a bit.'

'I can't find it.' José was searching high and low in the distance.

'Not the red bucket, the blue bucket.'

'Get up and look yourself – you're the one who put them there.'

'Can't get up.' We were surrounded by darkness on all sides. It felt like there were thousands of eyes blinking at us from beyond the firelight.

'How many do you want to roast?' he asked softly.

'All of them. If we can't finish them, we can have them for breakfast tomorrow.'

As they began burying sweet potatoes in the hot ashes, I tucked into my sleeping bag, imagining they were burying seven dead people, all with the surname Mahmoud.

'Speaking of people at work,' Miguel began again. 'That engineer is another one of them.'

'Who?'

'The eldest son of the police chief.'

'He's irrelevant, Miguel,' I said.

'I've been here longer than you. He's relevant. You just haven't heard about it. Two people went to find the great San Diego sand dune, got lost and didn't come home. The father went to look for them with the police. Two days later, they found them in a grove. They hadn't died of dehydration or heat. Their car had run out of gas and got stuck there. One of them was fine but the other had gone totally crazy.'

'Ah, I heard he was a bit weird to begin with.'

'No way. He was fine when I first met him. Once they brought him back, he was properly mad, running all over the place and foaming at the mouth. He kept saying there was a ghost chasing him. They had to forcibly sedate him. He'd pass out for a while. Then, when no one was paying attention, he'd open his bloodshot eyes and go nuts again. Everyone was worn out after a few days of this. They saw that this wasn't going away. They brought him to see the *santón*. The *santón* told him to pray facing Mecca. His mother stepped in and said they were Catholic and would certainly not be praying to Mecca. But the priest in town also said it was a kind of psychological treatment and he might as well pray. If he got better from praying to Mecca, it would be God's will...'

'What a strange priest. The priest and *santón* in town have always been enemies...'

'Sanmao, don't change the subject.' Miguel stopped here unhappily.

'And then—'

'Then he prayed and prayed to Mecca. The djinni stopped following him and left. Amazingly, it let go of him.'

'Psychological treatment, you got that right. In the desert, just go with Mecca. Other religions don't work.' José was laughing again in disbelief.

Miguel ignored him. 'He lost a lot of weight after that,' he continued. 'He was always sullen and unhappy. Still died in less than six months.'

'He swallowed a gun in the dormitory. His younger brother just so happened to be getting married in Spain that day, so his parents were both gone. Right?' I asked quietly.

'Swallowed a gun?' Miguel looked at me, uncomprehending.

'I'm using a Chinese expression in Spanish. Didn't he put a handgun in his mouth and pull the trigger? That's swallowing a gun,' I said.

'I heard his girlfriend left him to marry his brother,' José said. 'That's why he didn't want to live. It has nothing to do with the djinni.'

'Says who?' I looked at José disapprovingly.

'Me.'

'Ay…' I sighed. 'The desert corps also talk about the djinni,' I added. 'They start spitting everywhere when they talk about it, like it's bad luck.'

'A few decades ago, I heard that the soldiers came across a caravan of camels with no people. They say it was one djinni paying respects to another!'

'That, I'm not afraid of,' I giggled. 'It's a friendly gesture.'

'Yadasi?' Manolín, who had long been silent, suddenly called out.

'Do you want a smoke?' Yadasi asked him.

'So where exactly is this djinni?' Manolín asked, his tone suspicious.

'How would I respond to this kind of question? The desert looks the same everywhere.' Yadasi started sounding kind of vague.

'The small sweet potatoes are ready,' José said softly from by the fire. 'Who wants one?'

'Toss one here,' I called out quietly. I half sat up and caught the one he threw to me. It was too hot to hold, so I tossed it to Miguel, who threw it over to Yadasi. 'Ha ha, now there's a hot potato no one can hold on to.' I started chuckling. Abruptly another one was coming at me. I grabbed it and stuck it in the sand. With this ruckus, the *yin* energy all around us seemed to dissipate. José was putting more dry brambles on the fire, and soon the flames leaped up again.

Right then there was a commotion in Jerry's tent, the sound of something getting knocked over, followed by baby Isabel's wailing.

'Jerry, what's the matter?' José called out.

'Sanmao threw herself against the back of the tent and woke up Isabel,' Tania cried pitifully. Their gas lamp lit up.

'No, I didn't. I'm over here.' I shivered when I heard what she said. Soon I couldn't stop shivering. Everyone went over to their tent to take a look. Only I stayed, half-upright by the fire.

'We were fast asleep. Then there was a smack on the side of the tent closest to the woods.' As Jerry explained, Miguel shone a flashlight around there.

'Hmm, there are claw marks here. A very clear set. Come look.'

I sat straight up when I heard Miguel say this. 'Quick, come over here,' I called to Tania while the men ran into the darkness. 'Come by the fire!'

Tania staggered her way over in a rush, her face white as snow. Isabel was no longer crying in her arms. 'A wolf? Are there coyotes here?' She sat with her back against me, also trembling uncontrollably.

'Of course not. There have never been any. Don't be afraid.' I kept my eyes on the group that was slowly returning to us. 'We have more than wolves to be afraid of…' I added.

'Sanmao, what time is it?'

'I don't know. Let's ask José when he gets back.'

'Four thirty,' Yadasi said quietly behind us.

I turned around and almost cried out in surprise. 'Hey, don't scare us like that. Didn't you go with the others to find out about the claw marks? How did you pop up behind us?' Tania was already afraid of Sahrawi people. She was even more terrified now.

'I… didn't go.' There seemed to be something off with Yadasi.

Just then the three others got back. 'A wild dog,' José said.

'How did a dog get over here?' I asked.

'How would I know?' José's tone also seemed strange. He must have grown more nervous. I gave him a look and ignored him.

A deep silence surrounded us. Jerry went back to his tent to get blankets and spread one on the ground. Tania lay down with Isabel and pulled up two blankets as cover. Jerry stroked her hair. 'Back to sleep!' he whispered. Tania closed her eyes again.

We gingerly peeled the sweet potatoes. The fire had dwindled when we took out the smaller ones. Now it was spread weakly on the ground. 'Add firewood!' I called out quietly to Miguel, who was sitting by the fire. He threw on a few dry brambles.

All grew silent again. I sprawled out with my chin propped on my palms, watching the flames dance and jump. Yadasi also lay down. Manolín still sat cross-legged. Miguel was intently focused on stoking the fire.

'Yadasi, won't you show us the way to the djinni?' Manolín reopened the conversation that had long fallen to the wayside.

Yadasi didn't speak.

'If you won't, then maybe ol' Demon Eyes in town will?' Miguel inserted himself into the silence.

'Hanna took that foreigner once and his wife died,' I said. 'Who has the guts to bring anyone any more?'

'Stop talking rubbish,' José said under his breath. 'Hanna didn't die, the journalist didn't die. It was his wife, who didn't even go, who died…'

'The journalist – he did die,' Manolín said. No one knew such a thing had happened. We froze in place. 'In a car accident. Almost a year ago.'

'How do you know?'

'The magazine he worked for published a little announcement. I just happened to stumble upon it. It said a lot of good things about all that he did in his life.'

'Are you guys talking about the djinni?' Jerry asked Yadasi, joining the conversation. He motioned at us not to speak any further. Tania wasn't asleep yet. Her eyes kept opening and closing.

The sun was rising in the desert, but it was still dark where we were. The sky wouldn't grow light until seven or eight in the morning. The night was yet long.

'Speaking of Demon Eyes, did she really see something?' Miguel asked Yadasi in a low voice.

'No one else saw it, just her. At first she didn't realise. Then one time it followed her to a funeral. In broad daylight, she became confused and grabbed someone to ask, "Hey, where did all those flocks of goats and tents come from?" She pointed at the empty land and said, "See, those people are striking camp and getting ready to go, they're leading their camels…"'

'Bullshit. I don't believe it.'

'Bullshit or not, it's true. A dead man who she didn't recognise asked her to pass along a message. When she went back to town and spoke to his relatives, she found there really was someone in their family who had died many years ago. He asked who his daughter Shaia'a had married.'

'We have these kinds of people in China, too. They're all frauds!'

'Demon Eyes doesn't need money. She has enough already.'

'She's seen the djinni?'

'She said the djinni was sitting on a tree branch, shaking and shuddering and watching the burial beneath. It even smiled and waved at her. Demon Eyes was so frightened by this that she brought her own camel to sacrifice.'

'That's right, and there are people who say that the sacrificial altar is never full!' Miguel said. 'The altar is also weird. It looks just like a flat block of stone, not even as big as a table. One slaughtered camel wouldn't fit on it. But forget that. You could put the flesh of ten camels there and it would still never be full.'

'The djinni is greedy!' I said quietly.

A strange wind rose out of nowhere just then. I saw the fire, which was nearing its end, burst up and over towards me. José dragged me back, half tumbling. The fire receded as I stared at it. A cold and prickly feeling spread from my back through my entire body.

'Please, change the topic,' Tania moaned, covering her eyes. All of us sat stiffly after that burst of flame. The *yin* energy grew stronger still. The flames gradually grew dimmer. Everyone looked at the fire, sinking into silence once more.

After a while, Miguel said, 'Did anyone see the performance of *The Lion in Winter* in town?'

'I saw it twice.'

'Was it good?'

'Depends on your mood. I liked it, but José didn't.'

'A matter of taste in theatre,' José said.

Speaking of drama, there came a sound like roaring waves from the forest behind us. 'Stop talking,' I called.

'Now we can't talk again.' Miguel gave me a strange look.

'Macbeth.' I pointed at the woods behind me.

'You really love free association,' Miguel said, laughing all of a sudden. 'Is there anything in the world we can't be afraid of?'

'There's still something weird going on. Ask Manolín. He went in there too.' Manolín didn't deny or confirm anything. 'I think it can move,' I went on.

'What can move?'

'The forest!'

'You're crazy! Your imagination is running wild.'

I flipped over. Flames had just leapt out at me. Now the fire had died down on its own. Cold gloom seeped into our bones. The chill all around us grew heavier.

'Time to get more firewood!' José stood up.

'Use the gas lamp!' Yadasi said. There was a flicker of unease in his eyes. He kept shifting his gaze beyond the fire. We grew quiet for a while. The fire finally died down to a dark little pile. The gas lamp shone a pale white light on everyone's face. We all moved in a little bit closer to each other.

'Yadasi, are there really crystals here?' Jerry tried his best to change the subject, his arms around Tania.

'Last time I found a huge one. It was just on the ground here. Sanmao wanted to come because of it.'

'You came last time just to find crystals?' I couldn't help but grow suspicious. It felt like a metal claw had seized me, almost choking me with terror. In a flash, I understood. I understood where we'd been sitting all night. It all became clear.

Yadasi saw the look on my face. He knew that I knew. Averting his gaze, he said, 'I came before because of something else.'

'You...'

Finally the thing I least wanted to confirm was confirmed. My nerves were shattered in an instant. I opened my mouth, looking at Manolín. I took a deep breath. We were the only two who had gone into the woods. I almost began screaming in fright. A look in Manolín's eyes, so slight it was almost imperceptible, made me bite my lip. He also understood, then. He had known long before we had come to this cursed place.

Miguel didn't realise the huge shock that had come over me in just a few seconds. He unexpectedly started talking about it again. 'One time, the ground didn't crack, but a person died. Everyone thought it was strange. They still carried the body to burial. Afterwards, Demon Eyes, who hadn't gone with them, started going crazy at home, eating dirt and rolling around. She insisted that the person wasn't dead and the djinni wanted the people to take him out. Everyone ignored her. She caused a ruckus for a whole day and night, really going berserk. Finally they went and dug up the grave. Originally they'd buried the body with the mouth facing up. When they opened the grave, the mouth was facing down and the cloth around the body was ripped to shreds. The fabric around the head had been completely dry, but the corners of the mouth were wet and sticky when they dug it up. He'd been buried alive.'

'Jesus Christ, do us a favour, stop talking!' I shrieked. With this, the baby also started screaming, crying and kicking. A wind started blowing again. In the distance, there was a loud sigh in the night that slowly drifted towards us. The wind couldn't disperse that deep and muffled tone. Lifting my head, I saw that the moon had started to come out. The forest behind us cast dark shadows, rustling its way over to us, bit by bit.

'What are you yelling about, crazy?' José cried. He stood up and began walking away.

'Where are you going?'

'To sleep. Are you all done—'

'Come back, I'm begging you.'

Surprisingly, José started laughing loudly from the darkness. Blending in with the other noise, everything felt even more off kilter. What sounded like ghostly laughter was coming from José.

I crawled over to Yadasi and gave him a hard pinch on the shoulder. 'You're awful,' I whispered. 'Bringing us to this cursed place.'

'Didn't I grant your wish from earlier?' He cast a sidelong glance at me.

'Don't say it out loud.' I pinched him again. 'Tania will go nuts if she finds out.'

'What are you two talking about?' Tania cried, her voice unsteady. 'Is something wrong?'

The sighing sound floated towards us again. Terrified, I lost my senses. I actually grabbed a sweet potato and hurled it in the direction of the woods. 'Ghost – shut your mouth!' I screamed. 'We're not afraid of you!'

'Sanmao, you're being paranoid,' Miguel laughed contentedly, not knowing the whole story.

'Go to sleep!' Yadasi stood up and went over to his tent.

'José!' I called again. 'José…' The beam of a flashlight shone out from the little tent. 'Shine a light for me,' I cried. 'I'm coming.' I ran over there as fast as I could, dragging my sleeping bag. Once everyone had separated and entered their tents, I threw myself to José's side and grabbed hold of him, trembling.

'José, José, this whole time, we've been on the djinni's land. You, me…'

'I know.'

'When did you know?'

'The same time as you.'

'I didn't say anything… Ah – the djinni made you telepathic!'

'Sanmao, there is no djinni.'

'Yes, there is… Those scary sighs…'

'No, there isn't. No. Say it. No. There. Isn't.'

'Yes. There. Is. You didn't go into the woods, it doesn't count. For me, yes, there is, there is. I went into the woods…'

José sighed and put his arms around me. I fell silent. 'Go to sleep!' he whispered.

'Listen…' I whispered back. 'Listen…'

'Sleep!' he said again.

I lay there unmoving. Fatigue poured over me. I don't know when but I fell into a deep slumber.

When I woke up, José wasn't by my side. His sleeping bag had been folded neatly and set by my feet. The sun had long since risen. It was still cold. The air was filled with the freshness of a morning mist. Everything came alive. Crimson rays of light cast a warm stain on the desert. There were small red berries growing on the wild brambles. A wild bird I didn't recognise was flapping and flying low in the sky.

I crawled out, all dishevelled, and looked over at the forest again. In the daylight, it looked like an inconspicuous clump of trees covered in sand and dust. It looked more drab than mysterious.

'Ahem!' I called out to José and Yadasi, who were digging out the sweet potatoes. Yadasi hesitantly looked over at me.

'Don't eat all the sweet potatoes,' I said crisply. 'Save one for Tania so we can convince her to come next time.'

'What about you?'

'I don't want any. I'll drink tea.'

Looking at Yadasi, I repaid him with a bright smile.

Milestones in the Life of Sanmao

Born Chen Ping on 26 March 1943 (the twenty-first day of the second lunar month) in Chongqing, Sichuan province. Ancestral home in Dinghai, Zhejiang province.

Young Sanmao shows great passion for literature, reading *Dream of the Red Chamber* in the fifth grade. By middle school, she has read through many classic works from around the world.

Takes a leave of absence in the second year of middle school. Receives careful guidance from her parents on classical poetry and prose and English, setting a sturdy foundation. Studies art under the tutelage of Gu Fusheng and Shao Youxuan.

Receives special permission from Chang Chi-yun, founder of the Chinese Culture University, to attend classes in the philosophy department as a visiting student in 1964. Receives excellent marks in classes.

Drops out of school again in 1967 and travels to Spain alone. Within three years, attends Universidad de Madrid and the Goethe Institute, then works at the law library at the University of Illinois. Very beneficial for her life experiences and linguistic training.

Returns to Taiwan in 1970. Teaches in the German and philosophy departments at the Chinese Culture University at the invitation of Chang Chi-yun. Later, due to the sudden death of her fiancé, she leaves Taiwan again and returns to Spain, reuniting with José, who has held a torch for her for six years.

In 1974, conducts civil marriage with José in the local court of the Spanish Sahara.

Life in the desert stimulates her latent talent for writing. Encouraged by Ping Xintao, then editor-in-chief of the *United Daily News*, she writes a steady stream of works and begins to collect them for publication in book form. *Stories of the Sahara*, the first volume, is published in May 1976.

On 30 September 1979, her husband José dies in a diving accident. With the support of her parents, Sanmao returns to Taiwan.

In 1981, Sanmao decides to end her fourteen years of vagabonding and settle down in Taiwan.

In November of the same year, *United Daily News* sponsors her to travel through Latin America for half a year. She writes *Over River and Mountain* upon her return and travels around Taiwan on a book tour.

Afterward, Sanmao teaches in the arts and literature workshop at the Chinese Culture University. Her courses include 'Writing the Novel' and 'Writing the Essay'. The students receive her with great pleasure.

Due to health reasons, she leaves the faculty of the arts and literature workshop in 1984. Writing and giving talks becomes her main focus.

Returns to her hometown in mainland China for the first time in April 1989. Discovers she has many readers on the mainland. Pays a special visit to the renowned Zhang Leping, creator of the cartoon character Sanmao, a long-held desire.

Undertakes the writing of a screenplay in 1990. Completes her first Chinese screenplay and her last work, *Red Dust*.

Dies on 4 January 1991, at the age of forty-seven.

In July 2000, Sanmao's possessions enter into the preparatory office of the National Centre for the Research and Preservation of Cultural Assets. Current address is National Taiwan Cultural Centre, 1 Zhongzheng Road, Zhongxi District, Tainan.

Sanmao Memorial Hall is established in Dinghai, Zhejiang in December 2000, planned by Fu Wenwei, faculty at Hangzhou University's Tourism Institute, and his wife.

In 2010, the new *Collected Works of Sanmao* is released by Crown Publishing.

Translator's Note

The notion of a mother tongue or native language can be more complex than it seems. I was born in China and lived there until age four, speaking nothing but the twangy southwestern Mandarin of my rural surroundings in Hubei province. Then I had a brief stint in Denmark (where I was taught *putonghua*, or standard Mandarin) before immigrating to the United States with my parents at age five. English quickly superseded Chinese in my life out of practicality and necessity. Though I would continue to attend Chinese language school for a few hours every Saturday until age fifteen or so, my progress in literacy effectively ground to a halt due to structural limitations. Admittedly, by the time I was a teenager in suburban Ohio, I harboured an intense distaste for anything associated with China or Chinese culture. Like many first generation immigrants, I was compelled to reject my background, vying instead for conformity and the inoffensive monolingualism of Americanness.

Eventually, I went to grad school with a vague idea to research and write about Chinese language cinema, building upon my undergraduate studies in film and television production. It was around this time, in my early twenties, when I truly began to restore and reinvigorate my linguistic aptitude for Chinese. A few years later, I was gifted a copy of *Stories of the Sahara*. One of the first things that drew me to this book was Sanmao's eminent readability, even for a Chinese-American like myself who grew up largely without deep knowledge of or access to Chinese literature.

I recount all of this in order to give context to my own initial encounter with Sanmao, how enchanted I was by her voice, reaching across space and time to jolt my senses in New York City over forty years after she wrote the pieces collected in *Stories of the Sahara*. It's hard to describe how moving it was to read an entire book in Chinese and feel such an intense emotional resonance with the writer's sensitivities and observations, her humour and heartache. I knew from the outset that I wanted to translate this work into English. And, many years later, on the tail end of this circuitous journey, I'm incredibly honoured by the opportunity to have a hand in introducing this remarkable woman to English language readers around the world.

STRUCTURE AND MECHANICS

Vernacular Chinese can be deceptively simple to read, while still presenting many a forked road for the translator to consider. A single utterance of the exclamatory character *yi*, for example, can imply surprise, confusion or curiosity, depending on context. Subjects are often elided or ambiguous in casual prose. It is common to see complex thoughts conveyed through a multiplicity of clauses separated by commas alone, rather than the discrete sentences they naturally become when rendered in English. Dialogue tags, including relevant physical movements or expressions, are usually inserted only before or after a character speaks, rather than breaking up a long remark in the middle.

In all such instances, I have chosen the most straightforward way to present what I have interpreted as Sanmao's intention or narrative strategy while also conforming to the expectations and standards of English language prose.

STYLE

A hallmark of Sanmao's writing style is her personal tone – almost confessional, some might call it – which situates the reader as a friend and confidante, bearing witness to her tales of adventure and intrigue. The vast majority of the stories in this book originally appeared in Taiwanese print publications such as the *United Daily News*, garnering immense popularity for their unvarnished style, warm-blooded ethos and fascinating sketches of the hinterlands and its denizens.

Sanmao's lively voice has aged well, but the rawness and off-the-cuff quality of her work are apparent in many repetitive phrases or constructions, as well as some abrupt or unclear narrative turns. My editors and I have chosen to judiciously trim down overuse of phrases like 'suddenly', for example, while preserving the original structure of her narrative flow as much as possible. Despite the profound empathy with which the writer viewed almost everyone in her life, there are quite a few instances where her judgments of others, especially the Sahrawi characters, may come off as insensitive at best, derogatory or racist at worst. Instead of expunging or explaining these moments away, we have chosen instead to preserve the integrity of the whole work, elements of discomfort and all.

SPANISH AND ARABIC

The vast majority of proper names and many phrases in the original are transliterated from Spanish or Hassaniya Arabic into Chinese. Some of these are easily identifiable or verifiable names with a standard (or precedent) of romanisation, such as José, El Aaiún, Fatima, Muhammad and so on. Others characters, mostly Sahrawi, have names that do not necessarily conform to a standard or recognisable romanisation. I have translated these with an eye toward consistency, based on variations that were suggested to me by my native Sahrawi colleagues.

The usage of Arabic words like *khaima* (tent) or *Salaam alaikum* (good day) are accompanied by the explanations Sanmao inserted for the benefit of the Chinese reader. Meanwhile, there are some words or ideas that were not rendered in transliterated Spanish originally, but that I have opted to use in order to add flavour to the text: *sopa de mariscos*, the Hotel Nacional, *cobarde*, *Dios mío*, etc.

CULTURAL AND LITERARY ALLUSIONS

The touchstones of film and pop culture from the 1960s to 1970s are apparent in Sanmao's writing, some of which have clearly lapsed into obscurity more than others. We have chosen not to footnote the allusions to books, movies or TV shows such as *Born Free*, *Zorba the Greek*, *Mad Woman*, *Jonathan Livingston Seagull*, etc.

More tricky are the references to Chinese literature. Sanmao was a prolific reader and clearly well versed in the canonical literature of Chinese history. For excerpts of pre-modern Chinese poetry, we have used modern renditions by other translators of Chinese with proper attributions. For passing mentions of books, we have footnoted only when necessary in chapters with a density of references, such as 'My Great Mother-in-Law'.

Chinese language is rife with *chengyu*, four character idioms that condense a great deal of metaphorical, symbolic or even narrative signification into a pithy linguistic flourish. For the majority of these, I have opted for a conceptual translation into English, rendering them into phrases like 'a hedge between keeps friendships green' or 'have my cake and eat it, too'. A more direct translation is employed when the Chinese expression lacks an English language equivalent, usually in instances where the phrase itself is couched in an explanation of a particular sentiment or can be easily understood based on context.

Notes

NICE NEIGHBOURS

1 Albert Schweitzer (14 January 1875 – 4 September 1965) was an Alsatian humanitarian and philosopher who in 1913 founded a hospital in Lambaréné, Central Africa.

A LADDER

1 Li Shangyin, 'The Brocade Zither', translated by Chloe Garcia Roberts.
2 Excerpt from 'The Ugly Page/Picking Mulberries' by Xin Qiji, translated by Andrew W. F. Wong.

HEARTH AND HOME

1 From an untitled poem by Wang Wei.
2 From Ma Zhiyuan's 'Autumn Thoughts', translated by Andrew W. F. Wong.

MY GREAT MOTHER-IN-LAW

1 Told by an anonymous poet of the Han Dynasty (AD 196–219), *Southeast Fly the Peacocks* is the tragic love story of a young couple whose marriage was broken up by the man's proprietorial mother. When the woman was forced to marry someone else, the lovers killed themselves in order to live together in the next world.

2 A pun on the poem 'Pure Serene Music' by Southern Tang poet Li Yu, who lived in the tenth century.

3 Excerpt from 'Farewells on Grassland' by renowned poet and government official Bai Juyi (Po Chü-i), translated by Hugh Grigg.

4 In the *History of Song*, Neo-Confucian scholar Yang Shi and a companion visit the Confucian philosopher Cheng Yi. They find Cheng Yi meditating, his eyes closed, and respectfully wait outside the door in the snow. When Cheng finally comes out of his meditation, a foot of snow has gathered about them.

5 A couplet from the poem 'Climbing a Terrace' by renowned Tang poet Du Fu.

6 The closure of Bai's poem 'Farewells on Grassland'.

CRYING CAMELS

1 From *Dream of the Red Chamber*, volume 1, translated by David Hawkes.

Translator's Acknowledgements

All told, this translation has been a labour of love, bridging several epochs in my own life and supported by the time, effort and kindness of countless friends and colleagues. I was first introduced to Sanmao back in 2011, thanks to the most propitious birthday gift of *Stories of the Sahara* from Jacob Dreyer. Gray Tan was a helpful interlocutor long before the book translation became a viable project. Eventually, both Gray and Jade Fu of the Grayhawk Agency were instrumental in connecting me with Bloomsbury.

During a trip to Spain in 2016, I was able to spend time with Angeles Bela Quero, niece of José, and greatly enjoyed our conversation in Madrid, with translation support by Cassandra Sicre. While visiting the island of Gran Canaria, where Sanmao and José lived in the late 1970s, I was greeted with warm hospitality by Nancy Chang, a friend from that era, and her husband Daniel Chung. They brought me to Sanmao's former abode in the town of Telde and introduced me to her neighbour Candy Santa Cabrera, who spoke vividly of her recollections of Sanmao.

My confidence in the translation was bolstered tremendously through continuous discussion of linguistic nuances with a small crew of native Chinese speakers based in New York and elsewhere: Wenting Gu, Echo Yu He, Manchuang Nadia Ho and Ivy Ma. My parents Dechun Fu and Lihua Liu, as well as my sister, Ellen Fu, also contributed their own insights into certain tricky turns of phrase. I can't emphasise enough how much I benefited from reviewing, chapter by chapter, sentence by sentence, an early draft of the manuscript with Annelous Stiggelbout, the Dutch translator of *Sahara*. I also greatly appreciated the warmth and camaraderie of my fellow Sanmao translators Sara Rovira (Catalan) and Irene Tor Carroggio (Spanish/Catalan).

Initial guidance on the transliteration of Arabic names was provided by Dongxin Zou. Through the introductions of Alice Ella Finden and Carmen Gómez Martín, I was able to consult with a few native Sahrawi colleagues – Brahim B. Ali, Bahia Awah and Limam Boisha – whose patience and thoughtful interlocutions paved the way to more than one 'eureka' moment.

The editorial crew at Bloomsbury have been a pleasure to work with. I would like to thank Alexa von Hirschberg, Imogen Denny and most especially Marigold Atkey, who shared astute comments and many wonderful suggestions throughout the stories as we spent much of the past two years volleying the manuscript back and forth across the Atlantic. Katherine Ailes helped polish up the whole thing with her keen eye on copy editing. It was truly a team effort and I couldn't have done it without everyone named above. This project was also nurtured by the kindness and support of my partner, Christopher Yosuke Ishikawa.

Last but not least, I am grateful to Sanmao's family for their warmth and generosity, and I owe a debt of gratitude to Chen Ping herself, or Echo Chan, as she is alternately known. As the woman who invented and embodied Sanmao as pen name, persona and character, Echo filled the hearts of multiple generations of Chinese readers with wonderment for the great big world in which we all live. Now, over forty years after the original publication of these Saharan stories and twenty-five years since her untimely passing, Echo lives again in new translations of some of her earliest work. I'm certain she would have delighted in the opportunity to befriend even more people across cultures and languages. Though she is no longer with us, I hope my belated translation, among the others published in recent years, will give her some solace and allow her to rest contentedly, at last, amid the olive trees of her dreams.

Mike Fu
New York City, 2019

Note on the Author

Sanmao, born Chen Ping, was a novelist, writer and translator. Born in China, she grew up in Taiwan. After a stint in Europe, she moved to the Sahara Desert with her Spanish husband, a scuba diver and underwater engineer. She committed suicide in 1991.

Note on the Translator

Mike Fu is a Brooklyn-based writer, translator and editor. He is a co-founder and editor of *The Shanghai Literary Review*, a transnational English language journal for arts and literature, and the assistant dean for global initiatives at Parsons School of Design.

Note on the Type

The text of this book is set Adobe Garamond. It is one of several versions of Garamond based on the designs of Claude Garamond. It is thought that Garamond based his font on Bembo, cut in 1495 by Francesco Griffo in collaboration with the Italian printer Aldus Manutius. Garamond types were first used in books printed in Paris around 1532. Many of the present-day versions of this type are based on the Typi Academiae of Jean Jannon cut in Sedan in 1615.

Claude Garamond was born in Paris in 1480. He learned how to cut type from his father and by the age of fifteen he was able to fashion steel punches the size of a pica with great precision. At the age of sixty he was commissioned by King Francis I to design a Greek alphabet, and for this he was given the honourable title of royal type founder. He died in 1561.